UNION

Your Journey to Germany

HEADQUARTERS
BRITISH ARMY OF THE RHINE

Voyage I.

AUGUST 1946

OFFICERS INSIGNIA
Dienstgradabzeichen der britischen Offiziere

Field Marshal	General	Lieutenant General	Major General	Brigadier	Colonel	Lieutenant Colonel	Major	Captain	Lieutenant	Second Lieutenant
Feldmarschall	*General*	*Generalltn.*	*Generalmajor*	*Brigade Gen.*	*Oberst*	*Oberstltn.*	*Major*	*Hauptmann*	*Oberltn.*	*Leutnant*

Army Commander	Corps Commander	Divisional Commander	Brigade Commander
Armee-Commandeur	*Corps-Commandeur*	*Divisions-Commandeur*	*Brigade-Commandeur*

COMMANDERS PENNANTS
Flown from bonnet of Commanders Car.
Commandeur-Stander
geführt am Kühler des Commandeur-Wagens

A Strange
Enemy People

By the same author

Scapa Flow
(with Malcolm Brown)

The Great Inflation: Germany 1919–23
(with William Guttmann)

The Unnecessary War:
Whitehall and the German Resistance to Hitler

A STRANGE
ENEMY PEOPLE

Germans under the British, 1945–1950

Patricia Meehan

Peter Owen Publishers
London and Chester Springs

PETER OWEN PUBLISHERS
73 Kenway Road, London SW5 0RE

Peter Owen books are distributed in the USA by
Dufour Editions Inc., Chester Springs, PA 19425-0007

First published in Great Britain 2001
© Patricia Meehan 2001

ISBN 0 7206 1115 6

A catalogue record for this book is available from
the British Library.

Printed and bound in Great Britain by
MPG Books Ltd, Bodmin, Cornwall

Contents

List of Illustrations

Between pages 156 and 157

The surrender of Hamburg, 3 May 1945

Defeated officer among the ruins © *Hulton Getty*

White flags of surrender in the streets of Cologne © *Soldier magazine*

The Potsdam Conference, July 1945 © *Imperial War Museum*

Tanks entering Aachen © *Soldier magazine*

Refugees fleeing Aachen during the fight for the city © *Hulton Getty*

Refugees struggling across a bombed railway bridge © *Soldier magazine*

German male civilians placed under arbitrary arrest

A homeless family living in a ruined house © *Soldier magazine*

Women salvaging bricks from the rubble of Dresden © *Hulton Getty*

Edicts of Military Government being nailed to a wall
   © *Imperial War Museum*

Citizens studying regulations issued by the British authorities
   © *Hulton Getty*

German homes requisitioned for the accommodation of British
   families © *Illustrated London News Picture Library*

British officers assessing bomb damage to buildings

The first party of wives arriving from Britain
   © *Illustrated London News Picture Library*

A well-turned-out British family in a German street © *Soldier magazine*

A NAAFI shop for the exclusive use of the British © *Soldier magazine*

Soldiers on leave throwing their travel rations from a train to hungry
   German civilians © *Soldier magazine*

A German woman searches for food in the dustbins of a British home
   © *Illustrated London News Picture Library*

Hungry families growing vegetables in a bombed-out building
   © *Illustrated London News Picture Library*

Mass hunger demonstrations in the Ruhr, February 1947
   © *North Rhine–Westphalia State Archive*

A Control Commission officer and his German secretary; many such
secretaries doubled as interpreters and were suspected by the
Germans of wielding undue influence

British Armed Forces voucher

Inside front cover:
Identity Card issued to members of the Control Commission in the
British Zone of Germany; instructions issued to British wives
travelling to Germany to join their husbands; a guide to equivalent
Army insignia to enable Germans to recognize the rank of any
British officer from whom they might receive orders

Inside back cover:
Instructions to troops forbidding contact between British and
Germans issued by Field-Marshal Montgomery and designed to be
carried in the pocket; ordinances and edicts relating to curfews,
political meetings, the black market and elections displayed in both
German and English

You are going into Germany. You are about to meet a strange people in a strange enemy country.
    – Official handout to British Occupation personnel

Introduction

THE PRINCIPLES upon which the Occupation of defeated Germany was to be carried out were laid down at the Big Three Conference at Potsdam in July 1945. These principles were in due course ignored, manipulated, flouted, abandoned and over-zealously adhered to. The territory to be apportioned as a zone of occupation to each of the Allies had been agreed during the war. Of the Western Allies' allocation it was said that the Americans got the scenery, the French got the wine, and the British got the ruins.

The British Zone covered the extensively ravaged areas of the industrial Ruhr and the important port of Hamburg. When the British took control of north-west Germany it was in unimaginable chaos. In one of the great sophisticated nations of Europe, people were living in holes in the ground, dug out from beneath millions of tons of rubble which had once been historic cities or flourishing industrial communities. The simple necessities of life no longer existed and might never have been invented. Official estimates for the length of Occupation varied from ten to twenty to fifty years. Handfuls of Military Government officers worked miracles in bringing some order to the chaos.

Each within its own zone, the Allied powers set about creating a Germany in their own image. The British slipped easily into the imperial mode. When British wives, together with their children, were eventually allowed to join their husbands in Germany, Prime Minister Clement Attlee reminded them that 'they will be looked on by the Germans as representatives of the British Empire' and their behaviour should reflect how 'this Empire' should be regarded.[1] In the House of Commons a Member recommended, 'The model which the Germans would most easily understand and which would train them until they undertake responsibility would be our colonial form of Government.'[2] Another spoke of viceroys and governor-generals.[3] India was the yardstick against which British performance in Germany should be measured.

Thousands of British administrators arrived in a country about which they knew nothing, among a former enemy people whom most of them had never seen. In official government handbooks, which ranged from the anthropological to the socially bizarre, the newcomers were indoctrinated about the alien tribe among whom they would be living. The Army was similarly armed by military psychologists. The calculated alienation, through these tracts, of those who were to administer Occupied Germany helped to create a climate of 'anything goes' in which widespread corruption flourished.

An overblown bureaucracy bedevilled the British administration in Germany. Control was splintered into divisions, subdivisions, branches, commissions, subcommissions. The Germans themselves were astonished at the extent of British red tape. As they were not given any responsibility or allowed to work without supervision, every German employed was duplicated by a British administrator. This called for a vast army of officials. Initial military government was taken over by the civilians of – to give it its full title – the Control Commission for Germany and Austria (British Element). Hastily and almost indiscriminately recruited, its members included dedicated professionals, former colonial officers, demobbed servicemen unwilling to return to 'civvy street', former temporary civil servants, carpetbaggers and crooks. Ignorance of the language led to what the Germans called 'government by interpreter'. Parliamentary pressure at home eventually brought about the scaling down of the original force of 26,000 and the extension of executive power to the Germans.

In the first months after the surrender, a non-fraternization order forbade any human contact with Germans outside the strict course of duty. A Foreign Office official pointed out that this meant it would be the conquerors who would be the prisoners while the defeated would lead normal human lives. The writer Stephen Spender remembered hearing a German child suggest to another that they should throw an apple to the poor British soldier behind his barbed-wire fence.[4] Within a short time the policy collapsed under the pressure of humanity and common sense.

Nevertheless, a policy of segregation remained. The British lived completely separate lives from the Germans. To borrow a phrase from the Bard of Empire, it was a case of:

> All the people like us are We,
> And every one else is They.

It was an inward-looking, elitist society. Alcohol was cheap and freely available for the occupiers. There was a liberal allocation of free and duty-free cigarettes. Food supplies, although dull, were more generous than rations at home. Domestic servants were supplied for a nominal charge. There was much leisure time but little to do with it beyond frequenting British clubs and meeting the same people all the time. British and Germans shared cinemas and concert halls – although not at the same time. But, for all its tedious artificiality, the British lifestyle in Germany was an escape from the monotony and grinding austerity of post-war Britain.

The clock started again for the Germans in June 1948, when currency reform launched economic revival and a return to normality. With real money in circulation, the vast black market collapsed. The cigarette – with a recognized, if illegal, market value – was no longer the main unit of currency.

With Soviet Russia beginning to replace Germany as Enemy Number One there had to be new alignments in the West. Friendship with the Germans became not only permitted but positively mandatory. But many individual Britons had already made their own accommodations with the people among whom they were living, independently of the cynicism of power politics or the ravings of official handbooks. Deep had called to deep, and the best among the top echelons of the Control Commission had already found opposite numbers among the Germans with whom they could work constructively. Often they found themselves siding with 'their' Germans against a government in London which was often prejudiced, uncaring or obtuse. Many British families, too, had discovered a common humanity with their German neighbours. Countless acts of personal kindness were prompted by the hardship and suffering which they began to be aware of around them. To return to Kipling:

> . . . if you cross over the sea,
> Instead of over the way,
> You may end by (think of it!) looking on We
> As only a sort of They!

The British had taken over control in Germany in the appalling conditions of what the Germans themselves called 'Year Zero'. Five years later a newly created, fully democratic Federal Republic was on the road to recovery. During those critical five years the British were to influence, for better or for worse, all the most important developments in German life.

In the course of making a television documentary series on the British Occupation some years ago, I was fortunate in being able to talk to most of the key figures then surviving. I also received hundreds of letters from men and women who, like myself, had had the unique experience of living and working in Occupied Germany and still vividly remembered it. The Germans whom I interviewed, living now in a prosperous and flourishing democracy, preferred to dwell only on the happier aspects of the Occupation. In spite of the many problems and often misbegotten policies which the records reveal, they remembered best the common endeavour with the British, their former enemies, to bring their country back from the abyss.

I
Unconditional surrender

THE END, when it came, was a fumble. There was none of the
theatre of humiliation staged on the battleship *Missouri* at the
end of the war with Japan. There was no Allied foot on the neck
of a defeated nation: there was no government left to yield. It
had obliterated itself in the ruins of the capital. For some in
Germany the news simply came through an announcement in
halting German by a British officer from a town-hall balcony.
On 7 May 1945 the forces of the Third Reich surrendered in a
small schoolhouse in Reims on terms short of unconditional
surrender which put the Allied governments in a flurry. An
instrument of surrender, laboriously crafted during the war,
had been deposited in a filing cabinet at Supreme Headquarters – and forgotten. When the historic moment came, a document was hastily put together by staff officers There had to
be two more staged ceremonies in Berlin before they got it
right.

The slogan 'Unconditional Surrender' had been the banner
under which the Allied armies – or rather the Western Allied
armies – had been fighting since it was devised at the Casablanca
Conference in 1943. Stalin, who had not been present, thought it
bad tactics To its authors, Roosevelt and Churchill, it carried an
emotional charge which overshadowed any consideration of
its eventual implementation. The enlightened Regional Commissioner for Hamburg, Sir Vaughan Berry, reflected years later,
'I suppose it's absolute heresy to say so, but my belief was that the
British government during the war had no policy beyond unconditional surrender. What they were to *do* with the unconditional
surrender when they'd got it – I really don't think they'd thought
about it.'[1] The head of Political Warfare Department, Richard

Crossman, defined the 'Unconditional Surrender' slogan as 'a formula to avoid discussing the future of Germany'.[2]

The concept of 'unconditional surrender' had no precedent. By convention, surrender would normally be followed by an armistice under which the victors would suspend hostilities in return for compliance with certain terms by the vanquished. The Hague Convention conferred limited powers upon the – strictly temporary – belligerent occupiers of enemy territory. The purpose of such empowerment was to ensure public order and safety and prevent the outbreak of disease. But it was obvious that the Allies would require powers which went far beyond the Hague rules. No terms were to be offered to Nazi Germany. Surrender would merely be the first step in an unprecedented takeover of the whole country and nation.[3] The instrument of surrender drafted during the last years of the war proposed to demand from a German government powers not allowed for in international law. The ceding of such powers would vest in the Allies the *de facto* government of Germany while permitting *de jure* sovereignty to subsist in a German government.

But, in the absence of any responsible German authority to yield these wide powers, the only method by which the Allies could acquire them would be by the assumption of sovereignty. But this implied annexation, and the Foreign Office decreed that there was no intention to annex Germany. There should, it was felt in Whitehall, be a position in between: subjugation but no annexation. The concept might be new to international law, but the law was not something that could be altered only by legislation: it could develop to meet change of circumstances. 'It will in time be recognised', loftily declared the legal advisers of the Foreign Office, 'that International Law has been modified accordingly.'[4]

Not all British lawyers took such a cavalier attitude. Brigadier Andrew Clark KC, chief of the Legal Division of the Control Commission which was to administer the Occupation, set out his opinion after scrutinizing the draft of the Declaration of Defeat and Assumption of Sovereignty proposed by the Foreign Office. The preamble to the Declaration read, 'The governments of the United Kingdom, the United States and the USSR hereby assume supreme authority, with respect to Germany, including all the powers possessed by the German government, High Command and any state, municipal or local government.' This, wrote Clark, amounted to government of Germany *de facto* and *de jure* and effected the destruction of Germany as an independent state. Sovereignty was not vested in the High Command, who would have no power to grant it to the Allies. Nor was it extinguished by the absence of a head of state or government. In such a case it reverted to the people. No one except a new German government chosen by the people was capable of granting rights in excess of those of an occupying power laid down in international law. The Foreign Office were claiming that, for political reasons, the Allies were *not* assuming sovereignty:

> But if this is not an assumption of sovereignty, what is? . . . If this is agreed then the Declaration can have no effect whatever beyond announcing an intention wholly incompatible with international law . . . [The Declaration] should be clearly framed as a declaration of intention. The fact that this intention is not justified in international law – that it is really necessary for political reasons – should be openly faced.

Other eminent lawyers – Walter Monckton and Lord Somervell, the Attorney-General – had 'expressed concurrence' with Clark. This assertion was reinforced in a private handwritten letter by Clark to General Kirby at Control Commission Headquarters. He had discussed the matter with Somervell 'who agrees with the legal position but visualizes political difficulties'.[5]

These 'political difficulties' were smartly dealt with. If hitherto accepted principles of international law were to be considered inapplicable to the German case, then new legal principles must be formulated 'which it is considered politically necessary to substitute in their place'.[6] The Foreign Secretary,

Anthony Eden, put the question to the Lord Chancellor, Lord Simon, and law officers, who provided a looked-for answer. They reiterated the view that international law was a 'growing body of doctrine, the contents of which may legitimately vary with circumstances'. They could not regard international law as limiting the powers of the Allies to those of mere belligerent occupation.[7]

But the carefully constructed British-made base for supreme Allied authority over Germany was to continue to be a matter of controversy among international lawyers. Nor in the heart of the British Establishment itself was it clearly understood and accepted. A year after the end of the war the Legal Adviser to the Foreign Office wrote in a memorandum to German Department of

> a tendency amongst our legal people in Germany to take a rather different view of the present curious legal position from ourselves, and of course, as we think here, a slightly mistaken view . . . The present position of Germany is undoubtedly *sui generis* but that makes it all the more important that both our people in Germany and we here should keep in touch so that we say the same thing about it.[8]

The Legal Adviser at Control Commission Headquarters in Germany was trying to do just that when he informed the Foreign Office that – nothing to the contrary having issued from official sources – he had advised Political Department in October 1945 that it was 'probable' that the war had ended on the date of the signing of the Declaration of Defeat – that is, on 5 June 1945. He had therefore been considerably taken aback, he wrote, to see in *The Times* of 4 April 1946 that the Foreign Secretary had signed a certificate that 'His Majesty is still in a state of war with Germany'. Could the Foreign Office please elucidate? As the Allied Control Council was the supreme governing authority in Germany, how could Germany still be at war?[9]

There was an element of pish-tush in the reply by the Foreign Office Legal Adviser, W. E. Beckett. The author of the letter from Control Commission Headquarters, he wrote, 'seems to me to be the type of mind that sees difficulties and fails to see the way round them'.[10] He then proceeded to enlighten his hapless colleague in Lübbecke about the curious matter of the Foreign Secretary's certificate.

A German engineer, Karl Kuchenmeister, had moved to Manchester five years before Hitler came to power, establishing a successful business which had supplied much-needed machine tools to the British defence industry. In 1939 he had applied for naturalization, but when war broke out he was interned and then dispatched with other internees to Canada. He survived the sinking of their ship, the SS *Arandorra Star*, off the Isle of Man. Arriving back in England, he had been put in prison. He was still there, spending eighteen hours a day in a cell in Brixton. The Manchester business community had rallied strongly to his defence, although in vain, and his case was raised in the House of Commons. The Home Secretary, Chuter Ede, insisted he should be deported to Germany as an enemy alien.

Kuchenmeister applied for habeas corpus. His counsel argued that, as the Allied Control Council ruled Germany, the German state had ceased to exist and therefore former German nationals had ceased to be enemy aliens. As the British government – that is, the Crown – was a member of the Control Council, the King could not be at war with himself. The Foreign Office, which could always 'see the way round' difficulties, provided a way out. The Foreign Secretary, Ernest Bevin, issued a certificate to the court: 'No treaty of peace or declaration by the Allied Powers having been made terminating the state of war with Germany, His Majesty is still in a state of war with Germany, although, as provided in the declaration of surrender, all active hostilities have ceased.'[11]

In the letter from Lübbecke which had raised this issue, the poor man who could see only difficulties had further posed the simple question 'Are the other Allies still at war with Germany?' The Foreign Office simply shrugged this off: 'I imagine yes, but that after all is a question for them . . .'

It had been early agreed between the Big Three powers – Britain, the United States and the Soviet Union – that Berlin should be the seat of the Allied Control Council, the governing body for the whole of Germany. The Council would consist of the commanders-in-chief from the three zones. The city should be divided into separate sectors, as the country had been divided into zones. But, for various reasons, one important consideration was overlooked: Berlin was in the centre of the Soviet Zone. No provision was made to ensure freedom of access from the Western Zones to the city. This omission came home to roost in 1948 with the Russian blockade of Berlin, overcome in the end triumphantly by the Berlin Airlift.

The Declaration of Defeat and Assumption of Sovereignty establishing the government of defeated Germany was signed with considerable military ceremony in Berlin on 5 June 1945. Supreme authority would be exercised by each of the four commanders-in-chief (France was now included) severally in his own zone and jointly, in matters affecting Germany as a whole, as the Allied Control Council sitting in Berlin. Each would also carry the additional title of Military Governor. The four Governors were, initially, Montgomery, Eisenhower, Zhukov and Koenig – all battlefield commanders. Each had a deputy Military Governor upon whom the hands-on task of administration devolved. The Allied governments shared joint responsibility for Greater Berlin, with individual responsibility for their own sectors. For Germany as a whole, the political and economic requirements demanded by the Allies were laid down by the Big Three at their final meeting in Potsdam, the historic suburb of Berlin, in July 1945. The Potsdam Agreement conferred upon the Allied authorities control of every facet of German life.

While the instrument of surrender was still being hammered out by the representatives of the Big Three powers in the last years of the war, the British Foreign Office had been pursuing its own ideas about the disposition of the vast numbers of German troops whom unconditional surrender would deliver to the untender mercies of their conquerors. Once again international law was an early casualty.

Would it not be desirable, mused the mandarins, to define the status of German troops who might be retained for labour purposes, whether for the Allied forces in Germany or for their governments at home? 'Leaving aside the technical question whether we *can* take prisoners once active hostilities have ceased,' the status of the prisoner of war under the Geneva Convention entailed various rights, privileges and immunities. The use which could be made of these men would be 'considerably hampered' by such a status. The Foreign Office was uncertain whether it was feasible to specify their exact status. In general they would rank as persons whose services Germany provided for reconstruction purposes under the Armistice: 'They will really be forced labourers, but I can see no need to say so.'[12] The then Foreign Secretary, Anthony Eden, reported to the War Cabinet, 'The Allies would be possessed of full and complete authority inside Germany and will thus be empowered to make compulsory use of German labour, military or civilian, for whatever purposes they deem proper.'[13]

These smooth assumptions received a jolt. Brigadier Andrew Clark KC (who was later to challenge the proposed Declaration of Defeat) took issue with the Draft Instrument of Surrender in no uncertain terms:

> I view with trepidation the proposed misuse of prisoners of war and the cynical disregard evinced in this paper for the protective provisions not only of the Geneva Convention which was ratified by His Majesty's Government as recently as 1930 but also of established international law. The proposals in this paper are retrograde steps which, if once taken, will swiftly lead us back to the barbaric conditions of the Middle Ages when POW were treated as slaves.

If this was an attempt to contract out of the Prisoner-of-War Convention, Clark continued, it was not possible to do so legally.

Article 2(b) of the draft declared that German armed forces shall *at the discretion* of the Allies be declared to be prisoners of war 'and shall be subject to such considerations and directions as may be prescribed'. But, if these men were declared to be prisoners of war, such 'conditions and directions as may be prescribed' could only be those prescribed by the Geneva Convention. Clark urged the representatives of the Services to stand up for the maintenance of international rules on prisoners of war and not permit them to be sacrificed for political considerations. What was 'euphemistically referred to as a deviation' from the precise terms of an international convention was in effect a repudiation of the cardinal principles of international law on the subject. 'If the proposed course is adopted the whole structure protecting the status of prisoners-of-war is blown sky-high.'[14]

Clark's arguments were dismissed by a colleague who summed up what the policy was really about. 'The object of using the phrase "prisoner-of-war" was purely political, i.e. to impress indelibly on the German consciousness that their armed forces have been defeated this time. It was not the object to produce any particular status other than that of a "defeated enemy", if there is such a status.' In other words, it was a matter of semantics. They were not *real* prisoners of war and therefore had no claim on the Geneva Convention.[15]

In March 1945 the Supreme Commander, General Eisenhower, sent a memorandum to the Combined Chiefs of Staff. If the German forces were to be designated prisoners of war, the problem of feeding them would be immense and the provision of rations impossible. Eisenhower intended therefore to treat all surrendered members of the German armed forces in Germany as disarmed troops pending discharge. Approval was requested: existing plans had been prepared upon this basis.

The Foreign Office urgently alerted the War Cabinet. Once German soldiers had been discharged, it would no longer be possible to make them prisoners of war. And if they were *not* prisoners it would be impossible to use them as labour outside Germany. It was therefore urgently necessary to calculate how much German labour was required for the United Kingdom. These estimates should not be too low: the number suggested was 520,000. That number must be excluded from the designation 'disarmed pending discharge'.[16]

These thousands of prisoners were to be screened politically and categorized accordingly – 'white', 'grey' or 'black'. But there was an acute shortage of German-speaking British personnel to handle the immense task. It was agreed that Dutch, Norwegian or Czech German-speakers could be used. These should be trained by a few experienced interrogators. The director of Education Branch of the Control Commission suggested using schoolmasters during the holidays and at weekends. They could be trained at special courses during the summer holidays. Given the consequences of their categorization to individuals, it was a brutally *ad hoc* solution.

By July 1945, 10,000 prisoners of war in Britain had been cleared by Intelligence not only as anti-Nazi but also as likely to exercise a good positive influence on other Germans. But they were not to be repatriated. They were to be retained as labour in the United Kingdom.

By the end of the year the dearth of manual labour inside Germany became so acute that Employment and Labour Division felt compelled by sheer urgency 'to leave political considerations in the background and to concentrate simply on fit bodies'. A total of 425,921 vacancies for work of urgent priority for the Military Government could not be filled. The total holding of prisoners of war by the British was at the time 434,735. Manpower Division suggested that prisoners repatriated from Britain could be replaced there by the 45,000 Germans held as security suspects in civilian internment camps and by the 60,000 Nazis dismissed from their posts. The authorities in Germany were only too anxious to get rid of them. However, these were largely civilians, and export of civilians for reparations was barred by international agreements. Furthermore, the government at home refused to take 'black' prisoners into Britain.

They might disseminate Nazi ideas, warned Churchill's adviser Desmond Morton.

The Army in Germany noted resentment 'among those who wish us well' that the burden of reparations labour abroad fell upon those unfortunate enough to be taken prisoners as members of the armed forces, while those imprisoned, interned or dismissed as Nazis escaped. 'Thus the anti-Nazi soldier does reparations abroad while the undeportable Nazi civilian remains at home.'[17] The Parliamentary Select Committee on Estimates (British Expenditure in Germany), reporting after a visit to Germany in 1946, commented on 'the problem of the continued absence of German prisoners-of-war. Your Committee can only report, without comment, that this matter is having a bad effect on German morale and is retarding the recovery of her economy.'[18]

In August 1946 80,000 prisoners from Britain and the Dominions were due to be repatriated. In order to ensure that a maximum reserve of replacement labour was maintained, the Army Chief of Staff ordered that all prisoners arriving for discharge from outside the British Zone would be sorted for suitability as reparations labour. They would not be allowed home. Only the medically unfit would be discharged. The remainder would be transferred to, and retained in, transit camps or 'holding areas' and discharged on a 'head-for-head' basis as others arrived, so that a full holding was always available to replace any repatriation of 'whites' from the United Kingdom. The Control Commission took a brisk view of the advantages for these men for whom captivity had no visible end. Over in Britain they would be fed, housed and employed, whereas in Germany food and housing would be difficult for some time. And there was always 'the prospect of seeing a new country and learning a new language'.[19]

The holding camps to which these unreleased prisoners were consigned were administered by 'A' Branch of Headquarters, British Army of the Rhine (HQ BAOR). The conditions were appalling. Early in 1947 revelations of conditions in the camps were beginning to emerge from the accounts of former prisoners through the Soviet press and radio in Berlin. One prisoner returning from Egypt declared, 'We had heard a little about conditions in German release camps, but Münsterlager was far worse than we expected.' There were four electric bulbs in the whole camp; no fuel for the stoves; no straw mattresses. The hot meal consisted of thin watery soup, owing to the corruption of the German staff handling the food. It was claimed that the administration of the camp had been handed over to the German *Dienstgruppen*: – a labour force of ex-soldiers working under British military control: many of the guards were former members of Nazi military units. A banner with the slogan 'With Hitler through thick and thin' greeted all returning prisoners. One former inmate had produced a camp order dated May 1946 which had been issued by an SS *Obersturmführer*. Such reports were grist to the mill of Stalin's claim that the British were maintaining the German Army in existence for sinister purposes. The knee-jerk reaction on the British side to these reports was that they were Soviet-inspired lies. However, the Chief of Staff, HQ BAOR, was forced to admit that there was 'some foundation of truth' in the allegations.

An investigation was ordered by the military authorities. It was established that the staff of British officers were mostly old men and the running of the camp was indeed left to unsupervised members of the *Dienstgruppen*. None of these had been screened by Intelligence. The inspection further revealed that in one section there had originally been no bedding at all: men were sleeping on straw on the ground. There was one washroom per 500 men, without soap or towels. At the time of the inspection even this facility was frozen up completely and men were washing in the snow. For thousands of men in another section, washing facilities consisted of a trough of running water, also frozen up. There was no light whatever in 90 per cent of the huts. In the sickroom there was one storm lantern. Here, too, corruption by the camp staff meant that the 'hot meal' was a thin gruel. The head of the *Dienstgruppen* in the camp had built himself a house at Cuxhaven with material transported from the camp in British Army transport with permission of a British officer. A sample of prisoners interviewed had never seen a British officer, and the sight of a British NCO was rare.[20]

The report of the investigation, dated 2 April 1947, was sent to the Commander-in-Chief's Political Adviser in Berlin. His main reaction was relief that no accusations had been made, either quadripartitely or from Moscow alone, regarding British employment of unscreened *Dienstgruppen* with Nazi tendencies.

Other investigations followed. In view of the conditions in the camps and the frequent visits of Members of Parliament to the zone, questions might be asked and, if so, 'we [the British occupation authorities and the British government] are vulnerable'.[21] One MP commented that it was the British staff who really needed screening, not the Germans.

The whole question of prisoners of war was causing considerable disquiet in Britain. The presence two years after the end of the war of so many hundreds of thousands of men still in captivity was attracting hostile reactions. A Foreign Office brief for the British delegation to the Council of Foreign Ministers meeting in Moscow in March 1947 noted the 'immense rising uneasiness in British public and press about keeping POW here so long after the conclusion of hostilities'. There were many Parliamentary Questions being put. 'Public opinion was now difficult, even dangerous, to ignore.'[22] Most of the 300,000 prisoners in Britain were engaged on agricultural work (although Oliver Harvey MP complained about German prisoners 'hanging about the parks of London where they do nothing but arouse undeserved sympathy').[23]

But the anxiety in Whitehall to maintain the level of prisoners in Britain is revealed in Foreign Office exchanges in this same month of March 1947. The Control Office for Germany happened to put forward an unexceptional Bill which would provide for British subjects sentenced by Military Government courts in Germany to serve their sentence in the United Kingdom. The Foreign Office Legal Department immediately scented the danger inherent in any probing of legal matters relating to Occupied Germany. This would inevitably reopen that awkward question about the existence of a state of war which had already clouded the brows of the law lords. Beckett of the Foreign Office warned that 'there are various Members on both sides of the House who are trying to catch the Government out in supposed legal inconsistencies, because they want to establish that we are not at war with Germany in order to say that we cannot continue to keep German POW any longer'. His Majesty's Government was saying at one and the same time that Britain was technically at war with Germany and yet that the government of Germany was in fact the four Allied Commanders-in-Chief in Council. The Attorney-General and the Lord Chancellor, wrote Beckett, should be prepared in their respective Houses to dispute this alleged incompatibility. If they were not so prepared, the Bill must be withdrawn. It did not weigh in importance with the issues which would arise if, as a result of the debates, 'Government representatives had to admit that we were not technically at war with Germany; that various things, e.g. detention of POW, which were being done on the faith that we were, were being wrongly done. And that the Foreign Secretary's Certificate was wrong.'[24] The Bill was dropped by Cabinet the following day.

Two years after the end of the war, the British alone were still holding just under half a million German prisoners, including thousands in the Middle East. In the brief for the Moscow conference already referred to, Foreign Office advisers urged the Foreign Secretary not to 'advocate, defend or agree to any definite proposals for repatriation which go beyond our present programme, based on economic grounds of considerable importance to this country'. Nor should he display 'any signs of being ashamed of our own policy'. The Foreign Office admitted, however, that 'the impression in the public mind is that there is something not quite right about keeping so many POW away from their own country so long after hostilities. We are morally bound to observe the spirit of the Geneva Convention as stated in the House of Commons.' This meant undoubtedly that prisoners of war should be repatriated.[25]

The prisoner-of-war question was finally resolved by the Council of Foreign Ministers. It was stipulated that all prisoners of war must be returned to Germany by 31 December 1948. They must go home and be formally discharged. Afterwards they should be allowed the same facilities to return to Britain as members of the European Volunteer Workers scheme such as the Poles, with proper contracts of employment.

The withholding for so long of so many men from their homeland and families was to have a fearful effect on the social fabric of Germany during the first post-war years. In addition to those who had been killed in the fighting, hundreds of thousands more were held indefinitely in Russia, many of whom would never return. This distortion of society coupled with the conditions of severe deprivation – particularly hunger – was to bring about a moral crisis among the British serving in Germany which eventually had to be dealt with at the highest level.

Now, with defeat declared and sovereignty assumed, the Western Allies, who had set their sights so undeviatingly on unconditional surrender to the exclusion of any other options, had got what they wanted – but also, as they were to discover, rather more than they had bargained for. Victory was not to be the end of anything except the fighting.

2
Year Zero

THE NINETEENTH-CENTURY historian Lord Macaulay once con-
jured up a vision of a future time when some traveller from New
Zealand should, in the midst of a vast solitude, take his stand on
a broken arch of London Bridge to sketch the ruins of St Paul's.
A comparable vision, for the inhabitants of Germany, became a
reality in 1945. The poet Stephen Spender, who travelled
through Germany on an official mission immediately after the
capitulation, wrote, 'In the destroyed German towns one often
feels haunted by the ghost of a tremendous noise. It is impossible not to imagine the rocking explosions, the hammering of
the sky upon the earth, which must have caused all this.'[1] The
Allies had indeed created a desert and called it peace. Early in
1945 Lord Cherwell, Paymaster-General and Churchill's special
adviser, had put forward to the War Cabinet his own ideas about
what should be done with Germany after surrender. The Foreign
Office had responded acidly, 'The paper says nothing about the
difficulties of administering a desert traversed by swarms of
unemployed nomads. This is not of course Lord Cherwell's
responsibility but it will at some time become that of the Foreign
Office.'[2] That time was about to come.

The Germans, their country no longer a battlefield, emerged
from the ruins. One observer perceived a new race of troglodytes
inhabiting Europe from Aachen to the Volga. Thousands upon
thousands were living in cellars. Over the piles of rubble to
which the towns had been reduced, over the wrecked bridges and
blocked waterways, the tangle of twisted metal which had been a
railway system, swarmed millions of human beings. While it was
still possible, hundreds of thousands of refugees had already fled
westward in the face of the Soviet advance. Hordes of foreign

slave labourers, freed from the years of terrible captivity, took to the roads – those from the West to find their way home; those from the East unwilling to return there. Within a few days of the surrender an intelligence officer reported to SHAEF – Supreme Headquarters Allied Expeditionary Force – 'The sheer number of foreign workers and their apparently uncontrolled movement along every highway and byway of Germany is staggering to the eye.'[3] There were parents and children hunting for each other; former Nazis seeking to submerge themselves in places where they would not be recognized; criminals and bandits; refugees looking for shelter, for work, for food.

The correspondent of *The Times* wrote that perhaps the most striking spectacle of all along the roads was the German prisoner-of-war camps, 'like vast old-time armies in bivouac, stretching often over square miles of country, with the smoke of a myriad camp fires rising from them'. Millions of *Wehrmacht* troops – passive prisoners at the end of their tether – waited in their cages until they should be discharged to swell the human tides. In the chaos of displacement of civilian life caused by the bombing, people began to search for one other, not knowing who was alive and who was dead. A message on a doorpost or on a pile of bricks where once there had been a home indicated where surviving occupants could be found – often many miles away. Sometimes these scraps were gathered together on a board where discharged members of the *Wehrmacht* returning to what had been their home town would search for information.

The first detachments of Military Government, going about their business in the uncharted seas of rubble, had to pick out landmarks for themselves: a still-standing church steeple, perhaps, or a distinctive mound of masonry. Patrols had to keep to the middle of the road to avoid the hazard of falling masonry, which often came down without warning, dislodged by the vibration of feet marching in step. At 10.30 at night the curfew would sound – the awful crescendo of the air-raid siren. Silence would fall on the ghostly cities of dreadful night.

When the British entered Germany they came into a land

which had been sophisticated, modern, developed, much like their own but which was now utterly deprived of virtually every private necessity and public amenity. In the devastated cities, deprivation was almost primordial. It was as if the accustomed paraphernalia of modern life had never been invented. There were none of the things usually taken for granted – not even the time of day: there were no functioning public clocks. Water supply was a standpipe in the ruins for a few hours a day and any sort of container that could hold liquid. There were no knives and forks, pots and pans, pins and needles, darning wool or sewing cotton, scissors, shoelaces, soap, or household medicines. (A year later the allocation of sewing cotton was one reel per family every fourteen months.)[4] The lack of household goods and the endless search for their replacement were a source of exhaustion and exasperation. Germany became a nation of rag-and-bone men. It was commonplace on the streets to see people pulling small trailers, cobbled together out of scrap wood and ready to accommodate any lucky find or acquisition. Everyone, even the children, seemed to carry either a rucksack or a briefcase. Only by scavenging was there any possibility of repair or renewal. The Germans called this 'Year Zero'.

The policy of launching the bombing campaign on civilians in the towns, in order to destroy morale, rather than on primarily industrial targets had been strongly advocated by Political Warfare Department as being more effective for the prosecution of the war. It was a policy of which Air Vice-Marshal Arthur Harris, as head of Bomber Command, was to become the enthusiastic executant. But in a paper in 1941 the department stressed, 'So long as we maintain the fiction that we bomb exclusively military targets, it is impossible to enhance by propaganda the excellent effect on civilian morale of our raids.'[5] A number of relatively small towns of 100,000–200,000 inhabitants were to be singled out for special treatment. 'In bombing these towns attention should be concentrated on working class houses . . .' A comment on this memorandum sounded a note of caution: 'Although HMG have accepted the principle of bombing civilians for morale effect, it is probably still wise to pretend to the world that it is military or economic targets we are really attacking.'[6] By the winter of 1942 the department was still pressing for attacks to be concentrated on 'short-term morale targets'.[7] Morale in Germany, however, seemed to be holding up pretty well. A month after D-Day the problem was still occupying the attention of the Joint Chiefs of Staff. Daylight bombing by the Americans could destroy five small towns of 20,000 inhabitants in one operation, probably totalling thirty a month.[8] But the Air Staff deplored the fact that 'even 100 towns of 20,000 would contain only 3% of the population'.[9] By the last year of the war, ambitions had been revised upwards and the major cities of Germany were being obliterated.

A 'Strategic Bombing Survey' was set up by President Roosevelt in November 1944. Its remit was to determine the direct and indirect effect of bombing upon the attitudes, behaviour and health of the German civilian population with particular reference to the capacity of the people to give effective support to the war effort. The operation was manned by 350 officers, 500 GIs and 300 civilians (the economists J.K. Galbraith, Fritz Schumacher and Nicholas Kaldor were members of the team). They operated from a headquarters in London until the Allies entered Germany, when a forward HQ followed behind the advancing armies. They amassed quantities of statistical and technical material, including German government documents. Thousands of Germans were interrogated, including virtually all surviving political and military leaders.

An image of Armageddon flickers through dry statistics.[10] The most heavily populated areas lay in what was now the British Zone. Hamburg was the second largest city, in terms of population, after Berlin. Between 24 and 29 July 1943 it had been the target of five heavy area raids by the RAF. The nights of the 23rd and 24th became known to the inhabitants as 'the Catastrophe'. In those two summer nights 43,000 were killed and 37,000 were injured. A column of hot air rose two and a half miles high above the city from a base of a mile and a half in diameter.

The fire storm caused a vacuum which collapsed buildings: 56 million square feet of dwellings were destroyed; 750,000 people became homeless. Also destroyed were seventy-five churches; seventeen hospitals; ninety-seven schools; twenty-seven cultural premises (archives, museums, libraries). It was, in Air Vice-Marshal Harris's own words, a scene of unimaginable devastation. The raid of 27/28 July was directed against the densely built-up, thickly populated, residential and small-factory area of East Hamburg. As a result, there were 41,800 known dead.[11]

In Wuppertal during that same summer of 1943 153,000 homes were lost. The fire burned for forty-eight hours before cooling off. In Krefeld 171,000 were killed, 40 per cent of homes were destroyed, and 72,600 were made homeless. In Darmstadt the enormous fire was beyond human control and the wind of the conflagration was felt four miles away; 85 per cent of Cologne was destroyed and 80–90 per cent of Hanover.[12] (In 1945 a British Military Government housing officer reported, 'Cologne proved to be one of the most interesting places you could wish to see if you want to see bomb damage to houses at its best.')[13] In Krefeld 41 per cent of houses were destroyed and 91,000 were made homeless. Attacks in the Ruhr took place with such frequency that there seemed to be little time to do anything else but run from home to air-raid shelter and back again. According to a housewife in Duisburg, there was no time to wash the children or to eat.

The pattern of the area raids was that high-explosive bombs were dropped first, which drove people into their shelters. These were followed by incendiary bombs, When people emerged to fight the fires, more high explosives were dropped, people fled again to the cellars, and the fire could rage unchecked. The most successful incendiaries in these raids were the thirty-pound bombs, which contained phosphorus and could not be put out by water. Everyone, including the fire guards, was afraid to go near them. Fire passed from one burning human being to another if they touched. In Hamburg those who leaped into the canals found the inextinguishable fire floating on the surface. A great vacuum was caused in which balls of fire hurtled through the streets, scattering burning debris and sparks which spread the conflagration. Flames were sucked into the cellars and burned the occupants. In more merciful instances, carbon monoxide seeped in and asphyxiated them.[14]

The total number of lives lost in Hamburg would never be accurately known. The Strategic Bombing Survey estimated 100,000; the municipal authorities 150,000. In the United Kingdom, deaths of civilians due to the operations of war from 1939 to 1945 were registered as 100,927.[15]

To put in perspective, the effect of five days' bombing on *one* German city, Hamburg: 6,200 acres were destroyed compared with London's 600 acres and Coventry's 100 acres. One of the city fathers of Düsseldorf, Dr Walter Hensel, returning from his prisoner-of-war camp, at first sight could only think that his home town would have to be abandoned and rebuilt on a different site. The rebuilding of cities was considered by the Allies to be a task of such magnitude that it could be regarded only as a long-term policy extending, at a minimum, to fifty years.

The SHAEF intelligence officer previously quoted had reported, 'There are very few cities in which the three main utilities – gas, water and electricity – are still functioning. In *no* city visited were all three functioning everywhere at the same time.'[16] People were crammed into every available area of living space – a cellar still accessible beneath the rubble, or perhaps a room left suspended in a teetering ruin and reached by ladder, offering the shelter of at least three walls and a ceiling. Thousands lived in the windowless 'bunkers' – the massive concrete air-raid shelters, warrens of concrete passages without heating, their ventilation systems no longer functioning. The publisher Victor Gollancz, who chronicled in relentless detail the horrors of living conditions in the British Zone, wrote of 'a solid and continuous wall of congealed bad breath'.

The Political Adviser to the Commander-in-Chief, Christopher Steel, wrote to the Prime Minister that he foresaw some kind of explosion: 'The German population cannot be expected to continue much longer under the terrible conditions in which they are now living.'[18] There had in fact been an explosion of a kind – a population explosion. The Allies had accepted that German minorities in countries which had been the victims of Nazi aggression would assuredly be expelled when the war ended. In June 1944 the Cabinet Armistice and Post-War Committee recommended that 'transfer of population would have to be spread over a minimum period of five years' and should not begin 'less than a year from the termination of hostilities'. The problem of resettlement in Germany would be considerably eased, continued the Committee, if, at the period when transfers were taking place, some millions of active Germans 'should happen to be engaged' as organized labour in devastated areas outside Germany – for example, the USSR.[19]

On 27 July 1946 J. B. Hynd – as Chancellor of the Duchy of Lancaster the man responsible for the British Zone – wrote a memorandum for the Cabinet. The governments of the states in the East had in fact begun to eject the German populations immediately after the surrender in a headlong and disorderly manner 'without any apparent regard to humanitarian considerations'. (Richard Stokes MP described it in the House as 'sending millions of people across Europe like a creeping Belsen'.[20]) To date, wrote Hynd, 1.5 million from Poland and over 1 million from other zones of Germany had arrived in the British Zone, adding to the 350,000 displaced persons already there. Apart from accommodation, there were also great difficulties in resettling these refugees, as they brought very little with them and few consumer goods were available in the zone. Meanwhile, concluded Hynd, 'the British Zone is gradually reaching a condition of over-crowding such as has never been experienced before in a community so predominantly urban and industrial, but where industry is practically at a standstill'.[21]

The prospect of too many Germans – and not merely in the British Zone of Occupation – had already been a matter for discussion during the war. In 1943 a forecast of the future population of Germany had been drawn up by Research Department of the Foreign Office. If certain assumptions of fertility rates were accepted, there would be half the number of births in 1979 as in 1944, 'which would mean the end of Germany as an aggressive and expansive military power'. Even so, minuted O'Neill of German Department:

> There are still going to be too many Germans in the world as this century draws to its close . . . I think we can agree that it will be in the interests of this country if the German birth-rate declines . . . I hope it will not seem too shocking if I suggest that we might consider whether there are any means at our disposal for assisting the decline of the German birth-rate after the war . . .

Colleagues in German Department contributed their thoughts:

> At first sight I feel it is a kind of thing the Russians might tackle more effectively than ourselves . . . It looks as though we ought to encourage the Russians and others to import as reconstruction workers as many Germans, including women, as possible for as long as possible . . .

O'Neill offered more specific solutions: repeal existing German family legislation and take steps to see that adequate supplies of contraceptives were available at the earliest stage after the war.

> I am well aware of the danger of recommendations such as these – namely, that if the Germans become aware we are deliberately seeking to depress their birth-rate, they will probably breed all the more to spite us. Because it would at once reveal our intentions, we could probably never afford to press for another measure which might contribute to the desired result – the legislation of abortion in Germany.[22]

But, when the time came, the British were to have other things to think about than social engineering.

When Field Marshal Montgomery was appointed Military Governor and Commander-in-Chief of the British Zone in May 1945, he had under his control 2 million soldiers awaiting discharge and some 20 million civilians. He was in his element. He announced himself to his people:

> I have been appointed by the British Government to command and control the area occupied by the British Army. My immediate object is to establish a simple and orderly life for the whole community. The first step will be to see that the population has (a) food, (b) housing, (c) freedom from disease. All this will mean much hard work for everyone. The population will be told what to do. I shall expect it to be done willingly and efficiently.

It seemed so straightforward, that 'first step'. But for the next few years all steps would seem to lead backwards.

A most immediate and pressing problem for Montgomery was the hordes of 'DPs' – displaced persons, the former slave labourers – at large in the zone. Throughout the summer Russians and Poles with little means of reaching home, and many not wanting to go, roamed the countryside in marauding gangs murdering, raping and pillaging, driven by hunger and by vengeance. The Army could not be everywhere at once, and the British were losing prestige through their apparent inability to keep order. In August the Commander-in-Chief wrote to the Foreign Secretary that what he was dealing with was organized terrorism. He had given instructions for drastic measures, including shooting at sight of offenders caught in the act. Other thorns in Montgomery's side were the contingents of Belgian and Dutch troops who had no Military Government responsibilities. Their discipline was bad, he complained: officers and men considered looting and taking goods across their respective frontiers quite permissible.[23]

In December 1944, in a paper entitled 'Some Considerations concerning SHAEF policy towards the German Civil Population',

Richard Crossman of Political Warfare Department had set out the policy which the British wished to see enforced on defeated Germany. This stipulated that the troops were to 'regard all Germans as potentially dangerous, as sharing in guilt, as a people apart'. Instead of being careful in their contacts with Germans, British troops were to have no such contacts at all. Crossman expressed his own opinion that having no communication with a 'guilty' nation would lead to lapses of behaviour and lack of respect for other human beings.[24] Attlee, the then Deputy Prime Minister, shared this unease. In a Cabinet memorandum he wrote, 'The policy is right, but it should not in my view be interpreted to enjoin the treatment of all Germans as sub-human by occupying troops and the exhibition by them of behaviour indistinguishable from that of the Nazis.'[25]

In March 1945, with the Allies poised on the west bank of the Rhine, Montgomery spelt out the policy of non-fraternization to all officers and men of 21st Army Group in a wordy *Letter by the Commander-in-Chief on Non-Fraternisation*. This took the form of a pocket-sized booklet to be carried by each serviceman. The text began at the end of the First World War and brought German history up to date. The core of the message enjoined:

> You must keep clear of Germans – man, woman and child – unless you meet them in the course of duty. You must not walk with them or shake hands or visit their homes. You must not play games with them or share any social event with them. In short, you must not fraternise with Germans at all.

The Germans themselves were bewildered. After defeat and surrender they had expected harshness but not this wall of silence. Montgomery, at his most headmasterly, explained to the population:

> You have wondered, no doubt, why our soldiers do not smile when you wave your hands, or say 'Good Morning' in the

streets, or play with the children. It is because our soldiers
are obeying orders. You do not like it. Nor do our soldiers. We
are a naturally friendly and forgiving people. But the orders
were necessary and I will tell you why.

He then proceeded to take his German readers back to 1914 and
forward to the present situation. 'This we have ordered, this we
have done, to save the world from another war . . . You are to read
this to your children . . . Tell them why it is that the British soldier does not smile.'[26]

Eisenhower, however, was against this aspect of policy from
the start. How were we to influence the Germans, he asked, if we
could not talk to little children? In the first weeks of the Occupation he prevailed upon the US government to relax the rules
to exclude children. Montgomery pressed the British War Minister, Sir James Grigg, to make a similar concession for children
under eight years old, in order that British forces should come
into line with the Americans, but without success. Soldiers could
be, and indeed were, put on a charge for 'permitting children to
climb on Army vehicles or congregate round military premises'.
At last, on 12 June, Montgomery was empowered to issue a brief
amendment to his previous order: 'Members of the British
Forces in Germany will be allowed to speak to, and play with,
little children.'

That same month, in a briefing note for the British delegation at the following month's Potsdam Conference, Montgomery stressed that non-fraternization was becoming a
boomerang. The British could not expect a contented zone if
they maintained the present aloof and negative attitude. They
could not know what was really going on unless they had real
contact with the people. The Germans should not be forbidden
to hold meetings in towns and villages to discuss anything they
liked – they could always be monitored for Nazi talk. The Germans must be given information and hope.[27] They had, wrote
Montgomery, no mental targets to focus on. 'They merely know
we do not like them and will soon begin to suspect that we do not

ourselves know what to do with them.'[28] (In 1944, Anthony Eden's private secretary, Oliver Harvey, had entered in his diary, on the historic date of 11 November, that 'neither AE nor the PM have yet given serious thought even to the future of Germany. Bad enough in the PM but worse in the Foreign Secretary.'[29])

On 6 July Churchill, unhappy with the operation of the non-fraternization policy, informed the Cabinet that he had that day sent a message to the Commander-in-Chief, Field Marshal Montgomery, inviting his comments. Montgomery replied to the Prime Minister by return. He had himself, he wrote, been urging relaxation of the policy, although with little success. It had taken him some time to get War Offfice approval for lifting the ban on little children, even after the Americans had done so. British and American troops had been living side by side in many towns. The American had been allowed to talk to the children: the British soldiers would have been arrested if they attempted to do so. The whole situation, concluded Montgomery, was absurd and very awkward: 'The Allies crossed the Rhine on 23rd March and for four months we have not spoken to Germans, except on duty.'[30] Churchill reported Montgomery's views to the Cabinet. By a Cabinet decision of 9 July 1945 it was rather grudgingly agreed that there should be a relaxation of the strict policy, so long as it was 'gradual' and did not directly encourage fraternization.[31]

On 14 July Montgomery was able to issue yet another amendment to his troops (who were now assembling quite a collection of these *Letters*): 'You may now engage in conversation with adult Germans in the streets and in public places', although German homes were out of bounds.[32] On 25 September Montgomery issued his final *Letter*: all non-fraternization orders were cancelled by the Allied Control Council, except for marriage with Germans or the billeting of troops in German homes.

A glimpse of the attitudes which non-fraternization engendered emerges from an order issued as late as October 1946 by the then Commander-in-Chief, Major-General Brian Robertson. The original order that 'male Germans will always give right of way to British personnel; if necessary, the latter will elbow them out of the way' must now be revised. Henceforward: 'The forcing of German males off the pavement will not be resorted to except when Germans are deliberately obstructing normal passage.'[33]

The lifting of the ban did not please everyone. Troutbeck of the Foreign Office was unhappy at the thought of British and German jockeys riding alongside each other and deplored the idea of Occupation troops and Germans going to the same race meetings and betting on the same tote. The Services opposed it from a rather loftier standpoint. His Majesty's Government was still in a state of war with Germany and it did not seem becoming that His Majesty's officers and officials should fraternize indiscriminately with His Majesty's enemies.[34] As will be seen, among senior ranks – and particularly their wives – an attitude of non-fraternization was to persist against which even official policy was scarcely able to prevail.

The puritanical policy of non-fraternization was maintained only by the British and Americans. The long-sighted Soviets were playing their own game, which did not involve alienating the natives. Churchill summed it up when the implications of the policy came home to him: 'We are dignified and insulting. The Russians are boon companions and enslavers. I never realised such follies were being committed.'[35]

In November 1945 the Foreign Office set out starkly the principles governing the Occupation of Germany: 'The primary purpose of the Occupation is destructive and preventive and our measures of destruction and prevention are only limited by consideration for (1) the security and well-being of the forces of Occupation, (2) prevention of unrest among the German people, (3) broad considerations of humanity.' It was not exactly a clarion call to rally the crusading Britons who were coming to set Germany to rights.

3
'Charlie Chaplin's Grenadiers'

IN THE planning during the war it had been assumed that the task of Occupation would be to restore as normal conditions as possible to a defeated Germany. The training given to Military Government officers was to be no different from that given to those taking over liberated territories. The attitude would be that of armies forcibly releasing a people from subjection and not simply conquering it. But in the autumn of 1944 that policy had been violently transformed. Military Government was told that apart from the narrowest military requirements, nothing should be done to assist the Germans. Germany was not to be kept as a 'going concern'. The German people must fend for themselves as best they could.[1] However, this piece of policy-making was soon to be submerged in the realities of a devastated Germany.

As the Allies fought their way across the Reich, General Eisenhower ordered that no community should be left without Allied Occupation. The head of Political Warfare Division, SHAEF, after a reconnaissance through Germany in April 1945, reported that 'in many small communities Allied authority is represented only by a bewildered unit of tactical troops; doing nothing because they have neither training nor mandate – just holding on until competent authority arrives'.[2] The Military Government units which relieved them consisted largely of army officers unfit for active service or retired. While the war lasted, the best abilities of the Army were otherwise engaged. The training of these Military Government units in Britain had been devoted as much – or more – to army organization and weapon training as to the nature of the situation which they would face in Germany. Much of the indoctrination relied on the experience of the 'AMGOT' (Allied Military Government of Occupied Territories) teams in Italy, where the situation was very different, and, even more irrelevantly, on conditions at the end of the First World War.

As more territory fell into Allied hands, so more units were needed. A Foreign Office memorandum recorded, 'Officers had to be pressed into service for Mil. Gov. without any previous training or qualifications other than availability and an hour's orientation on the aims of military government.'[3] Nevertheless, many of these Military Government detachments, faced with unimagined chaos and devastation, performed heroically, working round the clock to organize food and shelter for their prostrate enemies.

A German who was a child at the time remembered his town being taken by the British. The first troops to enter had been Highlanders, and the impression on the small child was that all British soldiers were six foot tall and had red hair. An incredible number of people jammed the small town, which lacked resources and accommodation. There were several distinct categories: the local population; refugees from the East who just ended up there, having run out of money or having been halted by the British; former members of the *Wehrmacht*; former Allied prisoners of war; and British troops.

The atmosphere of an enemy-occupied country was captured by a writer who had known Germany before the war and had returned to serve in the Occupation. The Germans reminded him of army recruits who know that whatever they do will be wrong. If they were cooperative, both occupiers and occupied might sneer at them as collaborators. If they were uncooperative the occupiers' worst impressions would be confirmed. The solution was to be as unobtrusive as possible: 'They were a people walking about on tiptoe.' It was not possible to know which of the intruders had real power, so it was as well to be deferential to all. Any member of the Occupation forces might carry an arrest order or – a real disaster – a requisitioning notice to turn a family out of its home. Some people, the writer found, were inclined to salute anybody in a foreign uniform or even any civilian who was not speaking German or was speaking it badly.[4]

It was the duty of every town major to confirm or reappoint the burgomaster and to select civic officials to carry out the administration. Instructions were that such men must have a 'clean' record as non-Nazis. It was a formidable task for British officers pitchforked into a strange and alien community without intimate knowledge of the unique situation. There was guidance available in some quarters, however. The US Strategic Bombing Survey found 'hardly any German city which failed to reveal evidence of the existence of one or more [opposition] groups, varying in size, political tendency, courage and scale'.[5] The report by the SHAEF intelligence officer already quoted echoed this: 'There are in nearly every city some groups of genuinely anti-Nazi Germans who can be of enormous value to the Occupying authority. Where used, they have been of great value as informants and advisers.'[6] But at headquarters in London they knew better than intelligence officers in the field: non-Nazis, it was asserted, were also likely to be dangerous.

The resistance of the British Establishment to the idea of enlisting the help of anti-Nazis was illustrated by the experience of Christabel Bielenberg. An Englishwoman married to a German, she had lived in Germany since before the war. Her husband (who had been imprisoned in a concentration camp at the time of the 1944 July Plot against Hitler) and many of their friends were members of the anti-Nazi opposition. Arriving in England with her children at the end of the war, she approached a friend, David Astor, editor of the *Observer*, with an offer of help for those who were to shoulder the formidable task of running Germany. He organized a luncheon to which were invited senior members of the Control Commission and of the Army, some MPs and various newspaper editors. Aware of the problems for the British of separating the sheep from the goats, it was Mrs Bielenberg's idea to put them in touch with a nucleus of members of the opposition who were still surviving after the purges which had followed the attempt on Hitler's life. They in turn would guide the British on to a further half-a-dozen trustworthy people and so on, working, as the opposition itself had done, in cells. Eventually there would be a large network of reliable people who could be trusted and who would cooperate. Alas, she made no impact on her audience. She felt that she was dealing with children: they seemed to have no idea of what they were up against. Her suggestion was not taken up.[7]

The rejection of such an offer was unfortunate. Because they were all automatically suspect, German civilians were not accepted as partners by Military Government officers struggling with the colossal problems which needed to be tackled together. They were kept at arm's length. This was the sort of attitude experienced by Walter Hensel, a leading city official in Düsseldorf (appointed, of course, by the British authorities).[8] When he and the burgomaster went to call upon the city commander, they always had to stand three steps away in front of his desk. They felt, said Hensel, like the burghers of Calais. Naturally, this protocol was followed lower down the scale. Arriving ten minutes late for an appointment after negotiating the hazards of the ruined city, Hensel was told by a young British officer that if he came late next time he would be put in prison. The German riposted that he had spent two years in a Nazi jail and he did not suppose it would be worse with the British. The outcome of this spirited exchange was that the two men ended as friends.

Dr Hensel cast a curious sidelight on German perceptions of the occupiers. Whenever he visited a British officer whom he did not know, he would try to find out from the secretary where the man came from. If he was Scottish, Welsh or Irish he knew he would be easier to get on with.

In the weeks after the surrender, when the country was under solely military control, the exercise of total power when yoked to ignorance or prejudice could have considerable consequences. The dismissal of Konrad Adenauer from his position as Lord Mayor of Cologne is a famous example which later cast a shadow.[9] Adenauer was a leading politician, a towering figure in the Rhineland, who had been Deputy Lord Mayor of Cologne from 1909 to 1917 and then Lord Mayor from 1917 until 1933, when he was dismissed by the Nazis. He was restored to his position by the occupying American army, with whom he had got on well. But in June 1945 the British took over the area and the atmosphere changed.

The following month the Regional Commander of North Rhine Province, Colonel Hamilton, received a letter from a retired general, Sir Charles Fergusson, who had been a Military Government officer in Germany in 1918–19. He claimed to have known Adenauer then, describing him as clever, cunning, dangerous and a born intriguer who hated the British. Hamilton passed on this unsolicited testimonial to Brigadier John Barraclough, the local commander of 714 Military Government Detachment. Barraclough seized upon the unsubstantiated allegations as a chance to be rid of an awkward customer. However, this would be done ostensibly on the grounds of inefficiency: there was to be no mention of political undesirability. A press release stated that Adenauer had been dismissed from the position of lord mayor of Cologne on the grounds that he had 'not been sufficiently energetic in his pursuit of Mil. Gov. policy'. In his letter of dismissal, Barraclough told Adenauer that he was not satisfied with preparations for the coming winter: 'You have not fulfilled these responsibilities to my satisfaction . . . You will leave Cologne as soon as possible . . . You will take no further part in the administration or public life of Cologne or any other part of the North Rhine Province.' The Brigadier concluded, 'If you fail in any respect to observe the instructions contained in this letter you will be brought to trial by the Military Court.'

Adenauer appealed for permission to enter Cologne to escort his wife, who was attending a specialist there for treatment. He also raised the point that since the beginning of the Occupation his opinion on the future organization of Germany had been frequently sought by British, American and French politicians and journalists. Could he in future enter into such conversations? Colonel Hamilton ordered that Adenauer should *not* be allowed to accompany his wife and that no interviews should take place.

But later he wrote to Barraclough that Frau Adenauer was indeed dangerously ill and he had given permission for Adenauer to visit her in Cologne – but only 'on three days a week between stated hours'. The commander next received an enquiry from a leading member of the of the political party of which Adenauer was co-founder: the Christian Democratic Union. If he was *persona non grata* with the occupying power, Adenauer would have to be expelled from the party. Barraclough's testy reply to the chief liaison officer through whom the enquiry came was that this was an implied criticism of his own action: 'It might interest him to know that *no* German is *persona grata* with Mil. Gov.'

The disastrous misjudgement by the local commanders reached the ears of the Political Adviser to the Commander-in-Chief in Berlin, Christopher Steel. Aware of Adenauer's stature and potential importance to the future of democratic Germany, he moved swiftly. The head of Political Branch of Military Government, Lieutenant-Colonel Noel Annan, was dispatched to Adenauer to mend fences. Colonel Hamilton's knuckles were rapped: 'The ban on Dr Adenauer's political activity has now been raised and Dr Adenauer may take part in any regional political activity within or without Köln Regierungsbezirk. Dr Adenauer may now live in or visit Cologne whenever he wishes to do so.'

The action of this one British officer was to have momentous consequences. Relieved by the British edict of the crushing municipal problems of Cologne, Adenauer was free to take the helm of his party and enter the larger world of politics at the most critical period in the history of western Germany. But he was widely believed to have harboured a grudge against the British for some time afterwards.

At the Potsdam Conference it had been agreed that, although the establishment of a central German government was not contemplated for the time being, certain essential central German administrative departments headed by State Secretaries should be set up, covering such areas as finance, transport, communications, foreign trade and industry. Such departments would act under the direction of the four-power Allied Control Council in Berlin. This structure had been largely based on existing German ministries, which it had been taken for granted would still be functioning at the time of surrender.

It was the responsibility of the Allied Control Council to discharge the provisions of the Potsdam Agreement. But France had not been a participant at Potsdam and therefore declared herself not bound to do so. Even a hint of a centralized German government, of which such ministries might be a forerunner, was anathema to the French. France had her own intentions for Germany. So when, in October 1945, concrete proposals for such administrative departments were considered by the Allied Control Council, France vetoed them. (In the telling phrase of an American historian, the French consistently displayed 'the arrogant air of conquerors who had been placed in power by the arms of others'.)[10] The absence of a centralized administrative base meant that the occupiers had to construct their own bureaucracy.

When the machinery of control was established, the various branches of the Commission were perforce located where there were enough buildings standing to accommodate the offices and the personnel. The headquarters of 21st Army Group was settled in the spa town of Bad Oeynhausen in Westphalia, where it had been located when the war ended. It now became Headquarters, British Army of the Rhine, of which Montgomery, now Field Marshal, was Commander-in-Chief. With the Control Commission transferred from the Foreign Office to the War Office on 1 June, it was necessary for the executive to be stationed in as close proximity as possible to the Military Governor, Montgomery. The Commission initially moved its various divisional headquarters into other mostly undamaged (although seriously overcrowded) small towns in the area, mainly Lübbecke, Minden, Herford and Bünde, entailing the geographical separation of its component parts. There was criticism that the siting of the respective headquarters away from the devastated cities obscured the controllers' view of the reality of conditions in Germany. They also lacked the opportunity of meeting leading Germans. Local people viewed with a certain amusement the barbed wire with which the Control Commission nervously fenced its offices and quarters.

In Britain, recruitment for the Control Commission got off to a rather shaky start. In May 1944 the Foreign Office minuted, 'We have not yet really thought out . . . what qualifications the staff ought to have or how they are to be recruited.'[11] The conditions of service offered little inducement to the serious career-seeker. No one, even at government level, had any real idea how long the Occupation would last. As late as 1947 a Foreign Office paper was contemplating the necessity for a Control staff in Germany for not less than twenty years. Yet there were no long-term contracts or security of tenure.

As military demobilization got under way, recruitment became a matter of urgency. There were advertisements in the press and trawls through government departments. 'In the early days there were fewer candidates than vacancies. During that time we got in some of our weaker members,' wrote Sir Brian Robertson years later, with considerable understatement.[12] In its early stages the Control Commission became almost a refuge for the rootless and the insecure. One member summed up the service, rather sweepingly, as the Mecca of the maladjusted. Without doubt it attracted many who found themselves unable to adjust to the climate of peace. These included demobbed servicemen with nowhere to go; officers who were not equipped to match their wartime rank with an equivalent post in 'civvy street'; men whose marriages had broken down during the war; those who had acquired German girlfriends and wanted to stay in Germany; and former temporary civil servants no longer needed for wartime ministries. Faced with the greyness of austere post-war Britain, some servicemen preferred to return to the privileges and spurious status of life among the defeated enemy. For others who had been cooped up at home during the war years there was a prospect of travel and adventure.

The Control Commission was not part of the Civil Service but shared the same administrative structure. However, because of the military nature of the Occupation at the outset, it had to be integrated into a military framework. Every British civilian in Occupied Germany had to have an 'honorary' military rank according to which transport, accommodation and messing were allocated. A former private or corporal might return to Germany with the equivalent rank of warrant officer and the right to claim equivalent privileges. This infuriated the Army. There was even more resentment if a man had spent the war in a civilian job at home. When in due course the Army relinquished all Military Government responsibilities to the civilian Control Commission, the two British presences in the zone were almost as far apart from each other as from the Germans. They had separate clubs, sports and entertainment facilities and leave centres. The Army sneeringly converted the initials 'CCG' – 'Control Commission, Germany' – into 'Charlie Chaplin's Grenadiers' or 'Complete Chaos Guaranteed'. As civilians, many members of the Commission (although not perhaps those at the top) resented the fact that the system of pseudo-military ranks was maintained outside the office, further curtailing their already circumscribed social lives.

Military Government had begun as the responsibility of the Secretary of State for War, but it became clear that this would no longer be appropriate. However, the Foreign Office was reluctant to assume the burden of administering an organization approaching some 50,000 members. It was decided to appoint a junior Minister, with the sinecure office of Chancellor of the Duchy of Lancaster: ultimate ministerial responsibility would continue to rest with the Secretary of State for War. In October 1945 the Control Office for Germany and Austria was set up under J. B. Hynd, a former railwayman who at least had the edge on most of his colleagues in that he knew German, self-taught years earlier as a trade unionist. The choice of a political unknown was perhaps deliberate on the part of the new Labour government, which had come to power while the Potsdam Conference was still sitting.

The new Prime Minister, Clement Attlee, was not well disposed towards the Germans. He once confided in Lord Pakenham (who later succeeded Hynd) that he had always disliked them very much but that he and his wife had once had a nice German maid.[13] But Attlee was influenced, as were so many others, by having been an infantry officer in the trenches of the First World War. And his main preoccupation now was the welfare revolution which he was embarking upon at home. The new Foreign Secretary, Ernest Bevin, had never forgiven the Socialists in Germany for voting for war credits in 1914 and failing to oppose the Kaiser. The writer Terence Prittie was told by General Sir Brian Robertson that Bevin had said of the Germans, 'I try to be fair to them but I 'ates them, really.'[14]

Attlee and Bevin were absentee landlords. The only visit made to British Occupied Germany by the Prime Minister was during the time of the Berlin Airlift in 1948, when he went no further than the airfield – although he was persuaded to meet a few leading Berliners. It had been hoped that the Foreign Secretary would also visit the Airlift, but Bevin claimed he could not find the time and instead sent Herbert Morrison, Lord President of the Council, who stayed for just three days.

Positive antipathy towards the Germans was part of the official instruction of those British – military and civilian – who were to work and live among them. (There was a 'German Personality Research Branch' in the War Office.) An extremely long and deep paper on 'The German Character'[15] was prepared by Brigadier W. E. van Cutsem, a veteran of the First World War, a former War Office intelligence officer and now the Military Member of the Control Commission Selection Board. (It is perhaps worth mentioning that this officer, in a lecture to the Intelligence Corps in November 1941, declared that 'Communism is no longer the danger it was.') The influence of this document upon its readers could only be wholly negative:

The Germans are not divided into good and bad Germans . . . There are only good and bad elements in the German character, the latter of which generally predominate . . .

The Germans stress fanatical will-power, work and sacrifice, and they exalt death rather than life, all of which causes them to become subject to great strain, resulting in those familiar traits of lack of spontaneity, heaviness, morbid introspection, unhappiness and a fatalistic sense of ultimate doom, which in certain conditions culminate in breakdowns and mania and account for the high suicide rate . . .

The sadistic trait is not peculiar to the Nazis; the ordinary German, the husband and father, will derive pleasure in carrying out orders involving the infliction of torture and suffering. Yet in between he will take out the photo of his wife and children and slobber over it . . .

There was unlikely to be an outward show of hatred, but 'that it is there ready to be called forward in all its ferocity and bitterness, that we must never doubt'. After several thousand words – including such enlightening phrases as 'the need to compensate the inner doubt by a search for status and an endeavour to overvaluate self by outward expression' – the reader arrived at a more practical guide entitled 'Some Do's and Dont's':

Do give orders.	*Don't* make requests.
Do be firm.	*Don't* be weak.
Do see orders are carried out promptly and ensure severe punishment if they are not.	*Don't* try and be kind or conciliatory; it will be regarded as weakness.
Do drop immediately and heavily on any attempt to take charge or other forms of insolence.	*Don't* be put off or led into arguments.
Do play your part as a representative of a conquering power and keep the Germans in their place.	*Don't* show any aversion to another war if Germany does not learn her lesson this time.

Do display cold, correct and dignified curtness and aloofness.	*Don't* show hatred; the Germans will be flattered ...
Do use English in your official dealings with the Germans.	*Don't* try to air your knowledge of German.

Van Cutsem's paper was so well received by the authorities that, in spite of paper shortages, it was printed in large quantities. It was ordered that a copy should be given to every officer and NCO and every new member of the Control Commission staff on arrival in Germany. It was also circulated to all military units in Germany. Six months into the Occupation the Intelligence Group of the CCG was still recommending that 'we should continually plug the fact to all our personnel on the Control Commission that the German does not change his nature for a few months or a few years'.[16]

The policy of positively alienating the occupiers from the occupied was hardly likely to encourage in the former a sense of commitment to their task. It was also to have a demoralizing effect on British behaviour as the years went by and conditions in Germany went from bad to worse. The impression that 'anything goes' in respect of the Germans was eventually to bring about a moral crisis in the Occupation.

The bureaucracy of the British staggered even the Germans. Years afterwards, one German official said that he had worked as a German administrator and that was bad enough, but the British were far worse. Another claimed that 'British red tape excelled the German' – everybody felt that: it was not just his own impression. As the Germans were given no responsibility and were not allowed to work without supervision, this meant that every post was duplicated. Members of the CCG themselves complained that British administration was over-organized and too detailed in its supervision of the Germans. German administrative agencies, created as necessary adjuncts of control in some spheres – for example, food distribution – would transmit official British orders to the *Länder*, but before these could be enforced they had to be paralleled by similar orders sent direct to the *Land* through British channels. A poll of German officials revealed them to be 'swamped by British requests, instructions and directives'. Given the very low diet on which they had to subsist, it was almost impossible to cope with the workload.[17]

One of the main difficulties of control was that very few of the British administrators (with the exception of those in Education Branch) had any knowledge of German. The inevitable result was that business had to be conducted through interpreters – too often secretaries chosen as much for their charm as for their efficiency. The Germans called it 'government by interpreter' and resented it. Rightly so, as the dependence, indeed helplessness, of their British controllers allowed these women to wield considerable power and influence both inside and outside office hours, leading inevitably to corruption. Major-General Sir Alec Bishop later recalled how he had handled the problem. It was too much, perhaps, to expect that the British would be liked, but they should at least invoke respect. He took steps to remedy the situation in his own area. Calling his staff together, he insisted that they should set about learning German, as he himself was doing, and that in the meantime it would be wiser to employ as interpreters elderly ladies or, better still perhaps, men.[18]

In July 1946 the Parliamentary Select Committee on Estimates (British Expenditure in Germany) visited the British Zone to assess the running of it and its cost to the taxpayer. Starting in Berlin with General Sir Brian Robertson, the Deputy Military Governor, they toured the zone taking evidence from members of the Control Commission and from German officials. In Hamburg, with its own government, they received the burgomaster, Dr Rudolf Petersen, and leading members of the Senate. Petersen was a distinguished banker and businessman – conservative, English-speaking, with pre-war connections with Britain – and he and his colleagues had been appointed by the British as being politically irreproachable. The Germans' representation to the Committee covered various aspects of the

Occupation, but the question of duplication of work was in the forefront. Their impression was that there was a large number of Control personnel for whom jobs had to be found. These people had taken over a large number of tasks which were either being fulfilled already by the German administration or could easily be discharged by it. A task which the Control Commission took fifteen months to accomplish could be done in three by the Germans themselves. It would be better if the British confined themselves to supervision.[19]

The Select Committee had in fact made its own observations: 'The masses of papers on every desk in every British office one visits leaves one with the impression of harassed officials unable to reach reality through walls of files.'[20] An example of the obsessive 'over-controlling' which kept reality at arm's length can be cited from a paper by Research Department. The banning of whole categories of music might be necessary, and it was recommended that a list should be drawn up to which additions could be made. Constant attention would be required. For instance: 'We have discovered no reference to any special significance attached to "The Merry Widow". Yet Hitler's known penchant for it might suffice in a defeated Germany to invest its playing with a mystical meaning.' Brigadier van Cutsem suggested setting up a working party to monitor developments.[21] This sort of thing was a validation of the German criticism that jobs were being created simply to occupy British personnel.

Bearing in mind that the function of the Select Committee was to assess the efficiency of the Control Commission and to look for possible methods to reduce the cost to the British taxpayer, it is instructive to examine the fate of evidence given to it by German officials on this and other occasions. E. W. Playfair, the Head of Finance, wrote from Control Commission Headquarters in Norfolk House, London, to Sir Percy Mills, of the Economic and Industrial Planning Staff in Berlin, 'It is the Committee's decision what evidence will be published, but in practice they will not publish anything which we wish to suppress.' Sir Brian Robertson agreed with this:

It would be quite improper for publication to be given to any evidence from Germans. It would be damaging to the prestige of our administration if the Germans were led to feel that Parliament should prepare to receive and give publicity to their views of our efficiency. All such evidence is suspect from the very fact that it is German.

The great and the good colluded. The Control Office was allowed a sneak preview of the Select Committee's report: 'most unofficially of course but with the Committee's approval', wrote Playfair to Robertson. 'This was a "black market" transaction and should not be disclosed.' In their draft the Committee had recorded that they had 'taken evidence from Germans' and had quoted the Hamburg administration's complaints about duplication of work. 'These passages have now been changed to a form which we shall not find offensive.' The report was watered down to an unattributed version of the Hamburg senators' complaint: 'The German democrat feels that Germany should be governed by Germans, under control, and that he is the man for the job.'[22]

Although not allowed to govern, even under control, Germans were allowed a limited input. Early in 1946 the British had set up a Zonal Advisory Council, which consisted of the administrative heads of the *Länder* and representatives of the main political parties and of the trade unions. The Council had no executive powers. However, Occupation ordinances and directives could be discussed by the members, although the agenda had to be approved by the British authorities. Troutbeck of the Foreign Office commented sniffily after one session, 'This whole meeting has a slightly academic flavour – a number of leading men are being allowed to play at political democracy. Most of the resolutions are about the appalling material conditions in Germany and the inadequacy of the CCG.' Those present at that particular meeting had included Adenauer, the trade-union leader Hans Böckler, Petersen, and his formidable successor, Max Brauer.[23] But General Robertson considered that the Council fulfilled an important function. He ordered that its opinions should be sought (even if not adopted) and attended many of its meetings himself. At the same period a German Economic Advisory Board was set up. It had been realized early in the Occupation that the restarting of the German economy would be beyond the capability of the British alone.

At the close of 1946 the total number of British Control Commission personnel was 24,785; their American opposite numbers totalled 5,008. General Gerald Templer, Chief of Staff to the Military Governor, suggested an explanation of the enormous discrepancy: 'The Americans have mastered the art of Indirect Control. It is evident that we have not. Direct Control with a backward race is feasible and probably the only means to rule. This principle does not and cannot apply to a race which has attained the standard of education and scientific development of the Germans.'[24] But not everyone grasped this principle. A member of Political Branch noted that some of his colleagues in Military Government did indeed seem to assume the role of colonial officers in a rather forward-looking Bedouin country.

Certainly there was an influx into the Commission of those dispossessed colonial officers for whom a waning Empire no longer had any need. A former British administrator from Nigeria who arrived to take charge of one branch requested a list of staff under the headings 'European and non-European'. It was an aspect of British control of which the Germans were aware, and it was much resented. The leader of the Sozialdemokratische Partei Deutschlands (SPD), Kurt Schumacher, said that the only thing he regretted about India getting her independence was that the Indian Civil Service would now turn up in Germany – which to some extent did happen. Richard Crossman made the same point in the House of Commons: 'Is it really considered that we should treat the Germans as we have treated Indians in the past, as a colonial people? . . . I sometimes wonder whether some Honourable Members regard them as potential native troops for fighting somewhere or other.'[25]

Some ex-colonials were appointed Kreis Resident Officers,

which approximated to their former employment as District Officers. Other KROs were often retired senior army officers. As Military Government officers they had almost unlimited powers, although these later became only consultative and advisory. Some, in country areas, lived like eighteenth-century squires, with plenty of hunting and shooting and an almost feudal relationship with the local people. One KRO in an agricultural area forbade a May Day celebration because he considered it a socialist affair: there was quite enough of that sort of thing going on in England, and he was not going to have it in his area. Another greeted a newcomer to his staff with 'Not much shooting, I'm afraid.' The new man was more interested in political activity. 'There isn't any and don't you dare start it!'

The other side of this coin was a genuine paternalism. Many KROs held – and it was a tenable position – that not only Headquarters in Berlin but Zonal Headquarters as well were quite out of touch with reality. These men had both common sense and compassion. They took on higher authority on behalf of 'their' people and fought doughtily for them in many a fierce memorandum to Headquarters. A former political officer summed up: 'Although it was an awful nuisance to us at a higher level that they [the KROs] were doing what they liked, I find now when I go back to Germany that the people who are remembered best and in the most kindly fashion are just those people who really mixed with the population on the ground and got to see what the problems really were.'[26] A report to the Foreign Secretary in 1949 declared that 'their contribution to the existence of satisfactory social relations between British and Germans cannot be exaggerated'.[27]

On 1 May 1946 there was a major development in the organization of control when the Corps Commanders relinquished all Military Government responsibilities. Areas of control were no longer to be based on the location of military units but on German local-government areas or *Länder*. The Corps Commanders were replaced by four Regional Commissioners. General Sir Gordon Macready (Hanover and Lower Saxony) had been a member of the military mission to Berlin and of the Army Council at Versailles in 1918–19. Air Vice-Marshal H. V. de Crespigny (Schleswig-Holstein), an Australian, had been a distinguished First World War flyer. William Asbury (North Rhine–Westphalia) had been a senior local-government administrator in the Midlands and a Regional Commissioner for civil defence. H. V. (later Sir Vaughan) Berry (Hamburg) was a former merchant banker and member of the wartime Manpower Commission. Berry was undoubtedly the best qualified of the four. He knew Germany well. He had been a student in Germany before the First World War, had fought in the war and had served for six years in Intelligence in the previous Occupation, being a member of the Rhineland Commission from 1919 to 1925. His performance in his post was impressive. Publicly loyal to British policy, when he disagreed with it he challenged the authorities in forthright terms. He was much respected by the Germans for his capability, common sense, compassion and absolute integrity. He had known many of Hamburg's merchant princes before the war but now kept his distance. They in turn were not inclined to be associated with a Labour-government appointee – a socialist. But Berry welcomed students into his house for free discussions.

The new Commissioners arrived in Germany without any serious policy instruction at all. The first time they met each other was on the platform at Victoria station. The only specific instruction was, in Berry's own words, by 'some fool at the Foreign Office', who said that whenever they moved out of their own region they were to wear the Control Commission navy uniform ('like an air-raid warden's'), which Berry refused to do.[28] There is an interesting echo of this in the statement by the American general Lucius Clay. Writing five years after the event, he confessed that he found it amazing that, before leaving Washington to take up the important post of Deputy Military Governor of the US Zone, it had never occurred to him to call on the State Department. Even more amazing, no one had ever suggested that he should.[29]

With control having passed from military commanders to civilian commissioners, attitudes had to change accordingly. Berry, for instance, told his senior officers that of course they could summon a German official to attend at their offices at a specific time whenever they chose, but it would be very much better to agree a convenient time between them. And it would not do any harm if occasionally they went to the German's office instead. But such an enlightened attitude was not universally adopted.

The gross overmanning of the Control Commission and the proven venality of so many of its members increasingly made headlines in the British press and provoked questions in Parliament by Members jealous of Britain's reputation. A new MP, having spent the previous year as a Military Government officer, declared in his maiden speech, 'We have all too many of the wrong people, whose one aim in their life in Germany is to have as good a time as possible and to enrich themselves as much as possible.'[30] One official wrote to Sir Arthur Street, Parliamentary Under-Secretary at the Control Office in London, 'It is my opinion that those who planned the CCG had no idea what they were planning . . . Those inside are concerned with enlarging their staffs and no one outside knows anything of what goes on inside.'[31] An officer wrote to a colleague in another branch, 'We see little of people from high places and it is pathetic how ignorant they are of the work in the field.'[32] A professional in Economics Division explained to a friend at Headquarters why he was resigning:

> The worst features of the CCG are its complicated structure; the incompetence of many senior officers; far too many officers who know nothing about Germany, nothing about economics, little about administration. Because they do not understand the job they choose the wrong assistants. In many cases, disinclination to work, combined with desire to have a good time, breeds indifference to suffering: 'I don't care if the Germans starve.'

His job was very well paid, but he did not want it.[33] Another officer wrote to his MP expressing a similar resolution:

> The CCG was a rude shock to me . . . I had no idea it was really as bad as it is. It seems to me little short of a tragedy that we should be trying to administer Germany and teach the Germans the British way of life with such obviously unsuitable people and in such a very inefficient manner. I feel I cannot stay and keep my self respect.[34]

There were many letters in the press from those who had joined the service from serious motives and were distressed to find themselves in such company. A long and impassioned letter to the *Manchester Guardian* can be taken as representative. The writer had given up what he admitted was a well-paid job as an engineer officer in the Ruhr because, he felt, 'British interests could be better served by criticism and action from without than in remaining in a service which is daily bringing this country into greater discredit.' Large numbers of officers, he maintained, were experts with years of experience in various professions, yet they were employed on routine work which any intelligent clerk could do:

> The organization is so much occupied with administering itself that, at its upper levels at any rate, there is little opportunity or even desire to study the German problem at first hand . . . It is no exaggeration to say that the Commission has become weighed down and top-heavy with high ranking and largely redundant senior officers, many of whom have little or no qualifications for the posts which they hold.

The severest indictment of the Commission, he concluded, was to be found in the fact that increasing numbers of its best men were voluntarily quitting a service with which they had become ashamed to be associated.[35]

The Foreign Office privately endorsed this letter in an internal memorandum. The behaviour of large numbers of CCG officers had undeniably been bad – looting and drunkenness being the chief faults. Certain branches were also undeniably overstaffed. Very well-paid elderly British CCG officials were understandably anxious to hold on to jobs as long as they could, although the need for their services no longer existed. In a final burst of candour the writer concluded, 'The Russians have perhaps been more effective in their control of Germany than we have by having far fewer Mil. Gov. officers . . . who tend to be better and more authoritative than their British opposite numbers. And the Russians have never bothered to import a highly-paid army of retired drain-inspectors, unsuccessful businessmen and idle ex-policemen . . .'[36]

The Prime Minister was seriously concerned. While Bevin was attending the Foreign Ministers' Conference in New York in 1946, he sent him a Personal and Top Secret message:

> I am not happy about our set-up in Germany. There is widespread criticism in many quarters. There is also some misgiving as to the quality of some of the personnel in the Commission. It is admitted that some are first-class but there are, it is said, others whose conduct and quality is not up to standard . . . Montgomery has told me all is not well.[37]

In a Review of Policy produced in August 1946, Field-Marshal Montgomery, as Military Governor, had given some forthright advice. Except in respect of such matters as external trade, demilitarization and the dismantling of war plants, 'the best people to deal with the many difficulties which beset Germany to-day and await her in the future are not ourselves but the Germans. They know far better how to deal with their country's problems and they are not inferior to us either in intelligence or in determination.'[38]

This coincided with the previous advice of the Select Committee on Estimates that the authorities should devolve administrative and executive responsibility upon the Germans 'as fast as they can'. This admonition can hardly be said to have received urgent attention. Over two years later *The Times* reported that what impressed about the British administration was its 'sprawling character': 'We have this over-swollen administration with muddle and fuddle, inefficiency and frustration. First-class men and women were giving their all to make the machine work but there were others out there who could never hold equivalent jobs at home. The whole system surpasses the conception of the lengths to which bureaucracy can go.'[39]

By the following year the problem had still not been resolved. In April 1949 a somewhat anti-German paper on the situation in Germany was prepared for the Foreign Secretary by the Head of Political Division. It was rejected by Sir Brian Robertson, now Military Governor:

> I do not like this dispatch . . . The effect will be to convince men that the Germans are people in whom there is no element of good. The obvious conclusions to draw from this is that we should place no trust in them and should continue to control all their actions as extensively and for as long a time as possible. That is quite contrary to my idea of the correct policy in Germany.[40]

Four years after the end of the war, the argument by members of the Control Commission that the Germans could not be trusted was still current. The feeling had long been mutual.

4
'About as big a mess as it is possible to get into'

IN 1946, Richard Stokes MP put a Parliamentary Question to the Minister for German Affairs, J. B. Hynd. A German youth had been sentenced to death for displaying a picture of Hitler on his birthday. Would the Minister have the sentence quashed? It emerged that the Minister had no authority in the matter: authority was solely in the hands of the Commander-in-Chief. Was it to be understood, asked one Member, 'that people could be sentenced to death by British courts, or British authorities, without anybody in this House being responsible to the House?' In a rather uncomfortable answer, Hynd could only confirm that the Commander-in-Chief had indeed the ultimate power of life and death.[1]

In the early chaotic days after the surrender, when armed bands swarmed through the countryside committing murder and mayhem, the Army perforce often had to dispense summary justice. But in due course military courts were established by the Judge Advocate-General's Department. Such courts had the power to pass death sentences, subject to confirmation by the Commander-in-Chief. In addition to the usual capital offences, theft and the mere possession of any kind of firearm carried the death penalty. In many tragic cases the culprits were East Europeans from displaced-persons camps. Unwilling or unable to return to homelands now fallen into other hands, dehumanized by slave labour, they had survived only to meet their fate at the hands of the liberators.

The extent of the executions posed quite a problem in terms of cost-effectiveness. United Nations nationals – Poles, Russians, Czechs, Yugoslavs – had to be shot by Allied firing squads. The administrative costs of shooting were high. The Army disliked the job, and there had been cases where death was not instantaneous. It was impossible to draw on the intake of young National Servicemen coming out to Germany. Hanging, however, involved even more expense for the British taxpayer. Equipment which did not exist in Germany had to be installed. Albert Pierrepoint, the executioner, could attend only at lengthy intervals, which meant that prisoners were kept under sentence of death for an unacceptable length of time. With the readjustment of the apparatus between executions, it could take seven hours to hang six prisoners in pairs. Penal Branch pressed for the guillotine, already available in Germany, which could carry out six single executions in fourteen minutes. It was quick, certain and required no maintenance. No cost would fall on the British Exchequer. However, Legal Branch decided in 1947 that it was undesirable that a method *not* regarded as suitable for British offenders should be used in the case of those sentenced to death by British courts in a zone administered by the British.[2]

On 20 December 1945 the Allied Control Council in Berlin passed Control Council Law No. 10 specifying Punishment of Persons Guilty of War Crimes, Crimes against Peace and against Humanity. Punishments were to range from death through life imprisonment, hard labour, forfeiture of property and deprivation of civil rights. Control Council Directive No. 38 of 12 October 1946 codified the German nation into Groups of Persons Responsible.[3] These were identified as: (1) major offenders; (2) offenders (activists, militarists and profiteers); (3) lesser offenders; (4) followers; (5) persons exonerated (that is, those in the previous categories who could prove their innocence before a tribunal). The categories were further broken down into forty-eight subgroups, each beginning 'Anyone who . . .' The endeavour to leave no Nazi unturned resulted in some strangely unlegalistic language, indicting anyone who 'poisoned the spirit and soul of youth'; anyone who 'ridiculed, damaged or destroyed values of art or science'; anyone who 'took an attitude of hatred' towards opponents of Nazism at home or abroad; anyone who 'seems to be an offender, without however having manifested despicable or brutal conduct'.

The Potsdam Agreement had also laid down that those who could not be charged with any criminal offence but who were considered 'persons dangerous to the Occupation or its objectives' were to be arrested and *interned*. It was the effect of this catch-all clause which was to create among the Germans the feeling that nothing had changed: that they were still living under the Nazi regime. The object of internment was defined as 'neutralizing the activity of potentially dangerous persons'.[4]

Random sweeps carried out by military commanders in the first months after the capitulation had summarily netted thousands of individuals. In due course the Commander-in-Chief delegated the right of arrest to the Chief of Intelligence. He in turn had warrants issued to civilian intelligence officers, conferring upon them powers of arrest. And arrests became even more indiscriminate. Thousands upon thousands of men – prisoners of war as well as civilians – had been swept up into camps, held without charge or expectation of trial. Regular army officers and *Luftwaffe* pilots and technicians were considered to have expert knowledge which was 'an international menace'. By July 1946 some 66,000 persons were being held in custody. But no instructions had ever been given as to what was to be done with all these people. The Minister, Hynd, told a Cabinet committee that thousands of Germans were being deprived of their liberty without trial and, in most cases, without any charge having been laid against them: 'We are exposing ourselves to the accusation of employing against our opponents in Germany precisely those methods which we have condemned in the Nazis.' He proposed to separate these 'masses of people' into manageable proportions through a system of categorization.[5] But many internees could not even be categorized until, as decreed by Control Council Law No. 10, the Tribunal at Nuremberg had pronounced a verdict as to the criminality of various Nazi organizations.

Category I represented those brought to trial on criminal charges and, if convicted, either sentenced to death or imprisoned for a fixed term. Category II comprised so-called security suspects, both political and military, who would not be brought to trial as they had not committed criminal offences. They would be interned on the grounds that they were 'too dangerous to be at large'. In due course the internees would be dealt with by British review boards consisting of three officers, none of whom was required to be familiar with German affairs. They could be downgraded to Categories III to V, which did not involve internment but imposed various sanctions covering loss of office and civil rights and confiscation of property.

The civilian internment camps (CICs) into which Germans were consigned came under the authority of Headquarters, British Army of the Rhine. The screening process by which the disposal of those arrested was decided took the form initially of an interrogation. A report on the camps by the Bishop of Chichester, George Bell, noted that interrogations were usually carried out by 'European refugees in the British service who have also experienced cruel sufferings, either in person or by their next of kin. In a great many cases they do not even pretend to be impartial.' Interrogations were often brutal. Men who had not yet been found guilty of any thing were, according to the report, 'terribly beaten, kicked and so mishandled that traces could be seen weeks afterwards. The notorious Third Degree methods of using searchlights on victims and exposing them to high temperatures were also applied.'[6]

An MP told the House that 'prisoners' (that is, internees) were beaten unconscious by British officers and NCOs and that this had been confirmed by a British barrister who happened to be in Germany to defend a British guard against a charge of rape.[7] Many were kept in dark cellars to 'prepare them for interrogation'. The concentration-camp system of 'roll-call' was maintained, with men standing outside for hours in all weathers. If they dropped they were left there.[8]

The information elicited during interrogations in the camps was passed to review boards. The accused received a summons containing very often only a couple of words of explanation, such as 'ardent militarist', 'convinced Nazi' or 'dangerous if released'. The notes of the interrogation, which were neither read to the internee nor signed by him, were used as the basis of the review. The prosecutor, in many cases drawn from the same group as the interrogators, presented a case of which the accused had no previous knowledge and which was sometimes inadequately translated. The accused could not procure material for his defence, because he was allowed no contact with the outside world. Theoretically, the suspect was permitted a defence counsel but, as a Member of Parliament who raised the matter was told, the calling of witnesses was 'merely a time-wasting device' and the practice was discontinued. Review boards 'should not be bound by technical rules of evidence' and should apply to the greatest extent 'expeditious and non-technical procedure'.[9] As for internees not being told about the reasons for their categorization, 'it would not be possible to disclose all the information and the source of information on which the decision was based'.[10] There was no appeal against the verdict, and the conviction that judgement was arbitrary created a feeling of desperation among those who appeared before the review boards.

A particularly distressing aspect of this wholesale incarceration was the detention of children. In March, May and December 1946 the German Bishops' Conference petitioned the Allied Control Council on the question of children and young persons being arrested and held without charge, their whereabouts unknown. The petitions were unsuccessful. The number of children and young people in the internment camps ran into thousands and was increasing month by month. The burgomaster of one town reported 400 youngsters taken away, another 200. One small country parish had lost thirteen. It was claimed that the youngsters had been in the possession of arms, but the bishops pointed out that Germany had been a battlefield and rusty weapons were to be found lying about everywhere among the ruins. Some parents only learned from correspondence or from released prisoners that their children were in some particular prison. The bishops were still finding it necessary to press the matter in November 1947 – two and a half years after the end of the war.[11]

In September 1945 the German bishops appealed to the British Cardinal Bernard Griffin, who was visiting Germany, on behalf of the large numbers arrested by methods reminiscent of those of the Gestapo. People quite unconnected with the Nazi Party were being arrested. Many millions of Germans had suffered under the Nazis and opposed them as far as they were able; they were now classed as guilty. The German people were not universally guilty and must not be universally punished.[12] Churchill himself expressed this in Parliament: 'Indescribable crimes have been committed by Germany under Nazi rule. Justice must take its course, The guilty must be punished. But . . . I fall back on the declaration of Edmund Burke: I cannot frame an indictment against an entire people.'[13]

Preparatory to the transfer of supervision of the camps to Penal Branch of the Control Commission in April 1946, the Inspector of Civilian Internment Camps carried out an inspection. A summary of his findings reinforced the bishops' plea. The impression had been gained that in the early days investigations had been conducted with the object of seeing that no suspected person escaped internment. The majority of arrest warrants were found to have been signed by other ranks or not signed at all; yet such a document was the sole authority for holding the internee. Consideration was not being given to the release of individuals arrested on insufficient grounds, numbers of whom were still being held. Boys of sixteen years old had been seen in the camps.[14]

Some months later later the Deputy Military Governor, General Sir Brian Robertson, received a deputation, from British Churches this time, who complained that there were 'large numbers of old and harmless people in these camps who should be freed without delay'. 'I am afraid this is true,' noted Robertson. 'I consider that we should adopt rough and ready methods to clear the camps without delay of the more harmless elements.'[15] Still nothing was done. The Regional Commissioner for North Rhine–Westphalia, William Asbury, claimed that, in spite of the enormous numbers awaiting screening, review boards were averaging only about one case every six weeks. During the parliamentary debate on Germany in July 1946 the Member for Northampton declared, 'If this be our conception of justice to-day, then in a large sense we have lost this war because the principles of the Nazis are the principles which have won.'[16] Oliver Lyttleton, a former wartime Cabinet member, claimed, 'It seems to be a far from happy way of fostering democratic standards in Germany to tear up every provision of Magna Charta and Habeas Corpus.'[17]

Sir Brian Robertson acknowledged to Control Commission Headquarters in London in October 1946 that only a small fraction of the internees had been screened: 'Undoubtedly many thousands would be discharged immediately if their screening were completed. A most unsatisfactory situation and one liable to excite justified criticism.'[18] The members of the Select Committee which had visited Germany in 1946 were of the same opinion. They felt 'compelled to comment forcibly':

> There are now practically 40,000 prisoners confined in internment camps, some of whom have been there for over a year without trial; and this number is increased from time to time, equally without trial and on denunciations. If part of the object of the Occupation is to attract Germans to the British way of life, this is a singular method of setting about it.[19]

Wing Commander Norman Hulbert MP referred in the House to 'the appalling fact' that fifteen months after the cessation of hostilities 'we have 40,000 to 50,000 Germans still in concentration camps. I am afraid that concentration camps is the only right and proper description there is for these institutions.'[20] It is strange to find the phrase being used by the Select Committee on Estimates in a questionnaire to the authorities: 'What are the numbers of persons held in concentration camps?'

The Control Commission did not balk at the designation in replying.[21]

Indeed, the camps often were former concentration camps. Unfortunately, they had kept some of their former usages. To the Gestapo methods of incarceration without charge, trial or expectation of release were added appalling living conditions: near-starvation, ill-treatment and in some cases torture. A conference at HQ BAOR on 7 January 1946 had recorded that 'reports are being received that we are allowing internees to exist under conditions which were little better than those in German concentration camps'.[22] The same month the inspector reporting on the camps noted gross overcrowding: men sleeping on the floor or packed five at a time like sardines on beds constructed from old pieces of wood. Clothes were washed in the ablutions together with food utensils. And the ablutions had no protection from the weather. The majority of inmates were emaciated, with cases of hunger oedema. The death rate among ageing men in poor physical health would be very high and would, if it got out of hand as well it might, 'reproduce some of the more sensational features of the Nazi concentration camps'.[23]

In camp hospitals, operating theatres – where they existed – were without sterilizing or anaesthetic rooms. There was neither hospital bedding nor clothing: patients lay in bed in old clothes. In fact in all camps everyone slept in their clothes.

A nutritional survey carried out by Public Health Branch backed up the inspector's report: 'The non-workers' ration, unassisted, is a starvation one and leads to emaciation and ultimately death.' Inmates were classified as 'undernourished', 'clinically thin', 'emaciated', 'hunger oedema', 'died of starvation'. There was the possibility of 'an unpleasant and sordid scandal'.[24] In the House of Commons a Member demanded that 'the Pathé Gazette cameras' should be sent into the camps 'as they did with the liberated concentration camps'.

Time was not a healer. The following October, a further report by Public Health Branch on No. 7 CIC reported great overcrowding and very dark huts with no windows. There was little surface drainage and an insufficient water supply. The doctors' visit was followed by one by the Regional Commissioner, Asbury. He made his own report. He had found the conditions 'absolutely appalling':

> The number of internees is 9,220. The average space per man does not exceed 23 sq. ft. against an approved capacity of 45 sq. ft. The huts were not watertight. There was no heating. Latrines consist of one bucket per 45–50 men with only a canvas screen against the weather. Fuel deliveries are in arrears by 200 tons. The Army standard of water supply is 15 gallons per man per day. Here it is 25 litres. In 'A' compound there are 13 taps for 2,586 men. Amenities are practically nil. These conditions do not reflect any credit on the Control Commission.[25]

Three months later, in January 1947, the Deputy Military Governor noted, 'Serious alarm is being caused by the present position regarding the supply of essential requirements to maintain health, to prevent internees reaching a state of desperation in which attempts at mass escapes are made.'[26]

In the US Zone the Catholic charity Caritas and the Protestant Innere Mission had been allowed by the Americans to maintain a small office outside each camp with a list of the internees to which people could come in search of relatives or for news of their health. Even washing could be taken in and out on behalf of the inmates. A request by Cardinal Griffin to the military authorities, on behalf of the German bishops, for a similar facility in the British Zone was refused.[27] A year later Countess Bismarck, who with her husband had in 1944 been sent to a concentration camp after the July Plot against Hitler, asked to be allowed to set up a welfare committee for the civilian internment camps. After three months' cogitation the authorities decided that there was 'nothing to be gained by the formation of such a Committee'.[28] The internees would hardly have shared this view. Visits were cruelly short: half an hour every three months. (During the debate on Germany an MP stated that a mother of four had been imprisoned for a year because she had hidden in a ditch to snatch a word with her husband, on a working party from a camp.)[29]

In March 1946 the Commander-in-Chief held a conference about the disposal of those in Category II who were considered 'too infected by the Nazi or militarist disease' to be released into the community for about another ten years. In another twelve months, it was estimated, there would remain a 'hard core' of some 10,000. The disposal of these long-term internees was proposed by the establishment of 'settlements' where they could be joined by their families. These settlements should be situated on islands or peninsulas in the north of Germany, providing maximum security. A figure of 15,000 internees and dependants was envisaged. The native inhabitants would have to be agricultural workers and be 'of the hard-working, confident type, given to minding their own business'. Various of the North Friesian Islands were considered, but the Dutch and the Danes did not welcome such neighbours. The RAF also objected: it was carrying out 'Operation Backfire', learning German technique with long-range rockets by actual launches of rockets from the north-German coast.[30]

The whole 'Alcatraz' scheme was abandoned. Instead, in May 1947, a new establishment was created, on the mainland, near Bremen, known as Adelheide Civilian Internment Settlement. A former prisoner-of-war camp, it was in need of a vast amount of repair and reconstruction on which the inmates were expected to be put to work. They would continue to live behind barbed wire. There would after all be no accommodation for families. In due course wives and children would be allowed to stay for a few days at a time in hostels outside the wire, where the internee could join them.[31]

A population of 3,000 internees was expected at Adelheide. Of the first batch of 473 men consigned to the camp, thirteen were over the age of sixty, 136 were between fifty and sixty. Several had amputated limbs, and some thirty were suffering from chronic diseases of lung, heart, stomach and intestines. A general was transferred from Münsterlager Camp, unlikely to recover from head wounds and a physical and mental wreck.[32] Men arrived at Adelheide from other camps where they had seen bigger fish released through a seemingly random operation of the review boards. Some of the army officers had worked for two years assisting the British with the demobilization of the millions of defeated *Wehrmacht*. Now they were considered a threat to the security of the Occupation: letters of recommendation from high-ranking British officers did them no good. Fifty-six Hitler Youth Leaders – children when the war broke out or too young to vote in 1933 – were also considered too dangerous to be released into the population. As the internees had no income and were not paid for work done in the camp, they could do nothing to provide for their families, many of whom were refugees from the East. About a quarter of the men had been separated from their families for more than eight years. Compassionate leave was granted only when a relative was actually dying. And a man's mother and father were not counted as next of kin if he was married.

It was becoming increasingly obvious that matters could not be allowed to go on as they were. Members of Parliament were becoming more and more concerned about what was being carried out in Germany in the name of the British government. In a debate in the House of Lords on 12 November 1947, Lord Pakenham, who had succeeded J. B. Hynd as Minister for German Affairs, was pressed almost into incoherence by questions from noble lords. He was unable either to defend or adequately to explain the whole sorry business which he himself was doing his best to remedy.

On 12 January 1948 Sir Brian Robertson wrote to the head of the German Section of the Foreign Office on 'The Policy in the British Zone of Germany with regard to Detention without Trial'. Acknowledging that 'our methods had been somewhat rough and ready' in the past, he declared that 'it appears to me that now, almost three years after the end of hostilities, it is increasingly difficult to justify any procedures which are not compatible with the principles and practice of normal British Law'.[33] On 4 May 1948 Robertson reported to the Minister that steps taken had ensured 'a very appreciable hastening of the process of interrogation and review'. By 23 April 'there were no militarists left'. He agreed that 'your suggestion that disabled internees and young persons should have priority treatment is a good one and should have occurred to us before'.[34] So the concept of 'settlements' where people contagious to their fellow citizens would be indefinitely confined collapsed within a year of its inception.

Internees did not exactly walk free. In order to be let out of camp, they had to be downgraded by the review boards from Category II to III. Category III meant being debarred from public office and from voting and exclusion from the teaching, legal, police and journalistic professions and from employment in civil administration. There were also restrictions on residence and movement inside Germany. Persons who showed 'satisfactory evidence of reformation' could be further downgraded to Category IV, with its moderated sanctions, to the final exit through Category V. Categorization on release was provisional, and it was left to German panels to review the case and make a final decision. The internee would be given a form showing provisional categorization and its sanction but, according to Robertson's letter to the Minister, 'there is no indication on it of the specific reason *why* he was interned, but I do not think that this is necessary'.

If the British public were largely unaware of the fact of civilian internment and the manner in which it was conducted, the activities of other – secret – camps actually hit the headlines in the British press. Direct interrogation centres – DICs – had been set up in Germany manned by Intelligence staff transferred from the wartime DIC at Ham Common in Surrey. Administration was in the hands of Intelligence Division of the Control Commission. The main task was to anticipate and prevent the development of subversive movements such as the so-called 'Werewolves' which would threaten the security of the

Occupation. Suspects were picked up and put through interrogation. In fact, not surprisingly given the conditions in Germany, no such movements ever developed. A year after the end of the war there was a 'reorientation of objectives' when it was decided that any serious threat to the security of western Germany would come not from within but from without – from the East.[35] Intelligence-gathering was then directed towards the USSR.

Ex-inmates of DICs, because of their experiences of the interrogation techniques used, were considered to be 'in possession of knowledge which is harmful to the Allies and constitute a dangerous security threat to the Occupying Forces'. Even though 'otherwise unobjectionable', they were transferred to CICs as internees, to be held there indefinitely.[36] A senior official of Public Health Branch reported seeing half a dozen men, sent to No. 7 CIC after a spell at DIC Bad Nenndorf, who were all suffering from gross malnutrition. One was dying, and two were described by a doctor there as suffering from mental confusion. The official was told by doctors and others that the man who was dying had been brought into the camp shackled to another man, although he was already ill. Scars on the legs of two of the cases were said to be the result of the use of some instrument 'to facilitate questioning'.[37]

At the end of 1946, Intelligence Division was told that the practice of disposal into internment camps of prisoners from whom nothing further could be extracted was illegal. It was proposed to get round this difficulty by trying these cases in camera before Military Government courts, where 'a severe sentence should be imposed'. Those convicted could then be sent to prison. This shocking piece of cosmetic legalizing was demolished by Political Branch. It was contrary to the accepted principles of British justice that sentence of any kind should be imposed on people 'whose only crime is that they have had the misfortune to acquire a too detailed knowledge of our methods of interrogation'. However, it did offer a way round the problem – borrowed, suitably, from the Nazis. In August 1945 a report by Political Intelligence Division had recorded that persons released from Nazi concentration camps absolutely refused to give any account of their experiences, even in complete privacy, because of the threat hanging over them if they divulged anything of those experiences. This system was employed with such success by the Nazis when releasing inmates from concentration camps that very few people in Germany had any real idea of what went on in those camps.[38]

This claim was always dismissed when advanced by the Germans. Now it was accepted as the basis of a system which could indeed successfully stop mouths. Prisoners leaving the camps would have to sign an undertaking not to associate with the press, give information or interviews or discuss matters connected with the camp at the risk of being rearrested.[39]

One day in February 1947 two of the inmates of No. 74 DIC (Bad Nenndorf) were dumped at Rothenburg Internee Hospital.[40] Both died within hours. One patient was skeletal, suffering from frostbite, conscious but unable to speak. The medical officer at Bad Nenndorf had diagnosed 'dyspepsia'. The cause of death was certified as starvation and peritonitis. The other patient was unconscious, with no pulse, cold, skeletal and covered in 'thick cakes of dirt; frost-bite to arms and legs'. The medical officer had diagnosed 'debility'. The cause of death was certified as severe malnutrition and advanced pulmonary tuberculosis, almost certainly developed during his five months at the DIC. A third death had occurred in the camp – a prisoner arrested on suspicion of drug trafficking and thought to be connected with a 'subversive movement'. He committed suicide while undergoing periods of interrogation. He was found to have received injuries in air raids and to have been incapable of sustaining mental strain. As a result of these deaths and of allegations made by, or on behalf of, twenty-five former inmates, the Commander-in-Chief, Air Marshal Sir Sholto Douglas, appointed a Court of Inquiry to investigate the conduct of Bad Nenndorf camp.

The governor of No. 3 CIC was sent to Rothenburg Hospital

to obtain evidence. In addition to the details of the two deaths described, the German doctor in charge recited case after case received from the DICs. The governor was 'appalled by the revelations'. The doctor undertook to produce a report. In his own report the governor described one prisoner in the hospital as 'one of the most disgusting sights of my life'. He might have been one of the Belsen inmates: 'The man literally had no flesh on him.' On his spine was a huge festering sore – a result of lying on bare boards – which the British camp doctor had not even seen. The man who had died of TB had been taken to hospital, dying, in a jeep with only a canvas awning for cover. The stretcher was too long, and the jeep's flap could not be closed. The journey took three hours. He was not allowed to be transported in a military ambulance.

The Court of Inquiry took evidence in the camp and in Rothenburg Hospital. One patient had, on arrival at the camp on 27 November, been put into an unheated cell with a window pane missing. After eight days in solitary confinement he was interrogated several times and told that if he did not tell the truth he would not leave the place alive, that they did not care whether he left the camp a cripple or not at all. On 4 January he was put in a punishment cell. Buckets of cold water were thrown into it, which he had to mop up with a rag. His jacket and boots were removed and he had to stand with bleeding feet for about ten hours in extreme cold on a concrete floor. Finally he had to crawl on hands and knees to interrogation. He swallowed a spoon handle to try to damage himself. The British medical officer finally recognised frostbite and the prisoner was sent to Rothenburg, where he had four toes amputated. On 10 April he was still unable to walk. That month the court found that this prisoner had spent most of his time since 27 November 1946 in solitary confinement, which continued even in hospital. He was to be returned to the DIC when discharged from hospital.

The man whom the governor of No. 3 CIC had found 'the most disgusting sight' had a similar history of solitary confinement, deprivation of clothing in the intense cold and the throwing of buckets of cold water into his cell. After admission to the camp he had been held in solitary confinement for seven weeks before initial interrogation. He begged not be reported unfavourably to the DIC: 'If ever a man showed signs of fear, he did.' The court found him dangerously ill and not likely to recover for three months.

The court learned that the prisoner who had died of undiagnosed TB had been a prisoner of the Russians and had learned some Russian. Released in June 1945, he had been employed as an interpreter by the police in Dresden. After making his way to his home town in the British Zone he had tried to join the local police but had been picked up by the British and sent to Bad Nenndorf in July 1946 on suspicion of being a Russian agent. He had suffered the usual treatment in solitary confinement and in the icy punishment cell. An infected hand was treated without anaesthetic ('his cries could be heard all over the block'). He had been physically healthy when interviewed for the police in June 1946. After six months in Bad Nenndorf he had been carried out to die.

The Court of Inquiry found that the DIC lacked adequate control, supervision and guidance from superior authority. Mental pressure was expressly allowed, although not physical torture; however, it was difficult to draw a clear line between the two. Punishment cells were insufficiently controlled: men who were medically and mentally unfit were committed to them. Interrogators had admitted that they would keep prisoners standing to attention for several hours. Prisoners also claimed that on leaving the camp they were forced to sign receipts for valuables which were not actually returned to them. The Court of Inquiry summed up: 'The officials responsible for this treatment, including those who knowingly condoned it, are, in the opinion of the Court, unfit ever again to have such power placed in their hands without strict supervision.'

However, the court found that it was getting into deep waters. The discrepancies between the medical officer's diagnoses and the true physical state of the internees was 'so glaring' that they realized that their investigations had 'taken a very serious turn indeed'. The possibility was emerging of legal proceedings against members of the staff. Further investigations would have to be made by Public Safety Branch. The Commander-in-Chief immediately ordered the court to cease its investigations and suspended the Camp Commandant, the medical officer and three interrogators. Responsibility for the camp was transferred from Intelligence Division to Penal Branch of the Control Commission.

By this time the administration of the zone had become the direct responsibility of the Foreign Secretary. Ernest Bevin sent the Bad Nenndorf papers to his close adviser Hector McNeil, Minister of State at the Foreign Office. The latter was so disturbed that he decided, he told Bevin, to take the weekend to think before replying:

> Apart altogether from any normal emotional reaction to the incidents, I still think that if the substantial facts are given any currency it will cause us grave trouble in the House, will be a propaganda stick with which the Russians will beat us for a long time and will damage heavily the reputation of our Intelligence Services.
>
> I doubt if I can put too strongly the Parliamentary consequences of publicity. Our friends will be uncomfortable and our enemies will exult. Whenever we have any allegation to make about the political police methods of Eastern European states, it will be enough to call out in the House 'Bad Nenndorf' and no reply is left to us.

A full inquiry was ordered by the Commander-in-Chief and reported on 14 June 1947. It was found that there was sufficient evidence to prefer charges. The Commandant bore overriding responsibility for mistreatment of prisoners and the grossly negligent medical treatment of the sick. Considerations of manslaughter arose. The medical officer was also to be held responsible for internees discharged in a condition of chronic illness. The inquiry also found evidence that three interrogators – a British officer, a German-born naturalized British officer and a Dutch officer – had 'conspired to extract information from internees at all costs'. British and German guards had been instructed to carry out physical assaults on certain prisoners with the object of reducing them to a state of physical collapse and of making them more amenable to interrogation. It was decided to court-martial the three interrogation officers.

But the British officer had already been demobilized and had returned to England. The commander of BAOR ordered that court-martial proceedings be dropped. A technicality of military law prevented the interrogator's recall to Germany to stand trial before a Control Commission court. The Foreign Office felt that justice had not been done.

Meanwhile, the trial of the other two interrogators opened in Hanover on 2 March 1948 and that of the camp medical officer on 1 April. They were arraigned on counts of 'disgraceful conduct of a cruel nature'. The British press splashed over its pages reports making free use of the word 'torture' in their headlines. All the lurid evidence was reported in detail. Reaction from the press in Germany was surprising. The prestigious periodical *Die Zeit* considered it a good omen 'that in the middle of Germany a trial is being conducted against British officers, accused of having ill-treated German prisoners at Nenndorf'. All Germans should take the trouble to understand the full significance of the fact that

> these proceedings are taking place publicly on the initiative of the occupying power . . . Would it have been possible to institute such proceedings against members of the German forces, of the SS, the Party or the police? The trial in Hanover, demonstrating as it does that right must remain right whether it is for or against the British Army, is the finest proof of the superiority of democracy. There is no justice where there is no freedom.[41]

But matters were not quite as *Die Zeit* saw them. The Foreign Office was unhappy with the court-martial procedure under the Judge Advocate-General's Department. In both cases 'run-of-the-mill' prosecuting officers faced leading heavyweight defence counsel with very great experience of criminal work at the Bar. (Derek Curtis-Bennett was one.) These unequal confrontations made the Foreign Office uneasy. They confirmed the suspicion that 'there has been a lack of resolution in the Judge Advocate-General's Department to see that justice is done in this case'.[42] And so it would would seem.

The naturalized British officer was acquitted of all charges. Charges of manslaughter against the medical officer were dropped. He was also acquitted of all charges of 'Disgraceful conduct of a cruel kind', but found guilty of six charges of 'Neglect' and dismissed the service.

The trial of the Camp Commandant posed a particular problem. His solicitors informed the Foreign Office that the defence would refer to the existence and function of direct interrogation centres. But the Deputy Military Governor, Sir Brian Robertson, warned against any such reference in open court. The Russians should not get to know how their agents were apprehended and treated, since they would be enabled to take preventive measures. And deserters might be intimidated from coming over. Public reference to the special function of Bad Nenndorf in obtaining information about one of the other occupying powers would be a grave embarrassment to the government and grounds for an attack in the Allied Control Council.

The Commandant's court-martial opened in Hamburg on 8 June 1948 and was transferred to London. Of the four charges against him, he was acquitted of two of 'General neglect'. The other charges – of 'Disgraceful conduct of a cruel kind' – were, according to a brief notice in *The Times*, withdrawn with the consent of the court. The records of all three courts-martial are still closed.

Bad Nenndorf was closed down by the new Commander-in-Chief, General Sir Brian Robertson, in July 1947 and was replaced by No. 10 Disposal Centre, which was to be the only interrogation establishment in the British Zone. Revised regulations for the conduct of the centre had been drawn up by the Commander-in-Chief as an 'effective safeguard'. But when the Minister, Lord Pakenham, visited the centre soon afterwards he found that eleven of the eighteen interrogators there had previously been employed at Bad Nenndorf. The Minister suggested certain additional safeguards, but Sir Brian Robertson disagreed. He told the Foreign Office that he was strongly opposed to the employment of brutal methods but he was responsible for seeing that the centre served effectively the purpose for which it is maintained. 'If the conditions at No. 10 DC are to conform to those enforced by the Prison Commissioners in our enlightened country, and if justifiable cause of arrest is to be necessary in each case, then I believe we would do better to close No. 10 DC altogether.' A compromise was reached.[43]

In 1948 there were still about thirty to fifty death sentences a month being passed by Military Government courts (of which about one-third were quashed), although both the Foreign Office and the law lords were still shaky about the legal standing of the courts themselves.[44] In May it was finally decided that 'there is nothing further to be gained from repeated trials and executions' and that it was 'politically desirable to have buried the past by 1st September, 1948'. This would be the final date for the trial of alleged war criminals, whether or not they were in custody. In spite of questions in Parliament, there were to be no exceptions. Sir Brian Robertson agreed – otherwise 'there would be no end of the matter'.[45]

In 1954, as Germany stood on the brink of full sovereignty, Sir Alexander Maxwell, chairman of the Mixed Consultative Board of the British Zone, assisted by two colleagues, carried out a review of war-criminal cases in the British Zone. The review of sentences, he wrote, proved a 'humiliating experience'. Of about eighty cases examined, there were only twenty-five in which a conviction would have been justified. Possible war criminals were not properly screened before ever being brought to trial. There were quite disproportionate sentences on junior people carrying out orders of which they did not know the significance. Courts were not given adequate guidance: German defence counsel were accustomed to different procedures. There was anti-German feeling. All this showed British justice in a bad light. Sir Ivone Kirkpatrick, the High Commissioner, agreed: 'These trials are a disgrace to this country . . . It is a miserable chapter in our otherwise creditable judicial history.' Maxwell primarily blamed the War Office, who in 1945 insisted on being responsible for war-crimes trials: 'And part of the responsibility lies with Russell of Liverpool who for most of the time was the principal Judge Advocate-General in Germany.' The Foreign Office was also culpable. Maxwell refused to sit as the British member on a new Anglo-German Review Board which would be looking at cases in which the present board's recommendations had been rejected: 'Sir Alexander did not wish to find himself in the position of having to express the opinion that some of the Foreign Office decisions were mistaken.'[46]

It had been, as Ernest Bevin said, as big a mess as it was possible to get into.

5
'Necessary but impossible'

IN DECEMBER 1944 Richard Crossman of Political Warfare Department wrote to Deputy Prime Minister Attlee that the war of liberation begun on the beaches had ended: 'This winter we have begun a new war . . . in which we assume that a whole nation is and remains our enemy and must be conquered whether it wants to be liberated or not.'[1]

It had not begun like that. In a broadcast to the German people a few days after the outbreak of war, Prime Minister Chamberlain's tone was almost fraternal: 'We are not fighting against you, the German people, for whom we have no bitter feelings, but against a tyrannous and forsworn regime which has betrayed not only its own people but the whole of western civilisation and all that you and we hold dear.'[2] The Foreign Secretary, Lord Halifax, wrote to a correspondent that the war was 'not against the German people but against those who have, as it seems to us, so cruelly misled and deceived them. I should have no doubt at all . . . if only one could get rid of that regime, we ought to make as generous a peace as we could with the German people.'[3] Ridding the world of the Nazi warlord and his regime seemed, then, to assume an element of liberation for the German people themselves.

In his first proclamation to the German people as the attacking Allied armies drove into Germany, General Eisenhower, Allied Supreme Commander, declared, 'In the area of Germany occupied by the forces under my command, we shall obliterate Nazism and German militarism. We shall overthrow the Nazi rule, dissolve the Nazi Party and abolish the cruel, oppressive and discriminating laws and institutions which the Party has created.'[4] The armies entering Germany faced two tasks: to overpower her military might and to purge her political life. Well equipped for the former task, they were totally unequipped for the latter.

The handbook prepared by SHAEF for the guidance of the Occupation – known as JCS 1067[5] – had set out the scope of what was to be done. Final victory would bring about the extinction of the Nazi government, the abolition of Nazi laws and the disposal of the well-known Nazi leaders. All who had been more than nominal members of the party were to be removed and excluded from public office and important positions in private enterprise. This would cover finance, industry, commerce, agriculture, education, the press, publishing and news agencies. Active members were to be defined as having held office in the party from local to national level, participated in racial persecution or discrimination, been open believers in Nazi doctrines, or given substantial moral or material support to the party or its leaders.

One particular provision was to be the cause of many a headache to the occupiers: JCS 1067 had indicated that 'nominal' party members would not be excluded from employment in the categories listed. President Roosevelt would have none of it. There were to be no exceptions to the dismissal of *all* party members, however nominal, despite the demands of 'administrative necessity, convenience or expediency'. British 21st Army Group foresaw the problems which this rigid attitude would create and pleaded – in vain – for a more flexible and pragmatic attitude. It was pointed out to SHAEF that membership of the party had been virtually a condition of employment in many departments of the administration in Germany. If all those officials who had been party members were swept away it would mean somehow having to recruit and train whole new departments. But Roosevelt in faraway Washington was adamant.

The Potsdam Conference in July 1945, at which the Big Three agreed upon the treatment of Germany in defeat, reaffirmed the decisions of JCS 1067. In January 1946 Control Council Directive No. 24 was issued,[6] setting out for the Military

Government how 'denazification' was to be implemented. This first listed by title those whose position in the Third Reich called for mandatory dismissal and arrest. Second, it listed those whose dismissal was discretionary – who could remain at their posts until some politically acceptable person could be found to take over, even if not of equal capability. The categories for discretionary dismissal were so wide and so inclusive that it is difficult to see who was to be left out. They ranged from parents who had permitted their children to attend political institutes such as the Adolf Hitler schools to any individual who *had been* a member of an aristocratic Prussian, East Prussian, Pomeranian, Silesian or Mecklenburg family. (How one could cease to be a member of one's family was not explained.)

When Military Government officers entered Germany to take over from combat troops, their orders were to see that those in the offending categories were instantly removed from their posts. Subsequently, the Potsdam Conference decreed that all those removed from office should be replaced by persons who 'by their political and moral qualities are deemed capable of assisting in developing genuine democratic institutions in Germany'. But higher authority was insisting that few if any such persons existed. An official document issued to the troops for guidance stated, 'It must be affirmed that the Germans are not divided into two classes, good and bad Germans; there are only good and bad elements in the German character, the latter of which generally predominate.'[7] Patrick Gordon Walker MP subsequently expressed concern to Deputy Prime Minister Attlee about the consequences of 'the orders issued by military commanders in rather violent terms, depicting the Germans as an undistinguishable mass of sub-men'.[8] The Political Adviser to the Commander-in-Chief, Christopher Steel, added to the burden of those in the field who were supposed to be seeking out Germans of the right 'moral and political qualities'. In a personal letter to all detachment commanders in the British Zone, he abjured, 'Never think that because a man was a Social Democrat or Trades Unionist or a professing Christian . . . he is therefore beyond suspicion.' Such a man's past record must be examined to see if he had ever compromised himself.[9] In an order to his staff, General Macready, Regional Commissioner for the Hanover area, declared:

> Nazism is more than a political creed – it is designed to appeal to all the inherent German characteristics of militarism and domination. The nominal Nazi, approved by every test, is still a German. Although his enforced participation in Party activities may not have particularly appealed to his political sense, it no doubt provided a welcome outlet to other sides of his nature which are to our ideas equally objectionable . . . The next Hitler will not necessarily be a Nazi.[10]

Thus anyone who was exonerated from the crime of being a Nazi remained guilty of being a German.

The officials of the British Occupation upon whom had fallen the responsibility of 'cleansing' the population neither knew nor were allowed to know of the reality of life under the Nazi regime or of the opposition to that regime inside Germany. The only publicly known action against Hitler was the failed plot of 20 July 1944. This was dismissed in the press at the time as a purely military attempt – in the words of the *Daily Telegraph*, 'to replace the swastika with the jackboot'. In fact it had been a concerted action by military personnel *and* civilians. Among the thousands purged in the aftermath of the attempt, in addition to twenty generals and thirty-three colonels, were two ambassadors, seven diplomats, one minister, three Secretaries of State, the head of the Reich Criminal Police and several police presidents and presidents of provinces and districts.[11] But the British government had no intention of letting the existence of an opposition inside Germany be known. Eden, the then Foreign Secretary, had privately made that quite clear, as Richard Crossman testified in the House of Commons on the fifth anniversary of the plot:

I shall never forget the night when we got the news, after midnight, of the attempted assassination of Hitler and we had to decide what to say. Eden said: 'On no account was any distinction to be made between the men undertaking that revolt and the Nazis. They were all to be lumped together in our propaganda.'[12]

The existence of people of the requisite 'political and moral qualities', together with the nature of the pressure under which they lived, was well known to the British government. It was not information which was to be shared with the troops coming face to face with the Germans. From the dispatches of Sir Horace Rumbold, British ambassador at the time of Hitler's rise to power, through to the many personal reports of returning travellers with special connections in Germany – academics, journalists, businessmen, financiers, diplomats – the Foreign Office was aware over the years of a people increasingly disaffected; of individuals living in fear of a knock on the door and arbitrary arrest; of industry harassed by political interference; of education polluted by ideology; of churchmen silenced; and of the ruthless persecution of the Jews.

Twenty million voters in the last parliamentary election held in Germany before the war had denied Hitler an absolute majority. They were still out there, somewhere. Hitler had granted Himmler 'unlimited powers' to deal with the enemy within. In 1937 Himmler impressed upon an audience of senior army officers that it was essential for everyone in a responsible position to understand 'the vital importance of the internal battleground, which in case of war will mean life or death for us'. There must be more concentration camps. In case of war, 'mass arrests on an unprecedented scale will be necessary. Many political prisoners will have to be shot out of hand.' To neglect the 'internal battlefield' would lead to catastrophe. 'Thirty divisions of the Death's Head units of the SS are to form the nucleus of the considerably larger force we shall need to guarantee internal security and full control of the people.'[13]

A British-government informant who lived in Berlin described the many small circles or groups, 'more numerous than one could imagine. I have myself seen how, at the slightest suspicion or alarm, the scene has shifted literally in a split second from free comment and criticism to a kind of ultra-Nazism with the appropriate gestures, terms and accents . . .'[14] A letter which reached the Foreign Office via a neutral country from an undisclosed correspondent ('an intelligent and educated German') speaks directly from this experience:

> Who knows the man in Germany whose life has become one deadly dangerous game of hide and seek? Who only in the night, only behind closed doors, whispers with one or other of his friends? Who is aware that his children may never know that he is 'anti' – perhaps even his wife may not know. Who has burnt his favourite books, who has lost his best friends by emigration . . . He is the most isolated, the most forgotten man in Europe.[15]

The writer Sebastian Haffner, who escaped to England on the eve of war, described the Germany he left behind as 'a secret Germany, a shadow Germany, intangible but omnipresent'.[16]

The Morale Division of the US Strategic Bombing Survey, pursuing its investigations in the wake of the Allied advance into Germany in 1944, found evidence that opposition groups had existed among workers in most of the industrial cities during the war. Wherever possible, sabotage was carried out against aircraft and airfields; holes were punched in petrol tanks, and sand was put in cylinders. Quantities of material were wasted – for instance, by deliberately cutting U-boat parts to wrong designs or removing parts of torpedoes. Propaganda was distributed among the workers by leaflets and by word of mouth. Short-wave transmitters, moved about on lorries, kept the Gestapo busy even after the outbreak of war. Workers in a Berlin armaments factory broadcast to the city:

This war is not a just war, not a patriotic war, nor a war of liberation. It is an unjust war because it is not a war for the honour of Germany, of our people, but for the suppression of other peoples and for the conquest of foreign territories . . . The enemy is in our own country![17]

No wonder Himmler was worried.

In 1939, experienced saboteurs conducted a war of attrition during the building of the West Wall fortifications between France and Germany under Dr Fritz Todt. With a labour force which included men from all walks of life, professional as well as artisan, dragged from jobs and homes to work in appalling conditions, there was was fertile ground for sabotage. Go-slows and strikes were organized. In June 1939 there was a strike along the whole line from Gersweiller to Saarbrücken. But, as the organizers knew, desperately needed labour could not be shut up in concentration camps.[18] On the eve of the war, the British consul-general in Frankfurt reported to London on the state of the project. The construction was so bad and had so many weaknesses that after a personal inspection Hitler had ordered some of the engineers in charge to be executed.[19] The efforts of the clandestinely organized workers to sabotage the West Wall had been successful, but it was labour in vain. The British and French were never to attempt to breach it.

In the summer of 1939 the financier Hjalmar Schacht, who had served in the early years of Nazi government until he turned against Hitler, sent information to London via Switzerland about sabotage in industry. There was passive resistance in the factories, even in such leading companies as Leuna-Werke, the producer of vital synthetic fuel and rubber. But the most effective resistance was in the mines of the Ruhr and the Sudetenland. Goering had extended the working hours, but still production declined. The Gestapo was powerless to check workers underground.[20] Krupps, the famous armaments factory, was a centre of anti-Nazi activity among workers in the Ruhr. In December 1944 an intelligence source reported to SHAEF that in the predominantly Catholic Ruhr there was close connection between clergy and workers and what was described as 'spiritual sabotage'. There had been arrests of Krupps workmen and engineers together with seventy Catholic priests.[21]

The US Strategic Bombing Survey found that resistance had not been confined to the industrial sphere. Oppositional elements had operated within the system, even under the noses of the Nazi apparatchiks installed everywhere as spies. It was clear that the Detective Division in the police force contained substantial numbers of old supporters of the Republic – mainly former members of the SPD. The Gestapo was balked of its prey by impending victims having their names entered in the missing-persons files after they had been warned of impending arrest. It was known to 'insiders' that there were active cells in government agencies such as the Ministries of the Interior, Justice and Labour, in certain courts and prosecutors' offices and in local government. The head of the Berlin police, Count Wolf-Heinrich Helldorf, was himself a key figure in the anti-Nazi opposition.

Confirmation of this report and of the extent to which sand was thrown into the Nazi machine is contained in a letter by Helmut von Moltke, a leading member of the opposition, himself executed by the Nazis in 1944. He was writing from Sweden in 1943 to a distinguished friend in England, the All Souls Fellow Lionel Curtis. As an expert legal adviser to the Army, Moltke moved in influential circles and was in a position to observe:

> There is seldom a week when I do not notice something that must have been done in order to prevent a command from being executed or at least from becoming fully effective . . . and this is done in all walks of life. People who have been officially executed still live; others have been given sufficient warning to escape. This is especially so in occupied countries . . . People will perhaps come to realise that many thousands of lives have been saved by the intervention of some Germans.

Von Moltke also wrote of 'nineteen guillotines working at considerable speed without most people even knowing this fact, and practically nobody knows how many are beheaded per day . . . or the exact number of the concentration camps and their inhabitants'.[22]

Social Democrat politicians in exile managed to keep a record of the victims of the state – by name if possible. B. F. Heine, a Social Democrat in exile in England, wrote in 1942, 'The regime rages against its enemies at home with a frantic barbarity which resembles that displayed against its opponents in the occupied countries.' The German press revealed 'an endless chain of trials and convictions' for acts of the 'most elementary kindness' to French and Polish prisoners.[23] In July 1944 a Social Democrat source in Stockholm reported to London the many accounts of people discovering that friends or acquaintances had simply vanished from their workplace. There was no trial, not even a formal arrest. 'They are merely taken from their office or their home, shot and cremated. Their relatives are simply told by the Gestapo to send for the urn.'[24]

The redoubtable Bishop of Münster, Count Clemens August von Galen, proclaimed this openly from the pulpit of his cathedral in a sermon in July 1941. He spoke of the 'punitive measures of the Gestapo against innocent men, condemned without verdict or legal charge, without a chance of self-defence'. Such methods, he said, must call down divine punishment and destruction of the country. 'Soldiers will die for Germany but not for those who disgrace the name of Germany before God and man.'[25] The Bishop commended to the congregation a man 'respected by all, who had rendered signal service to the nation in the last War and had lain in a concentration camp for years' – Pastor Martin Niemöller. (Within two months von Galen's sermon had been dropped by the RAF as a leaflet over Germany.)

In the week following this sermon the Gestapo seized all religious houses in the province and turned the monks and nuns out on to the streets. The Bishop publicly denounced 'the attacks of our enemies within this country'. He announced in the cathedral that he had sent telegrams of protest to Minister-President of Prussia Goering, to the Minister of Home Affairs, to the Minister of Church Affairs and to the High Command of the Army. Above all he had sent a telegram to the Führer himself. He read out the text. He had begun by referring to the recent bombing of Münster by 'the external enemy' and then described 'the attacks of the enemy within this country'. In conclusion he had begged the Führer in the interests of justice 'to protect the freedom and property of German citizens against the arbitrary measures of the Gestapo'. At about the same time, the Bavarian bishops issued a Pastoral Letter (which would be read from all pulpits) fiercely denouncing the recent Nazi edicts on the forbidding of prayers in schools, the removal of crucifixes and the closing down of religious establishments.[26]

Other churchmen also did not hesitate to take their protests to the top. Cardinal Michael Faulhaber of Munich and the Lutheran Bishop of Stuttgart, Bishop Theophil Wurm, each visited the Reich Chancellery to protest against the depredations of the Gestapo. Bishop Wurm addressed the Evangelical Conference in similar terms. The Strategic Bombing Survey recorded that the Catholic Church, the Confessional Protestant Church and other small religious groups constituted a well-entrenched force of resistance to the encroachments of the state. A small but persistent stream of acts of defiance kept the authorities on edge.[27] In his letter to England (already quoted) von Moltke wrote, 'The most important part of the Churches' work has been the continuous process by which the whole clergy practically without exception have upheld the great principles in spite of all the intense propaganda and the pressure exerted against them . . . and the churches are full, Sunday after Sunday.'[28] Goebbels himself complained in his diary of the opposition of the Churches, 'which is giving us so much trouble'.[29]

Himmler yearned to have von Galen shot. But there was a problem. Intelligence from Germany, forwarded from the World Council of Churches in Geneva to the International Missionary Society in London (intercepted by the censor and passed to the

Foreign Office), revealed that Hitler, fearing the effect on the thousands of workers in Westphalia, would not consent. The Führer had now reined in the most radical elements of the party and decreed that for the time being no further measures should be taken against the Church.[30] ('I boil with rage,' Goebbels confided to his diary.[31]) The Strategic Bombing Survey noted: 'Thousands of lower clergy were in concentration camps but the most eminent spokesmen no Nazi dared touch.'

The story of the 'White Rose' organization[32] – particularly poignant because of the youth of those involved – was directly connected with Bishop von Galen's courageous stance. (It also shows how far afield his sermons were disseminated, without the help of the RAF.) In 1943 a copy of one of his sermons was thrust by an unknown hand through the letterbox of the Scholl family in Ulm. Hans Scholl was so inspired by its language that, together with his sister Sophie, he launched a clandestine movement to involve students all over Germany. The Scholls and their companions secretly produced leaflets attacking the moral obloquy of the regime, calling for passive resistance against the war, and urging German youth to 'avenge and atone for' Germany's crimes against the world. Captured by the Gestapo, the brother and sister and some of their companions were condemned to death by the same notorious Judge Roland Freisler who was later to convict those who were involved in the 1944 plot against Hitler. After their execution many buildings in Munich were daubed with the message 'The spirit lives.' (A copy of a White Rose leaflet eventually reached Churchill. He minuted, 'I do not at all wonder that Hitler's gang reacted in a murderous way against it.'[33])

During the war only senior officers of the *Wehrmacht* had the remotest – and it was indeed remote – chance of approaching anywhere near the Führer's person. Between 1940 and the ultimate failure of 20 July 1944 at least half a dozen attempts were made on Hitler's life. All were frustrated through circumstances outside the conspirators' control.[34] For most ordinary citizens opposed to the regime, passive resistance was the only option.

Bishop von Galen spoke for them:

> Against the enemy within our own country who tortures and
> strikes us, we cannot fight with weapons. There remains one
> kind of struggle: strong, persistent, dogged endurance. At
> this moment we are not the hammer but the anvil . . . The
> anvil cannot strike back. But if it is sufficiently tough, firm
> and hard it usually lasts longer than the hammer.[35]

Although the concept of collective guilt was never part of
official Allied policy, it pervaded the Occupation at all levels.
Speaking to a group of pilgrims at a national shrine in July 1945,
Bishop von Galen again spoke out, as he had done under the
Nazis, against perceived injustice. (All public utterances by
leading figures were monitored by Intelligence for possible sub-
version – just as in the old days.) His voice had been made known
abroad in the past, he said, while at home he had been attacked
and abused as a traitor to the Fatherland. On the strength of
that he felt he had the right to speak out now. 'I would like these
words to be heard beyond the frontiers of Germany':

> If it is suggested that the bulk of the German people and
> each one of us is guilty of the kind of atrocities committed by
> members of our nation, that is not just. If it is said that the
> entire German nation and each one of us appears equally
> guilty of the crimes committed at home and abroad and
> especially in concentration camps, then that is against many
> of us an untrue and unjust charge.[36]

The Bishop was severely censured by the British authorities.

Denazification was by its very nature beyond the ability of
outsiders to handle. Fabian von Schlabrendorff, a leader of the
anti-Nazi opposition who miraculously escaped execution
almost as it were at the foot of the scaffold, gave in retrospect a
perhaps understandably bitter view of his countrymen. The German people could be divided into three groups, he wrote: the

Nazis, the non-Nazis and the anti-Nazis. The non-Nazis were almost worse than the Nazis: 'their lack of backbone caused us more trouble than the wanton brutality of the Nazis'.[37] The Germans themselves knew the difference between the card-carrying paterfamilias trying to earn a living, persecuting no one, and the block warden reporting to the party. Yet the British and Americans insisted on shouldering the task of distinguishing them, treating as a judicial process what was essentially a matter of political judgement. The extirpation of Nazism root and branch had been expected, accepted, even welcomed in Germany. But, although it was possible to formulate rules for getting rid of Nazism, it was another thing to put the rules into practice. The major Nazi leaders could be dealt with. They were well known, and there were no doubts about either their identity or their culpability. But what of others? The problem was to identify them. There had been something like 8 million party members and half as many again in dependent party organizations. On this count some one-fifth of the population would have to be excluded from public life. As the Minister, J. B. Hynd, acknowledged in the House of Commons, 'It must have been extremely difficult for anyone to keep clear of all association with one or other branch of the Nazi Party or its subsidiary organizations.'[38] He instanced membership of the Hitler Youth, which had been compulsory. He did not mention that Control Council Directive No. 24 had placed Hitler Youth leaders in Category I, liable to be interned for fifteen years.

Some of the top people, even when supporters of the regime, had not been party members: they were too valuable in their particular spheres to be forced into unwilling membership. Conversely there were others – for instance, in the Civil Service – whose careers had been overtaken by the advent of National Socialism and who had been simply designated as party members. Some of these sober citizens had even suffered the indignity of having to wear fancy uniforms. All the leading members of the anti-Nazi resistance who could hope to operate effectively in a coup against the regime were men with responsible pos-

itions in society, in the Civil Service or in the senior ranks of the
Army, which provided them with both cover and opportunity.
They would, had they not received their own mandatory dis-
missal at the hands of Hitler's executioners, have fallen foul of
Directive No. 24.

Many ministries had been penetrated by party trusties who
spied upon the established staff. Many officials kept their heads
down lest worse should befall and their jobs pass into the hands
of militant Nazis. Older teachers tried to stand between their
charges and the worst excesses of Nazi indoctrination enthusi-
astically instilled by younger colleagues. But how could such
people ever hope to establish their innocence?

The blunt instrument of denazification was the *Fragebogen*.
This was a questionnaire consisting of some 130 items which
every applicant for public employment (and there was not much
of any other kind) had to complete. This applied to all jobs above
that of ordinary labourer. The questions ranged over all aspects
of life: military service; membership of a political party before
1933; religious affiliation or lack of it; all publications written,
compiled or edited since 1923; speeches other than those strictly
non-political; a record of employment showing sources and
amount of income for each year from 1930; any journeys abroad
since 1933. The applicant had to account for membership of any
of forty-four Nazi organizations. This list was in itself testimony
to the all-pervading intrusion of the party into every aspect of
the national life. And, just in case anything had been overlooked,
the *Fragebogen* called for details of 'any associations, society, fra-
ternity, union, syndicate chamber, institute, group, corporation,
club or other organization of any kind, whether social, political,
professional, educational, cultural, industrial, commercial or
honorary, with which you have ever been connected or associated'.

The difficulty of remembering so many details over such a
period of time, which had included the upheaval of the war
years, must have been formidable – perhaps sometimes insuperable. As an intelligence officer noted, 'Few places and people are

where they were or do what they did before the war . . . Dislocation dominates the surface of life.' Yet false statements, omissions and incomplete answers incurred prosecution and the risk of internment without trial.

These forms were checked where possible against party records, publications, newspapers, statements by informers. Just to check one single form must surely have involved very considerable time. Yet between March and July 1946 1 million *Fragebogen* were issued.[39] The accuracy of such checks must be a matter for speculation. A year after the end of the war Hynd spoke in the House of Commons of cases being cleared at the rate of 90,000–100,000 per month, which hardly seems possible, given that the Public Safety Branch officers who carried out the work for the most part knew neither German nor Germany and had as a rule gained their experience in police work in the Commonwealth. An unsatisfactory classification meant exclusion from all public service and from employment by the Military Government, which in turn meant virtual starvation, because employment ensured a ration card. A Control Commission officer, giving evidence before the Parliamentary Select Committee which visited Germany in July 1946, summed it up: 'There is a vast number of people affected, if only to the extent that they must go before a committee at some time or other. As long as they have to go before a committee, they don't know where they are.'[40] They might at any moment be thrown out of their homes, lose their furniture, everything. Someone thrown out of his job lost everything and became a beggar. Even study at university was barred. There was a danger of creating the nucleus of a nationalist proletariat.

Although denazification applied to everyone seeking employment above the level of general labourer, the 'big fish' usually had the contacts and resources to avoid the necessity of seeking work. They could stay hidden and live off the black market, or even escape from Germany altogether. The Germans themselves were well aware of this as they filled out their *Fragebogen* – sometimes, perforce, more than once, as British officials came and went. But the problems raised by denazification were not confined to the individual. There were serious repercussions on a larger scale. The well-documented situation in the coal industry can stand as an example.

Coal was, with food, the most vital, critical and contentious element of the whole Occupation of Germany. The British director of production in the Ruhr, mining engineer Henry Collins, found his already uphill task being considerably impeded by the operations of denazification.[41] In November 1945 he was shown a list of top men who were to be removed from their posts. Those involved in policy would not be a loss, but Collins was horrified to find there the names of key men in the mining industry. In January 1946 he submitted a report to Economics Division of the Control Commission. Denazification, carried out by relatively junior British officials, was removing men with a wealth of knowledge and experience of the utmost value. The constant feeling of insecurity among managerial staff of all grades was corroding the discipline without which safety and efficiency in the mines were impossible. One month later disaster struck.

At the Monopol Grinberg mine an explosion on 20 February took 402 lives, including those of three Britons. There was no German engineer left with the necessary knowledge of the mine to take charge of rescue and recovery. One senior man with ten years' first-hand knowledge of the workings of the mine had recently been dismissed as general director of another mine in the area. Collins drove to his house and begged him – as one mining engineer to another and with no assurances as to his future – to take charge, which he did. Subsequently, Field Marshal Montgomery, as Military Governor, wrote letters of appreciation to both British *and* German staff for their heroic work.

Shortly after the disaster Collins wrote another report, this time to Headquarters, entitled 'Safety in Mines as Affected by the Denazification Policy'. Monopol Grinberg had been an unprecedented catastrophe in the history of the industry, he wrote, and had demoralized men and management. British staff were at risk in their duties underground through loss of effective control by German technical management. The manner in which denazification was being implemented had denuded the industry of many of its competent officials, and those remaining were in such a state of uncertainty about their future that they were incapable of giving their best service. The complete and utter disruption of the German mining industry was a heavy price to pay for the inflexible formula of denazification. The only hope for the industry lay in the reinstatement of sufficient mining engineers to ensure the adequate staffing of all mines.

Montgomery's Chief of Staff, General Templer, immediately convened a meeting of denazification officers, which Collins attended. A letter was drafted, to be promulgated throughout the zone, stating that the policy of denazification as then implemented in the coal industry must cease. Dismissals could take place only after consultation with Collins.

But such flexibility was not in fact instituted in other areas, where commanders were still adhering to Directive No. 24. An order was issued by the Regional Commissioner for the Hanover area. General Macready was concerned with 'the conflict of interests within Mil. Gov. over the implementation of the policy by reason of the diverse, and frequently diametrically opposed, interests involved'. On the one hand, Public Safety Branch was concerned only with the process of denazification. On the other, the 'functional' officer in the field pleaded his inability to meet the demands of higher authority for production or services were he to comply with the rules involving dismissal of personnel in key positions. 'A deadlock would appear to have been reached,' wrote the general. He came down against the functional officers. Twelve months after the end of the war, exceptions which were necessary in the first months of chaos could no longer be allowed 'now that the initial emergency may be said to have passed' – which in fact it had not, by any means.[42]

As it dragged on, denazification alienated more and more people across all classes – particularly those who might have been looked to for support. In September 1946 Brigadier H. W. H.

Armytage, commander of Hamburg District, reported to General Sir Brian Robertson on consultations he had had on denazification with political and trade-union leaders. Opinion had been unanimous: 'They feel that it is unwise to mix demilitarization and denazification, on the grounds that no German will understand how a man who was a soldier but never a Nazi should be placed in the same category as a Nazi.' Robertson dismissed such delicacy of feeling out of hand.[43]

All clergy had to be denazified before being allowed to officiate again. Even Bishop von Galen, whose sermons the RAF had sent fluttering down over the Reich during the war, was obliged to submit to the process. The Churches, which had suffered persecution, could identify better than any British policeman any guilty among their own. (Cardinal Frings, later Archbishop of Cologne, told a congregation in Westminster Cathedral that only two out of over 2,000 priests in his Cologne diocese had defected to the Nazi Party.) They objected to their authority in what they saw as essentially a matter of spiritual discipline being usurped by lay – and foreign – officials. In pleading for help from Cardinal Griffin, on a visit from London in September 1945, the bishops pointed out that there had been no ordinations since 1940: the British had promised months ago to reopen the seminaries, but nothing had been done. The British authorities regulated matters which even the Nazis had never interfered with. Volumes of theological works had to be submitted for censorship, although most were standard texts from pre-Nazi days.[44] In August 1945 von Galen wrote to the Military Government about the difficulties arising from the order which forbade documents drawn up by episcopal authorities, or communications to the Pope or the Apostolic Nuncio, to be sent through the post because they were in Latin.[45]

Control Commission officials, mostly unaware of the Churches' record under the Nazi regime, approached matters from a purely political standpoint. Archbishop Frings was a thorn in the side of the British because of his persistent and uncompromising pursuit of the speedy restitution of religious rights and properties removed by the Nazis. Religious Affairs Branch considered, rather perversely, that he would never have become Archbishop unless he had been a friend of the regime. In fact, by the Archbishop's own account, his wartime consecration went publicly unrecorded, the only (accidental) reference to the event being a newspaper appeal by a woman who had lost her wallet, containing her soldier husband's photograph, at the ceremony in the cathedral. Religious Affairs Branch was alarmed when it learned that the Deputy Military Governor had instructed the Regional Commissioner, Asbury, that if it was felt at any time that discussion would be helpful he should invite the Cardinal to his house. And if he did not come the police should be sent to bring him in. 'This was a course which the Nazis themselves shrank from pursuing . . . the news would spread like a prairie fire through the Rhineland.'[46]

As time went by, the uncertainty and both the imprecision and the quality of the advice being given to Military Government tribunals by returning exiles and refugees – employed for their knowledge of the language but hardly for their objective judgement – alienated the population, which had initially accepted the purge of Nazism. A report by a Political Intelligence officer stated, 'An important section of Germans who have gone through appalling periods of persecution have an acute sense of responsibility on behalf of the German state and nation, but no acute sense of personal guilt and bitterly resent attempts to make them feel equally guilty with Nazis.'[47] Failure to acknowledge this element was serious, concluded the report, because it was from these people that future leaders would be drawn and they should be treated as allies.

This conclusion was shared by the Swiss Protestant theologian Karl Barth, who spent three months in the British Zone in 1946. At the invitation of the British authorities, he recorded his impressions. They were not good. Did the occupiers, he wondered, have any idea what the crowds of Germans they passed through were thinking? Were they in the least interested?

Do the Allies realise what disappointment their policy up to
date has caused, particularly to the fundamental opponents
of the Nazi system, up and down the country? Have they
taken sufficient trouble to search out those who opposed
Nazism from the beginning and who are therefore the really
useful elements of the population? Have they encouraged
these Germans, made use of their information about persons and conditions, brought them in to co-operate with the
building of the new Germany?[48]

There was only one answer to these questions.

Legislation degenerated into a morass of revisions and
amendments – it was no longer necessary to denazify the typist
and the gardener, only the *head* typist and the *head* gardener.
Concern about the *Fragebogen* even reached the House of Commons when (although not until 1947) it was realized that the
applicant was required to divulge how he had voted in the elections of 1932 and 1933. As a result of the revelation that they
were breaching the secrecy of the ballot box in Germany, the
government ordered the relevant questions to be deleted. In July
1946 German panels were set up to help with denazification, but
they were only advisory. Finally, in October 1947, two and a half
years after the end of the war, responsibility was handed over to
the *Länder*, with instructions to complete the process by 1 January 1948.

Denazification started too late – because there had not been
adequate planning in advance – and lasted too long – because
the forms when established were too elaborate and wide-reach-
ing. The Germans had a joke about Hitler's 'Thousand-Year
Reich': twelve years of Nazism and 888 years of denazification.
The contradiction between the actual experience of Germans
under the Nazi regime and the conception of this experience by
the British occupying their country was to be a source of conflict
throughout the Occupation. The attitude was at best failure, at
worst refusal, to recognize the reality of life under a dictatorship. Dr Walter Hensel had listened to the BBC German Service

during the war (which of course it was a capital offence to do) and had heard how well trained psychologically the Occupation forces would be when they came to Germany. But he was convinced that 'the most primitive knowledge just was not there'. His personal solution was to invite the denazification officer in Düsseldorf, Captain Mackintosh, to his home one evening and over a bottle of wine try to make him understand. 'You must try to imagine', he told his guest, 'what it would be like to live without air.'[49] But, in the words of an official British historian, even if the reality of the party's hold on the community was understood, 'the central difficulty was in knowing what judgement to pass upon the actions of persons held in its grip'.[50]

A tragic example was Dr Hans Korbel, director of Wolfsburg Hospital and medical officer for the workers of the state-owned Volkswagen factory.[51] He was arrested by the Americans in April 1945 and, after a year in prison, was charged in a British military court with 'wilful neglect'.

In 1943 Korbel had been given charge of a mother-and-baby unit for the workers at some distance from the VW factory. He had found it in an appalling state. Requests to the authorities for nursing help and supplies of food and medicine were refused. He fought in vain against the separation of the newly born from their mothers. The lack of breast-feeding and the paucity of other suitable nourishment led to a high degree of infant mortality. In the two years during which Korbel was in charge, 200 infants died. The *gauleiter* responsible committed suicide at the end of the war.

An impressive array of public figures hastened to Korbel's defence. Warm tributes to his high moral character and integrity were received from the Evangelical Bishop of Berlin, the Bishop of Hanover, Pastor Niemöller and the Catholic parish priest of Wolfsburg. Political opponents – Christian Democrat and Communist leaders in Hanover, Brunswick and Oldenburg, and the chairman of the local trade union – united in Korbel's support. Affidavits came from France. A professor described how French workers at the factory had petititioned the Americans for his release. Another affidavit from France, from Dr Ferdinand Porsche, testified to Korbel's efforts on behalf of starving Russian prisoners of war in a camp in the area. As inventor of the Volkswagen, Porsche had access to the Führer. He had taken the doctor's secret report and photographs to the top. Action had been taken.

In spite of the weight of evidence on his side, Korbel was found guilty and condemned to death. Representations were received from the *Land* superintendent, the Red Cross and Quaker Relief. The defence secured a stay of execution on the grounds that the affidavits from France had not been produced to the court until after sentence had been pronounced. Legal Department recommended 'further consideration of this point'. The Assistant Judge Advocate-General, Lord Russell of Liverpool, did not agree. Dr Korbel was hanged on 7 March 1947, two years after his arrest. The Foreign Office recorded an uneasy post mortem: 'The Germans concerned feel that this case provides a striking example of a growing number of cases in which there is miscarriage of justice due to a lack of understanding by the British of the situation in Germany as it was in the Nazi period.'

This lack of understanding resulted in an expectation – a demand almost – of a standard of conduct for purposes of denazification which was unrealistic. Countess Marion Döhnoff, founder of the respected periodical *Die Zeit* and herself an active member of the anti-Nazi resistance, expressed this in an article in the *Observer* at the time of the Nuremberg trials. Active resistance and a willingness to face martyrdom had come to be considered the norm – as the standard to be expected of everybody. Everyone who failed to reach that standard was to be condemned. Sebastian Haffner wrote in the same vein: 'It is easy from the high horse of assured and guaranteed civic rights to reproach these Germans with cowardice when they do not lay their heads on the block for their political convictions with the same unconcern with which other people throw a piece of paper into the ballot box.'[52]

Churchill understood. He expressed it in his own way in a debate in the House of Commons eighteen months after the end of the war. In a country handled as Germany had been, he said, the ordinary people had had little choice about what to do:

> I think some consideration should always be given to ordinary people. Everyone is not a Pastor Niemöller or a martyr, and when ordinary people are hurled this way and that, when the cruel hands of tyrants are laid upon them and vile systems of regimentation are imposed and enforced by espionage and other forms of cruelty, there are great numbers of people who will succumb. I thank God that in this island home of ours, we have never been put to the test.[53]

Denazification was once described as 'necessary but impossible'. Necessary in some form it may have been. Impossible it certainly was.

6
'The cesspool of Europe'

ON WHIT Sunday 1946 the Assistant Chaplain-General of the British Army of the Rhine, the Revd Geoffrey Druitt, conducted a service of dedication of the Garrison Church of St George, Charlottenburg, Berlin, before a congregation of the most senior officers of BAOR and Control Commission Headquarters.[1] Also present were representatives of the British press invited by the chaplain himself, who – in his own words – was 'out for trouble'. He had chosen the occasion to speak out, he later told his fellow chaplains, because 'backstage' efforts and moderated statements had failed in the past. Evil had been vocal and active without retaliation. Some 'bold and startling pronouncement' seemed the only way. His target was the conduct of the British administration and its representatives during the first year of Occupation.

He had been waiting and longing, the chaplain told his distinguished audience, for others to say what he was about to say, but he had waited in vain. So now he was going to speak himself, while there was time, as he put it, to call a halt. 'We must get our eyes open to the things that are really happening . . . We must see where we are and where we're heading for.' For more than a year the German people, living in the squalor and rubble of their ruined cities, had faced nothingness. Denied all power and independence, with no future prospects, occupied by nations unable to find any agreed policy, they could see neither a beginning nor an end 'and we shrug our shoulders and say, "They asked for it."'

This must be said – a sad proportion of the occupying armies are playing a shameful part in encouraging the rot. Too many are exploiting for financial gain the material needs of this conquered people. Too many are prostituting their women and girls by giving way to lust and easy temptation. Unless it pulls itself together, Rhine Army, as well as other Britishers, will leave a shameful heritage behind it . . . Germany will become a danger not as a military power but as the cesspool of Europe, and it will be big enough and deep enough to drown herself and her neighbours.

It was, given his position, an impressive performance. As he told his fellow chaplains, he had put his service career 'in the melting pot'. He had publicly mentioned the unmentionable: the Allies' inability to find an agreed policy for Germany. He had criticized the government at home. He had said all the things which were not supposed to be said 'in front of the Germans'. But he spoke as a man of God, standing aside from political considerations. His very real concern was not only for what he called 'the soul of Germany' but for the spiritual state of those who, at the surrender, had assumed total control and responsibility for the defeated people.

In a society so dramatically divided between the haves and the have-nots, corruption was inevitable and endemic. It was measured by the depth of deprivation. The ultimate corruption was human. The war, by death and imprisonment, had terribly reduced the male population. Most of those held in Russia never returned; those who did were practically at death's door. Population statistics recorded that at no time since perhaps the end of the Thirty Years War in 1648 had any community had such a disproportionate gender distribution: there were 2 million surplus women in the age group over twenty-one.[2] The old and the young needed feeding. Women were the breadwinners. Starving people could not afford morals. Once the fraternization ban was lifted – or even before – the occupiers, armed with their cigarettes and other goodies, found themselves in an almost free market. The incidence of venereal disease among both Occupation forces and Germans rose steadily. Penicillin had to be flown in from Britain. Sir Jack Drummond, nutritional adviser to the government, laid it on the line: 'Venereal Disease amongst the Occupation troops follows closely on the development of hunger amongst the population. I would go so far as to say that one can be taken as the measure of the other.'[3]

Britain was loath to acknowledge its bastards. Headquarters in Berlin advised the Foreign Office of the 'political undesirability of affiliation proceedings being held either in German or Control Commission Courts. These would have a most damaging effect on British prestige.' The Army agreed. As usual, it rallied round its own. The Commander-in-Chief, Sir Sholto Douglas, reported that service commanders were unanimous in resisting any such proposal. Troops would be placed in far too vulnerable a position vis-à-vis unscrupulous German women, 'whose promiscuity was generally appreciated'. Owing to short tours in Germany, the soldier father might be absent when the claim was made. 'The standard of morality of German women is so low that it would be difficult to bring home a claim with justice to a specific defendant.' The standard of morality of British servicemen was not called into question.[4]

Furthermore, it was argued, most claims referred to servicemen, and British soldiers were not subject to foreign courts. Decrees of such courts could not be enforced against the pay of servicemen. The Foreign Office added its own rider: any maintenance payment would be objectionable on financial grounds, as it would involve United Kingdom dollar expenditure. As the Foreign Office Minister wrote to a protesting Member of Parliament, 'This decision may involve hardship on certain German women but the alternative is to impose equal or greater hardship on British subjects.' In vain the Council for the Unmarried Mother and her Child pointed out that the children of Norwegian, Dutch and Danish mothers were paid maintenance while the Germans were in occupation of their countries; and the Americans paid up for their progeny in Britain.[5]

The chaplain's invitation to the press did not result in the high-profile reporting which he had hoped would influence public opinion. It was only when a report appeared in the *The Times* two months later that the authorities sat up and took notice. (A copy of the sermon had been sent to the paper by one of Druitt's colleagues.) The item was brief but did contain some of the most forceful of his castigations. From the Cabinet Office, General Hollis wrote to the Commander-in-Chief, 'Chiefs of Staff request you assemble your Service Commanders and investigate.'[6] The result, as anyone will remember who was there at the time, was a wave of obligatory so-called 'Leadership Courses' organized by the chaplains of the various denominations, for servicemen and civilians alike. The Army commander, General Sir Richard McCreery, sought to arouse spiritual awareness among his officers at Headquarters by ordering early-morning runs. The General hoped that smaller, 'homelier' messes, reduction in the supplies of liquor to bars and the forthcoming arrival of British families would introduce 'a healthier atmosphere'.[7]

But sexual morality was not the only cause for concern. While at home the Chancellor of the Exchequer, Hugh Dalton, groaned at the cost to the British taxpayers of sustaining the Germans, many of these taxpayers were ruthlessly enriching themselves in the 'Tom Tiddler's ground' which was Occupied Germany.

As in the days of the great German inflation of the 1920s, only 'things' (*Sachwerte*) had any true value for the population. Wages paid in marks were good only for public transactions such as rent, transport and the purchase of official food rations when available but not for procuring the real necessities of life. 'Are you working?' ran a current joke. 'How can I afford to work?' was the reply – 'I have a family to feed.' The cigarette became the actual – illegal – currency, with an established value of around five marks. Economics Branch claimed that, together with chocolate and alcohol derived from Allied stores, 'the cigarette is probably one of the biggest single threats to financial stability in the country'.[8] In the British Zone the troops had a free weekly issue of fifty cigarettes plus a further 200 at duty-free prices. There was also a personal issue of chocolate and soap which could be bought. By selling these articles directly to the Germans, servicemen acquired marks which they exchanged for sterling at the field cashier before going home on leave or on demobilization. Or they bought sterling postal orders which they sent home. Similarly, British Treasury notes changed hands at a high rate of exchange (the official rate was forty marks to the pound, although the mark was not negotiable outside Germany), and the results of these transactions were changed back again into sterling.

The troops were in effect sending home a great deal more than they were actually allowed to draw in pay in Germany. (By October 1945, for instance, American forces in Berlin alone had sent home $4 million more than they were entitled to in pay, even after paying their local expenses.) The Treasury was paying out vast quantities of sterling to purchase valueless marks. The British government was slow to realize the implications of this – as indeed was the American – and it was over a year after the end of the war before a system of British Armed Forces Vouchers (BAFVs) were issued for use in official establishments. These alone were exchangeable into and from sterling.

Cigarettes were never smoked by the ordinary Germans who acquired them: they were used in the black market for procuring whatever necessities could be had. Economics Branch noted that such transactions 'are so frequent and widespread and affect so many commodities required in daily life, that they have gradually become an integral part of it'.[9] For a British person to have paid a laundress, a hairdresser, a dressmaker, a gardener in legal but valueless marks instead of illegal cigarettes would in real terms have been unjust. Nevertheless, each cigarette used fuelled the black market, which burgeoned daily. As late as two years after the end of the war a Member of Parliament complained in the House of

the appalling moral vacuum which has been created. Toddlers are being sent out to pick up cigarette ends – for the black market; 10- or 11-year-olds are sent out to play with the troops and get cigarettes – for the black market; and girls from 14 to 16 are set out to solicit and get cigarettes – for the black market.[10]

Cigarettes or spirits or chocolate or coffee or soap – costing their British owners little – could be traded for cameras, binoculars, optical instruments, jewellery, porcelain, silver, paintings – any valuables which had survived the catastrophe. And troops were disposing not just of personal rations but of stolen army stores. Lack of accurate accounting and record-keeping and the continual turnover of military personnel through demobilization created endless possibilities for looting (or 'liberating', in the jargon of the times) both military and civilian goods. A public-safety officer reported, 'Black market operations flourish here [in Hamburg] as in no other part of the British Zone'; 3,000 black-market cases were awaiting trial in German courts.[11]

With the advent of the Control Commission with its mixed bag of recruits, military miscreants were reinforced by civilian ones. Public Safety Branch claimed that the situation regarding the black market was grave, 'and the task of keeping it under effective control is made more difficult by the illegal activities of the Control Commission'.[12] One case, which made it into *The Times*, involved eight senior CCG officers, one of whom had the equivalent rank of brigadier and two others that of colonel.[13] One of the accused had staffed his branch 'with friends and associates regardless of the grotesque lack of qualifications of some of them'. Another had only drawn four pounds in pay over eighteen months' service. Goods involved in the case included firearms, silver and rationed foods. The officers had control of raw material and fuel for factories and had the power to close factories down or earmark them for reparations. No German dared inform, but Scotland Yard investigators caught up with those responsible in the end.

In the first months of peace the taking away of private property had been officially condoned. Until 1 August 1945 any such action was ruled to be an 'incident of war' and no compensation would be paid.[14] 'To the victor the spoils.' Only the most distinguished victims earned a mention in the records. In March 1945 a party of British soldiers entered Schloss Glücksberg, the home of the Grand Duchess of Mecklenburg, a princess of the British royal house. Led by a major in Field Security and claiming to be in search of leading Nazis, they had helped themselves to jewels worth 25,000 marks and 10,000 marks in cash while the Grand Duchess and her family looked on. Appeals to the officer in charge were disregarded. When the war ended, an investigation was begun through BAOR. It was revealed that the officer involved had previously been involved in a looting affair in Flensburg and acquitted. Further investigations were considered impracticable, 'owing to the lapse of time and the demobilization of all material witnesses'.[15]

Of course any amount of low-level stealing of goods from the Germans, although perhaps a tragedy for their owners, went unremarked. More important disappearances of property, involving millions of marks, occurred through lack of supervision or responsible recording when large and historic properties were requisitioned.

The vast Krupps mansion, Villa Hügel, outside Essen, was taken over by the British Military Government as the headquarters of North German Coal Control. The house was full of treasures of every description: old-master paintings, silver, tapestries, antique furniture. Many of these were removed from the house and stored in outbuildings, looked after by German storemen under the supervision initially of the Army and subsequently of the CCG. Unbelievably, at no time was any inventory taken by the Occupation authorities. But the German custodian of the Krupp mansion had done so: in April 1945, in September 1946, in 1948 and in 1950. In 1952, when the British derequisitioned the villa, the custodian's records revealed property worth some 2 million Deutschmarks missing.[16]

An inquiry was hastily instigated, and Special Investigation Branch was instructed that it should be pursued 'with full vigour and without discrimination and should not be affected by the grade of any persons who may be involved'.[17] Depositions were taken from both Germans and British who had been in charge of the repositories in the outbuildings – even from those who had returned to Britain. A mass of property was recovered in Holland, whither it had been taken by a sergeant-interpreter of the Royal Netherlands Army who had been stationed at the villa, working for the British. He had removed valuable books, paintings and silver, easily transported by car over the frontier. Light-fingered Britons did not have the convenience of a land frontier with Germany, but evidence was given of items of furniture, carpets, cutlery and glassware having started the journey to the United Kingdom via the 'barge route' with its terminal on the Ruhr river at the conveniently adjacent town of Duisburg.[18]

German domestic servants employed by the British had helped themselves. As they were all local people, they were easily located. Former army and CCG personnel were pursued in Britain. Over 100 items were retrieved. The inquiries carried out in Britain upset the Foreign Office: 'The Secretary of State does not want to be faced with the unnecesssary task of answering questions that he initiated widespread investigations in the special interest of the former war criminal Krupp.' The High Commissioner in Germany, Sir Ivone Kirkpatrick, pointed out that it would have been rather more embarrassing had the German parliament discovered that the German taxpayer 'had been stung for a considerable sum because the British had looted on a massive scale and had declined to take steps to recover the loot'.[19]

The depredations at the Villa Hügel had arisen from the total lack of responsible control. But the activities at Schloss Bückeburg were on quite a different level. The owner was in the top rank of German nobility, and the British officers involved belonged to the highest echelons of the Occupation forces.[20]

Schloss Bückeburg in Westphalia had been the home of the Schaumberg-Lippe family for nearly eleven centuries. With its 200 rooms and historic treasures valued at millions of marks, the Schloss had been placed on the Official List of Protected Monuments under the supervision of the Monuments and Fine Arts

Branch of the Control Commission. But in April 1945 the head-quarters of BAFO (British Air Force of Occupation) was established in the nearby town of Bad Eilsen. The occupiers took over the Schloss by simply chalking over the door, 'Required by the RAF.' The owner, Prince Wolrad, was told he would not be arrested if he remained under house arrest some twenty miles away and placed the administration of the estate under RAF instructions. The Prince's entire property was to be regarded as belonging to the RAF.

Air Officer Commanding Air Vice-Marshal Sir Arthur Coningham detailed a flight lieutenant on his staff to acquire a residence for him in the area. The flight lieutenant lighted upon an empty property known locally as 'the Farmhouse', which he then set about furnishing from the Schloss. As various witnesses – British and German – later attested, from the end of April until June 1945 on average four or five lorries came every day to the Schloss. Material selected by the flight lieutenant was removed and transferred to the Farmhouse. Paintings, carpets and rugs, chandeliers, china and glass, even Gobelin tapestries, were taken. The Schloss custodian was promised an inventory when the furnishing of the residence was complete, but, in spite of repeated requests, none was supplied.

For safety during the war the Schaumberg-Lippe silver had been dispersed in thirty-eight boxes among the homes of members of staff. In view of the imminence of housing requisitioning, the Prince's agent had brought the silver back to the Schloss. These boxes were now ordered to be loaded into RAF lorries and transferred to the Farmhouse. According to the German staff supervisor and the RAF corporal in charge at the residence, twenty-two of the thirty-eight boxes were unpacked and the contents disposed about the house. The contents of the remaining sixteen were laid out in the cellar. On 25 June Air Vice-Marshal Coningham took up residence.

The Schloss and its collections had for months been, in the words of the local Military Government commander, a thorn in the side of Monuments and Fine Arts Branch (MFA). In June

MFA managed to secure the sealing of the two artistically most important rooms in the castle: the chapel and the *Goldener Saal*. The decoration of the latter was extremely fragile and had hitherto been perfectly preserved. On a return visit later, the local MFA officer discovered that the *Goldener Saal* had been reopened and was being used as an office.

In July Air Vice-Marshal Coningham left for France. He had a villa at Cannes on the Riviera, which he designated a 'rest home' for senior RAF officers. German servants helped RAF staff to pack silver, glass, porcelain, rugs, carpets, even tapestries into cases. These were loaded on to two lorries. The sergeant in charge then departed with them. The air vice-marshal had two Dakota aircraft allotted to him for his personal use. According to statements by his aircrew at the subsequent inquiry, one of these was used as a freight plane and made many flights to the South of France and England. Professor Geoffrey Webb of MFA recorded, 'We were very concerned that Coningham had his own private plane and we were afraid that objects might be removed out of the country.' This concern was conveyed at the time to the Political Adviser to the Chief of Air Staff, Air Vice-Marshal Arthur Tedder, at Headquarters in Berlin.

The night before he left for France, Coningham ordered that all the silver in the cellar was to be taken to the RAF Welfare Unit depot for distribution to senior officers for their own use. There it was unpacked and displayed on tables and shelves. Various senior officers visited the depot and chose pieces for themselves. These were signed for, but the receipts were vague – 'silver for eighteen persons', for instance.

Coningham was succeeded as Air Officer Commanding by Air Vice-Marshal Sholto Douglas, who took up residence at the Farmhouse for the next few months until he succeeded Montgomery as Commander-in-Chief of the zone. The Farmhouse was then taken over by his successor, Air Vice-Marshal Philip Wigglesworth.

The RAF was now brought up short by its own Financial Adviser. In a minute in August 1945 he sharply drew attention to the dangers of negligent control of such valuable property. A claim might accrue against the British government for property which had come under control of the occupying power and was later found to be missing. He referred particularly to Schloss Bückeburg.

In reply to a request for information about the silver sent to the Welfare Unit, Coningham replied from Cannes that 'the silver was a mass of dull stuff, wrongly listed or missing in many respects'. Some material – furniture, crockery and so on – which had been taken down to France had been found to be in excess of requirements for the officers' rest home and he was therefore returning it. The Assistant Inspector General of Public Safety subsequently noted, 'Sir Arthur did not, unfortunately, disclose that he had a considerable quantity of silver, china, carpets, etc. at Cannes.' (Ellis Waterhouse of MFA noted the 'unfortunate Goering-like' attitude of the air vice-marshal.)

At the beginning of January 1946, with the permission of Military Government, furniture, paintings, jewels and the remaining silver were removed from the Schloss to the mausoleum in the grounds, which had never been requisitioned by the RAF and to which it had no access. However, the custodian was forced to surrender the keys to the RAF, and further removals of property took place. The nobs of the Occupation were anxious to enjoy a princely lifestyle. Lady Sholto Douglas visited the mausoleum and ordered that nothing should be removed, as the contents would be required to equip the two residences of her husband, the new Military Governor. Three weeks later she arrived in her car and departed with seventy items of silver and sets of silver cutlery. A month later came a major on behalf of Sir William Strang, political adviser to the Military Governor at Berlin Headquarters. Thirty-two items were removed, one of which was a case of eighty-four wine glasses. In November a selection of sixty-two princely items were on their way to General Sir Gordon Macready, Regional Commissioner for Hanover and Lower Saxony.

The inquiry prompted by the RAF Financial Adviser and conducted by a Property Control officer, Howarth, continued meanwhile. Matters now took an unfortunate turn. Lord Rothermere had got wind of the story and had dispatched a *Daily Mail* correspondent to 'obtain information regarding certain irregularities committed by high-level British officers'. The reporter, Richard Greenough, a wartime RAF officer and former chief public-relations officer at the UN Relief and Rehabilitation Administration (UNRRA), arrived in Hanover on 4 July. Within the next few days he had interviewed the custodian, the Prince's agent, Prince Wolrad himself and the Duke of Brunswick. The latter was a cousin of the Prince and related to the British royal family, being a nephew of King Edward VII.

Greenough's article appeared on 8 July 1947. The reporter seemed extremely well informed. Names were named: Tedder, Douglas, Coningham, Wigglesworth, Strang were 'assisting in the enquiries'. The Duke of Brunswick had told him that the investigation had begun after he had sent a personal message to the King. (A retired RAF officer who had been stationed at BAFO GHQ remembered many years later 'the King's intervention about Schaumberg-Lippe'. As duty officer, he had answered the telephone one night to find the King himself at the other end demanding to know why things were not progressing. He was hastily put through to someone more superior.)[21]

The Commander-in-Chief, Sir Sholto Douglas, was assured by the acting Regional Commissioner for Hanover, Brigadier J. Lingham, that the report by Property Control 'would not be placed on file'. There were only six copies, and they would be kept under lock and key. 'It was intolerable', wrote Lingham, 'that names should be mentioned in connection with Schaumberg-Lippe in a way that seems to suggest that all was not as it should be.' The German press had raised some questions arising out of the *Daily Mail* article. They had been told that a routine check was taking place 'and that, for the rest, the article was a Press stunt'.

Sir Sholto Douglas, meanwhile, tipped off Sir Arthur Coningham. On 30 July Sir Arthur responded with an official letter from Cannes. As he was retiring from the RAF in November, he would like to return 'sundry articles of German furniture and equipment which were sent down there'. His villa had now been leased by the French government and was reverting to private hands. As originally it had not been completely furnished, he had arranged for staff to take down necessary equipment – table silver, ornaments, crockery, rugs. As this was in excess of requirements, 'a lot' had been returned in August 1946. He was now returning the remainder. A quantity of silver and three Gobelin tapestries were subsequently received at Bückeburg.

Meanwhile, further investigation was put into the hands of Assistant Inspector-General T. Hayward of Public Safety Branch – a CID inspector seconded from Scotland Yard. But before his report was finished Sir Sholto Douglas was gone.

Marshal of the Royal Air Force (he always insisted on his full title) Sir Sholto Douglas had succeeded Field-Marshal Montgomery as Commander-in-Chief in May 1946. There had been a discussion with the Foreign Secretary about possible resignation the following January, although his term of duty did not expire until October 1947. In May 1947 he had a meeting with Bevin. In June the Minister for German Affairs, Lord Pakenham, was informed that the Secretary of State 'had conveyed in general terms to Sir Sholto Douglas the fact that his services will be dispensed with'. The Foreign Office drafted some notes as a background to the announcement, 'to dispose tacitly of any question that Sir Sholto Douglas might be leaving Germany for any other reason than that his term of duty has come to an end'. Sir Sholto in his turn told a press conference, 'If you are expecting something sensational I am afraid you will be disappointed.' He had felt in need of a rest and a change of occupation.[22] He was succeeded by his deputy, General Sir Brian Robertson.

In December 1947 Inspector Hayward produced an interim report. Property missing included 166 carpets, 155 paintings and five Gobelin tapestries. Out of the original 6,442 pieces of silver contained in the thirty-eight boxes, 2,993 were missing. The new Commander-in-Chief, Sir Brian Robertson, ordered the investigation to continue. He would not close the inquiry until every effort had been made to trace the bulk of the property and bring to book anyone who might be responsible for the disappearance of large quantities of it: 'What we should aim to deal with is a large-scale looting and not a petty pilfering.'[23]

On 30 June 1948 Inspector Hayward produced his final report. The last missing Gobelin had been recovered from a former wing commander now working for the Air Ministry as a civilian. Interviewed by the RAF police, he claimed that he had thought it was of no value and had used it for packing purposes when he returned home. Hayward considered this 'a very poor answer to a charge of stealing'. With regard to property removed to the South of France, Hayward noted that, although there was a record of what had been returned from Cannes in August 1945 and later in 1947, 'We have no means of ascertaining whether all that was originally taken was in fact returned.' He had interviewed Coningham himself in London. 'Unfortunately he was about to leave by the morning plane for Paris and could spare me only a few minutes.'

Inspector Hayward stated that the investigation into the missing silver had come to the end of the line unless new information emerged. It was possible, he concluded, that at some future date responsibility for the losses might become an issue. The evidence assembled by his investigation 'indicates quite clearly where the responsibility lies'.

Earlier, in 1946, Economics Division of the Control Commission had reported to London that illegal trading, inside Germany and beyond its frontiers, had reached unprecedented proportions and threatened to ruin what little remained of the country's financial and economic structure. 'Nowhere has anything been experienced comparable with the developments in this field which have taken place in Germany during the past twelve months.'

A top-secret report was prepared by Economic Sub-Commission Headquarters and Public Safety Branch.[24] The findings were so staggering that it is worth reproducing here just some of the highlights.

Investigations had begun in Berlin, where it was discovered that 'a large number of illegal trading groups existed in which many Allied officers appeared to participate'. The total amounts involved led to a widening of the investigations, which, although covering 'no more than a small part of the ground', revealed an extent of black-market activities sufficient to present 'a major threat to the German and perhaps even European economy and financial stability'. The large number of Allied officers involved was 'a threat to Allied prestige and morale which might eventually have political repercussions'.

Before the war the Nazi government had placed under strict control all German assets in precious metals and stones. The movement and handling of these were prohibited without the sanction of the government agency Reichstelle für Edelmetalle (RfE). During the war such materials were acquired from occupied countries by government purchases on the black market, by expropriation of Jewish property, and by the organizations whose task it was to loot valuables for the SS and leading Nazis. The RfE extended its authority to these importations and to currency, shares, patents and works of art. Another agency was responsible for receiving and controlling radium, uranium and other radioactive minerals. From information received, it was estimated that in 1938 Germany had held twelve grams of radium; at the end of the war, twenty-five grams. (It was found that some eight grams were presently available on the black market in Berlin.) The RfE, its considerable deposits, the larger part of its staff and its records were dispersed to Thuringia during the first months of 1945. Various officials, individually responsible for stocks of valuables, moved from there – some to the West and others deeper into the east of Germany. After May 1945 contact between the various sections of the RfE ceased and thus an organization responsible for immense wealth had disintegrated and its assets had slipped beyond Allied control.

At this first stage of the investigations the amounts involved were somewhere in the neighbourhood of $300 million. The suspicion that specific British personnel had undertaken irregular investigations on their own behalf into the location of the precious metals necessitated the whole operation being placed on a top-secret basis and taken over by Intelligence. It was considered possible that certain personalities in British Military Government 'could not be taken fully into trust'. Sir Brian Robertson wrote to Christopher Steel, Political Adviser at Headquarters, that the operation was discovering 'a certain amount of peculation on the part of Allied officers'. He was glad to say there was no evidence of peculation by British officers on a large scale, 'though it will be surprising if we do not discover some instances where objects of value have adhered to the wrong fingers'. He was to be in for a shock.[25]

US Counter-Intelligence now joined British Intelligence in what was designated 'Operation Sparkler'. In view of the Soviets' approach to illegal trading 'their co-operation in a joint operation cannot be called upon'. Information from the directors of the Berlin Stadtkontorbank led to the discovery that 25,000 carats of precious and industrial diamonds with an estimated pre-war value of 50 million marks were lodged in the bank's vaults. Alas, the bank was located in the Russian Sector.

The ramifications of the black market were staggering. Americans with their German friends were organizing a large export and import business based in New York with agencies in Paris and Brussels. Germans involved included members of the Berlin administration holding key positions. Certain 'personalities' in black-market groups were former SS members. Other Allied officers and officials were involved in transactions covering deals in precious metals and stones, antiques, paintings, furs and clothing, carpets, and real-estate property. Optical instruments – cameras, binoculars, microscopes, photographic equipment – were obtained from stocks scattered throughout the zones and particularly in the British Sector of Berlin. They were traded for hundreds of millions of marks. Millions also changed hands in the purchase of radium by Yugoslavs and Czechs. Deals were 'reliably reported' in opium, cocaine, penicillin and other medicaments. Narcotics were obtained from abroad – from Switzerland, for instance. Drugs such as penicillin were obtained from British, American and other Allied personnel. Apart from French officers operating in Berlin and elsewhere in Germany, a special French group was 'manipulating trans-actions in drugs and medicinal preparations, particularly peni-cillin'. Shades of Harry Lime – already left far behind in this scale of things.

Motor fuel was easily obtained from Allied stores and 'is indeed mostly stored in the many garages in the centre of Berlin, mainly in the British sector'.

> Since German transport has shifted and is still carrying con-siderable consignments of valuables through all four zones of Germany and outside the Reich frontiers (for instance a whole plastics factory has been set up in Belgium by the American group, from machinery transported through the British Zone by Russian lorries) it is not unreasonable to suppose that this is being effected if not with the help, at least with the cognizance of certain Control Commission officials.

> Diamonds totalling some 34,000 carats from the Low Coun-tries had been distributed to various firms through Germany and also taken into Switzerland and Spain.

> Foodstuffs were mostly derived from the Allies' stores and from black-market sources in Denmark. Danes and Germans together were operating food rackets between Denmark and Germany. The Swedish Red Cross was selling foodstuffs on the black market. At least one Norwegian officer was involved with the Americans. Displaced persons who received food and cloth-ing from UNRRA and the Joint Jewish Relief Society were noto-rious for organizing selling agencies to dispose of these supplies. UNRRA transport was frequently used for the movement of

stolen stores and property. Two Chinese officers of senior rank appeared to be involved in the selling of foodstuffs.

With no frontier control inside Germany, there was vast smuggling activity in and out of the British Zone. In May 1947 the Regional Commissioner for Hamburg, Sir Vaughan Berry, reported the confiscation on the border of large hauls of cigarettes, coffee and spirits, together with 1.5 million Oxford units of penicillin and considerable amounts of morphine, opium and cocaine valued at between 50,000 and 200,000 marks. This was at a time when the average daily ration in hungry Hamburg over a four-week period was 1,000 calories (two of those weeks only reaching 850).

As late as 1948 illegal trading was continuing unabated. The Educational Adviser Robert Birley received a communication from a student who had gone 'underground' to monitor the black market. Best-sellers were cigarettes, tobacco, ration cards, chewing gum, watches and rings. Luxuries were chocolate, tea, cocoa, fruit, cameras and dogs. There was a brisk trade in narcotics – cocaine (sold by the kilo), morphine and opium – penicillin (for VD), quinine (for abortions) and contraceptives. 'You can buy anything,' he wrote: 'passports, visas, entry permits, foreign and DP identity papers and exit permits – which are not even forgeries.'[26]

The authors of the top-secret report emphasized that only a small proportion of the ground had so far been covered and that the bulk of the work had still to be done.

> The question of buying up of real estate in Berlin by foreigners is again a chapter by itself. It is our impression that the black market groups are so strong and numerous that no real estimates can yet be obtained as to how much real estate they have already purchased or as to the true extent of their holdings in the other commodities mentioned above.

> The authors had not investigated the subject of art treasures

but could report that these and museum pieces of Dutch and other foreign origins were being traded. Many, because of their priceless value, were not readily marketable in Europe, but there was considerable interest in the United States.

The report summarized its conclusions. The distinct impression was gained that the most varied and the most concentrated activity was to be found in the British Sector of Berlin and that, in addition to certain British Control Commission officers who were actually named, 'quite a large number of our own people are aware of what is going on . . . Each individual investigation unearthed some new aspect of this black picture and brought forth a further list of personalities who are involved in it.' Many rumours were circulating regarding the extent of British involvement. The fact that there had been no coordinated British action to uproot and destroy illegal marketing led to the assumption in many circles – which included some reliable German personalities – that the British authorities were willing to tolerate the current position until such time as a stabilized currency system could be introduced. 'The amounts involved in the British Sector of Berlin and the British Zone proper are likely to run into many millions of pounds and may be of sufficient consequence as to lead to a substantial reduction of the British Sterling expenditure on behalf of Germany.'

In October 1946 Prime Minister Attlee approved the appointment of a team of forty Scotland Yard detectives to investigate criminal activities among British personnel in Germany.[27] Although the establishment of a special inquiry was considered 'a matter of some urgency', typically much time and paper was expended in arguing about the salary and grading of the officers concerned. The CCG – spiritually if not legally part of the Civil Service – was obsessive about such matters.

In 1948 the chief of the Internal Affairs Directorate of the Control Commission, Julian Simpson, resigned amid some controversy – much aired in the German press – because he considered that the general behaviour of the armed forces and the

Control Commission did not match up to the high standard required and believed that an example should be made of certain senior members.[28]

In a debate in the House of Commons on British administration in Germany, Earl Winterton declared, 'Whether we like it or not, we have an immense moral responsibility for British Occupied Germany. It is with us day and night, and the sooner we, as a House, realize it and the sooner the country realizes it, the better . . .'[29]

7

'A strange people
in a strange enemy country'

A YEAR after the surrender the Cabinet took a momentous decision. In April 1946 the Armed Service Ministers and the Minister for German Affairs, J. B. Hynd, discussed the question of
reuniting wives, already separated for so long during the war
years, with husbands who were serving in Germany. The British
Zone had been designated by the Ministry of Defence a 'home
station'. This meant that families would normally have expected
to be accommodated in married quarters. But that was not possible on the Continent. Nevertheless, it was felt that it would be
wrong to keep families apart in peacetime. After weighing various options (such as increased frequency of home leave), the
Cabinet agreed that members of the forces and of the Control
Commission serving in north-west Germany with not less than
one year's service in prospect should be allowed to have their
wives and families with them. A memorandum was sent to the
Cabinet seeking a decision in principle, so that preparatory
steps might be taken, but with a caveat: it was felt that it would
be unwise to start any movement of families at the present time,
when there was such grave distress among the civil population of
Germany. The disregard of this warning was in due course to
have dire results. In June Cabinet approval was given for what
was to be known as 'Operation Union'.

In a memorandum to the three service chiefs, Prime Minister Attlee raised an admonitory finger. It was very important
that the British wives who were going out to join their husbands
in Germany should be well briefed before leaving:

First and most important, they should be told they will be
looked on by the Germans as representatives of the British

Empire and that on their behaviour and that of the children, far more than that of the armed forces, the Germans will judge the British and the British way of life. Therefore they must be meticulously careful all the time to behave as they wish this Empire to be regarded: good mannered and tactful, and they should take the greatest care of the houses in which they live, and the contents thereof; and not consider, just because it is German property, they can misuse it as they like.

Second, stipulated Attlee, they should be told something of Germany, Germans and their way of living.[1]

But the German way of living at that time was very far from that described in the official information booklet, *You Are Going into Germany*. The booklet's contents were totally irrelevant to the actuality that awaited the travellers.

'You are about to meet a strange people in a strange enemy country,' declared the author of this guidebook. 'It is necessary to know something about what sort of people they are.' The tone was not, as in earlier effusions prepared for the occupiers, aggressively hostile, although there was a stern résumé of the Nazi regime and its dastardly record. There was even a rather backhanded reference to opponents of the regime – 'of course there were Germans who were against the Nazis all along . . . but even those Germans who have been more or less anti-Nazi will have their axe to grind . . . There is no need for you to bother about German attempts to justify themselves.'

After some basic background on Germany's geography, climate, industry (destroyed) and (no longer existent) transport system, the text became more anthropological: 'When you meet the Germans you will probably think they are very much like us. They look like us, except that there are few of the wiry type and more big, fleshy, fair-haired men and women, especially in the North. But they are not really as much like us as they look.'

Then, under the heading 'How the Germans Live', there were some hugely irrelevant paragraphs on German cuisine.

The chief difference from English cooking was the treatment of vegetables. In place of 'the English boiled greens' the Germans served pickled white and red cabbage – 'very tasty if you eat them with *Wiener-Schnitzel* or *Schweinkotellet*'. Germans preferred pork and veal to beef and mutton and cooked them better. But the staple meat dish was the sausage, of which there were hundreds of varieties. The Germans 'are very fond of pastries with *Schlagsahne* (whipped cream) but it will be some time before such luxuries are obtainable again at the *Konditorei* (confectioner) . . . The Germans don't know how to make tea, but they are quite expert with coffee.' The many varieties of beer were extolled, but 'whiskey and gin will be scarce'. But life was not just fleshpots: 'The Germans are extremely fond of music. Beethoven, Bach, Brahms and Wagner were all Germans.'

The newcomers were forewarned about the ruins by means of a comparison. The Germans had dropped 7,500 tons of bombs on London in eleven months; 'we' had dropped 10,000 tons on Duisburg in two attacks between a Saturday and Sunday morning. But no prior warning could have prepared them for the unimaginable reality.

On 15 August 1946 the first contingent of 'Married Families' (as they were officially designated) set sail from Tilbury in the SS *Empire Halladale* and SS *Empire Trooper* (both former German ships) on the 424-mile journey to the port of Cuxhaven on the north-west coast of Germany. Organization by BAOR was flawless. Everything went without a hitch. Every possible problem or necessity on the voyage had been anticipated. Where travellers were to be directed by the first letter of their surname, special instructions were provided for those with double-barrelled surnames. Each person was given a Union Jack badge to be worn in Germany (although, as one woman said, they were sufficiently identified by being well dressed and well fed). All trains were colour-coded according to their routes, and each traveller received a coloured flag relating to her destination. There would be no misplaced wives turning up for the wrong husbands.

For the women leaving behind the dreariness of post-war

austerity Britain it was like a dream. The composition of the trains had been so calculated that each person had a corner seat. Cigarettes, sweets and magazines were available. On the long-distance trains sleeper accommodation was provided. Restaurant cars served meals. But the guidebook had not prepared them for the actual state of the country in which they were to set up their new homes and upon which they now gazed with excitement and happy anticipation from their corner seats.

As the first trains of Operation Union fanned out through Germany, the passengers saw at first hand the reality of a nation in defeat. Near the towns the tracks were lined, as usual, with people – mostly children – begging for food. For troops going on leave it had become almost a routine to throw out of the train windows the ration packs supplied for the journey. For some there was a particular pleasure in singling out an individual child and watching the package fall into a pair of eager hands. For the British women, this first sight of those who had for so long been simply the faceless enemy was a shock. One six-year-old, to the embarrassment of her mother, piped up, 'Those aren't Germans, are they? I thought Germans were animals.' The apprehension some of the early arrivals might have felt at the prospect of coming face to face with the enemy was dissipated by the sight of the thin, almost yellow-faced figures and the all-pervading air of hopelessness.

Eyes were further opened on the drive from the station. First there was the shock of the unimagined and unimaginable devastation. Drifting smoke from a pipe protruding from a pile of rubble, they learned, indicated that another kind of married family was living underneath. Astonishingly, here and there a line of washing straddled the ruins. The chatty guidebook had not prepared them for anything like this.

The failure (or refusal) to heed the warning against moving families into a Germany in circumstance of 'grave distress' began to have its dire effects.

As soon as Operation Union had been authorized, the Army had set about acquiring accommodation for the incoming families on a wide scale by ejecting the occupants of such housing as was still standing. The Army was, understandably but ruthlessly, determined that soldiers should have their families join them. But in October 1946, when the first families had already arrived, the Commander-in-Chief and Military Governor, Air Marshal Sir Sholto Douglas, informed the commanders of the three Services that the housing situation in the zone was 'unparalleled'. He wrote personally to the Commander of the British Army of the Rhine, General Sir Richard McCreery, to say that the situation in Hamburg was desperate. General Surtees, Commander of Hamburg District, was demanding 100 houses and 300 flats for Married Families and would be evicting 6,000 Germans. Yet Surtees was refusing to release barracks which could absorb the occupants of cellars and air-raid shelters. The Minister, Hynd, had given an undertaking that housing would not be requisitioned for British families unless similar alternative accommodation for its German occupants could be found. The Regional Commissioner for Hamburg, Sir Vaughan Berry, had now told him that the fulfilment of this pledge was quite impossible. Unmoved, General McCreery agreed that the situation arising out of the arrival of British families in Germany was indeed reaching a crisis but nevertheless insisted that Germany *must* count as a home station for the Army.[2] In the House of Commons the Minister's response to a Parliamentary Question on the problem was sublime: the Germans should be asked to 'move up a little and make room'.[3]

A report by British women's organizations, including the Townswomen's Guild and the National Association of Women's Institutes, had calculated that the living space allowed to each German after British requirements had been met would be four square metres – the floor space of two ordinary beds.[4] A letter to *The Times* signed by a score of distinguished Englishwomen deplored the requisitioning of homes in circumstances of such widespread distress.[5] Mrs Winston Churchill wrote separately to endorse their letter.

After a consultation between Berry and Generals McCreery

and Surtees, it was agreed that the situation in Hamburg would be reviewed every month. Berry wrote to the Commander-in-Chief, 'The Service authorities are now fully aware of the consequences, political and otherwise, of inflicting unnecessary hardship on the German population . . . If it does not work, I shall not hesitate to stop *all* evictions and to stop the inflow of families.'[6]

One of the scandals of requisitioning which did much damage to relations with the local population was the number of premises requisitioned and then left standing empty. Public Relations Branch in Buxtehude reported that, when they had tried to talk to the Germans about British democracy, fingers had been pointed at a street of thirty-two houses requisitioned eleven months previously and still standing empty.

Sometimes military exigency was responsible for such situations. In Schleswig-Holstein, for instance, barracks stood empty because 6th Airborne Regiment might arrive from Palestine and accommodation had to be kept available. But often the Army simply moved out of houses without derequisitioning them – sometimes through oversight; sometimes on the well-known Army principle of never giving up property once acquired; sometimes through callous unconcern. In the early days after the surrender the military entering a town simply took over any sizeable undamaged premises, usually for officers' messes, and expelled the occupants. As such actions were unofficial, there was no handing-over routine when the unit moved away. Even when premises had been officially acquired through the Town Major's office, once relinquished they could be left unoccupied for long periods or simply forgotten about. In Hamburg a block of 130 empty houses, evacuated by troops, continued to be guarded by German watchmen without anyone being aware of the situation. (In 1954 a Foreign Office brief noted that some houses in Germany were still under requisition after nine years.) Furniture would be 'requisitioned' by the Army, with units trawling areas of surviving housing with trucks and removing items which took their fancy. This might be stored in warehouses, overlooked and forgotten when personnel in charge were posted or demobilized, then pilfered by German and British civilian staff. Or items might be moved from house to house or town to town without any record being kept.

The Military Governor, Sir Sholto Douglas, ordered checks on all requisitioned property to ensure that the optimum use was made of it. The Army was requisitioning premises just to strip them of furniture for the Married Families and then leaving them unoccupied. No houses must be left empty.[7] In January 1947 he announced that he had under review the question of accommodation of Married Families and was not prepared to authorize any further large-scale requisitions of houses beyond those already planned.[8]

In the spring of that year there was a head-on clash between the town of Essen and the Occupation authorities. Essen, in the heart of the Ruhr, had been one of the most heavily bombed towns in the zone. An order was given for eighty families to be evicted to make room for the families of 76th Field Regiment, Royal Artillery. The town council forbade its housing officer to carry out the order and passed a resolution expressing regret at its inability to defend its citizens. Regional Commissioner Asbury informed the Minister-President of North Rhine–Westphalia that if the council refused to obey he would dismiss the burgomaster and the whole council if necessary. If this failed to produce results he would ask the Army to take control and enforce the evictions. He then warned Berlin of the steps he had taken, adding that it would be fatal to allow the Germans to think that the British authorities were bluffing. Headquarters was alarmed: 'You will no doubt consider the grave repercussions both in Germany and the United Kingdom which might result from use by British troops of physical force to effect evictions particularly where women and children are concerned.' Essen perforce eventually abandoned its resistance.[9]

Two months after the arrival of the first contingent of Operation Union, the Military Governor declared that many of the 23 million inhabitants of the British Zone were living in conditions that were intolerable.

Against this background of escalating distress, the British in Germany embarked upon what was to be nothing less than a folly of overwhelming proportions: the Hamburg Project. This single scheme encapsulated everything that was basically wrong with the Occupation: the failure of firm control from the top; the lack of forward thinking; the misappropriation of scarce resources; the sublime disregard in London for the reality of conditions in Germany; the almost unwitting lack of humanity.

At the end of 1945 Control Office Headquarters in London decided to concentrate in one location the headquarters of BAOR, the headquarters of British Naval Forces, the headquarters of the Control Commission and the various Zonal Executive offices which were scattered about in small relatively unscathed towns.[10] The plan was drawn up without any firm idea – official or unofficial – of how long the Occupation would last, how it would evolve or the actual numbers who would need to be accommodated. The only thing which seemed important was the prestige of the British imperium. The visiting Parliamentary Select Committee investigating expenditure in the zone was briefed in Berlin: 'The prestige of the Headquarters and indeed of the United Kingdom itself obviously demands more suitable accommodation than that which it occupies at present.'[11]

Various locations were canvassed, and Hamburg was the unlucky winner. Twelve tall buildings were to be erected (paid for by the Germans and reverting to them at some future date) in a central area of the city. But not only the offices were to be resited. All British personnel and families in the zone were to be absorbed into living accommodation in the same complex or near by. They would thus be removed from all contact with the natives. The plan was actually referred to in Foreign Office documents as a 'cantonment'. A whole area would be cleared of Germans and made exclusively British.

Approximately 750 houses would be demolished to clear the site for the construction of six-storey blocks consisting of hotels, clubs, theatres, shops and flats for single personnel. (It was reckoned that 38,200 Germans would lose their homes.) The armed

forces would take over existing barracks and in addition requisition 800 houses for quarters. It was estimated that 6,450 Germans would be evicted to provide 350 houses for senior officers.[12]
In the pleasant suburb of Blankenese on the Elbe, 4,100 houses
would be 'made available' for 17,000 single officers. Residents
who were without a trade or profession would simply be
deported to other parts of the zone. A country house would
become an officers' social club with a dance hall, a restaurant
seating 1,000, a bar, a lounge and a reading room. Another
country house would provide an officers' sports club with restaurant, bar, billiard room, four squash courts and twelve tennis
courts. There would be a social club for warrant officers and ser-
geants, with all amenities, including twelve tennis courts. There
would be riverside clubs for all ranks, for swimming and boating.
In barracks NAAFI clubs would be constructed for other ranks.
One barracks would have a club for 3,000 with dance floor,
restaurant and kitchen – in addition to eight tennis courts, one
hockey pitch and three playing fields. Another would have a
similar dining and dancing facility plus seven tennis courts and
three playing fields. Inside the enclave there would an other
ranks' social club. There would also be a cinema, and a garrison
theatre seating 1,200. Additional recreational facilities around
the city would provide six playing fields, six football grounds and
three rugby grounds.[13]

Seven large existing buildings in the commercial centre –
occupied by 562 German firms with 5,800 employees – would be
requisitioned as office accommodation and their occupants
evicted. Many of these offices were connected with key industries being started in the zone and by the city administration.
But what really caused the planners' brows to wrinkle was the
problem of providing lunch for 10,000 British personnel at
approximately the same time as close to their offices as possible.[14]

Military Government officers in Hamburg, already trying to
hold the line against a housing catastrophe, were appalled. The
city could not possibly absorb the 50,000–60,000 who would be

evicted. Current housing work consisted simply of weather-proofing existing accommodation: there was no new building. Now Hamburg would would lose 16,000 of its building workforce needed for housing projects. This would have serious repercussions on the rehousing and rebuilding of Hamburg and the opening up of industries essential to the British Zone. Vaughan Berry had been fiercely opposed to the Hamburg Project from the word go.

In February 1946 a swingeing memorandum had winged its way to Germany from London which might at least have given pause for thought if not actually put paid to the whole scheme. The head of Finance Division, Paul Chambers, wrote to General Kirby at Headquarters in Berlin, 'I must confess I am horrified at the size and ambition of the proposals and I feel I must at once bring certain aspects to your attention.' There would be questions in the House:

> I do not for one moment think that the scale of accommodation you have in mind will be regarded at home as economic and modest, having regard to the severe housing shortage at home as well as in Germany . . . The expenditure on a colossal scale which you have in mind will involve the diversion of building resources from the urgent task of repairing existing living conditions . . . If all the facts were known it is exceedingly doubtful whether a democratic government either in Germany or Britain would sanction the diversion of resources in this way.[15]

Nevertheless, in May all branches of Military Government were informed that the project was to go ahead.[16]

In May the details of the Hamburg Project were communicated to Burgomaster Petersen. A month later Press and Information Division was authorized to make it public. When the news became known, shock and horror spread throughout the community. There was an immediate and dramatic reaction. A deputation of women of all classes presented a petition to the burgomaster which they implored him to present to Military Government. It was known, they wrote, that it was the war aim of the Allies to banish injustice, distress, fear and hatred from the world. Prime Minister Churchill and President Roosevelt had declared that the Allies would always put humanity in the forefront. The petitioners could not believe that the eviction of people from the remaining parts of the city that were still habitable, amid the unimaginable misery, reflected this deep moral obligation:

> An English residential quarter of the kind planned, populated by healthy and well-fed human beings, amid the hunger and distress, is a symbol of unbearable contrast . . . We see in the Project the greatest danger for our future and that of our children and implore the Military Government to put humanity in the forefront of their planning. We entreat you, Burgomaster Petersen, to make it clear to the Military Government that misery must not be stretched to the limit of the unbearable.

It was earnestly hoped that at the very last moment the destructive plans might be abolished and a better and happier solution be found.[17] A crowd of about 500 gathered outside the town hall to support the delegation, The crowd soon increased to several thousand. A report to the Commander-in-Chief described the citizens as being 'in ugly mood and singing the German national anthem'.

The petition was duly forwarded to Military Government by Burgomaster Petersen, but it received short shrift. The head of Military Government in Hamburg, Brigadier Armytage, received orders from Berlin: 'Inform the Burgomeister that the Commander-in-Chief is dissatisfied with the behaviour of certain sections of the population. The Citizens are to be warned that disturbances of order will not be tolerated. Firm measures will be taken if this warning is not heeded.'[18]

Armytage duly carried out his orders but made his own

impassioned plea to Berlin on behalf of the stricken city. The housing situation would reach saturation point by 1 September. Some 30,000 people were living in unhealthy cellars, air-raid shelters and hutted camps. The conditions in which they were living had to be seen to be believed. Anything between 225,000 and 300,000 either had no beds or were sharing. TB was increasing rapidly: from 495 cases in January to 1,168 open and infectious cases notified in May. Over 1,000 old, infirm and feeble-minded persons were dying for lack of attention. 'It may well be that they are better off out of this world but that is not my way of doing things.' He requested that the move of HQ BAOR should be delayed. There should be no further evacuations from the enclave by doubling people up elsewhere. 'I don't propose to agree to any further evictions than those already referred to unless I receive direct orders from you to do so.'[19]

In September the regional economic officer warned the Regional Commissioner, 'The economic recovery of Hamburg is being very seriously retarded by the Hamburg Project.' In fact the project was having a major adverse effect on the economy of the whole zone. The concentration of building labour and materials in Hamburg was halting construction elsewhere. Particularly serious was the effect in the Ruhr, where housing for miners was urgently needed to assure the output of desperately needed coal. Furthermore, there was widespread absenteeism, among a population living in cavemen conditions, while workers tried to secure habitable and weatherproof shelter.[20]

The details of this lamentable affair were to be withheld from Parliament. A leading official of Control Commission Headquarters in London was a member of a Parliamentary Committee touring Germany. He forwarded an advance copy of their report to General Ian Erskine at Headquarters in Berlin: 'You will notice that the whole passage about the Hamburg Project has gone out: we thought it better so.'[21] However, the gaff was blown by Richard Stokes MP after a visit to Germany in which he had discovered the whole story. He erupted in the House of Commons:

Are we to see, in the midst of this devastation and in a state of things where men and women have nowhere to live but holes in the ground – what? A great big gin palace in the middle of Hamburg. For what I call the Hamburg Poona, for the British Raj. Is this to be done when everybody is suffering from cold and hunger and is it to be surrounded with soldiers carrying fixed bayonets and marching up and down outside?[22]

Intelligence Branch summed up the damage being done in no uncertain terms: 'Uncertainty and insecurity hangs over every Hamburg citizen, defeating attempts to restore healthy and constructive initiative among the citizens.'[23]

In December 1946 a high-level conference was held in Hamburg. *Officially*, the project was *not* being abandoned. The decision was taken to announce temporary suspension because of difficulties with supplies. In reality Vaughan Berry had been instructed to fly to London the following day to inform the Foreign Office that it had been agreed that the project *should* be abandoned. HQ BAOR decided that work on the foundations should be completed to the point where the steelwork began.

On 10 March 1947 the Hamburg Project was handed over to the Germans for flats (although these could not be expected to be ready until at least 1952).

A handwritten note in a Foreign Office file stands as the epitaph of the Hamburg Project:

Officially, project is being resumed on the original scheme and is working on top priority second only to coal mining. *Actually*, will be brought to the stage where it will not deteriorate when left unfinished. This is the general understanding, though no-one can say it on paper. Apparently it is a matter for Cabinet decision and it is expected they will eventually admit the scheme should not have been started and call a halt to it.[24]

It was decided that the German situation made further requisitioning on a large scale virtually impracticable, although in 1948 Operation Union was still far from complete. It was proposed that houses for British families should be built by the German authorities under mandatory order of the Control Commission.[25]

But the British already had their reservations about German house-building. The Germans had insisted that their houses traditionally had cellars, the surface of the ground being considered to be cold and damp. But the British Housing Office discerned a hidden agenda. Cellars would have been used as shelters during the war and thus 'probably saved an appreciable percentage of the population'. It was decided that elimination of cellars would have 'a psychological effect on the man in the street and be an additional deterrent to any future 'ambitions'.[26] Hitler, the architect *manqué*, had spared time from his 'ambitions' in November 1940 to make known *his* specification for the German home:

> It is the Führer's wish that the kitchen should be of the kitchen–living-room type with cooking stove. The Führer has settled the bath versus shower controversy in favour of the shower so that families for reasons of economy will not have to use the same bath water. A People's Refrigerator will be available for the preservation of food.[27]

The Führer thought of everything.

An apt description of the British in Germany was that they lived on a magic carpet where they could forget the conditions in which those below them had their existence, until brought to earth by some perhaps simple experience which shocked them into realization. Concern at this lack of awareness of the conditions in which the indigenous population was living was voiced by the Chief of Staff at HQ BAOR as late as the end of 1947. He thought it would be a good idea if parties of wives could be given tours of, for instance, the Ruhr or Hamburg.[28] Such sightseeing trips around the ruined cities might have been a revelation of a sort, but they would not have brought the viewers any closer to the lives of the citizens who lived there.

The British women had found their new lives not without drawbacks, particularly the Control Commission wives.[29] The domestic arrangements were the same for Control Commission and service families. The size of the quarters allocated – house or flat – was dictated by the husband's rank or equivalent rank. The quantity and quality of all crockery and cutlery were similarly regulated. All cooking utensils were the same. All quarters were curtained with the same floral material known as 'Married Families Chintz'. (This was useful in identifying all British-occupied premises from outside.) Furnishings were a mixture of Army issue and what the 'occupied' had been forced to leave behind.

All this was normal army quartering routine, but the civilian wives found it difficult to accept. For many, the sameness of their domestic surroundings was an irritation – they felt they had lost their individuality. They could not introduce any variation: there was nothing to be bought in Germany. Eventually, Married Families shops were opened by the NAAFI, which eased the situation. Food, too, came as army rations on a graduated scale, delivered by army trucks – often in unmanageable quantities, such as seven-pound tins of jam. But this diet could always be varied by eating out in British clubs. Buying any food from Germans, whether on open sale or through the black market, was strictly forbidden. To do so reduced the food available to the population and – as payment had to be made with cigarettes or chocolate or soap or other British goods – also fuelled the black market, which was a major problem. Nor, on the other hand, was it allowed to give any food from British rations to Germans: according to the letter of the law, not even a meal to a domestic servant in the house. This was a rule which naturally went mostly unobserved.

Perhaps the major impact on the generality of British women was the availability of domestic help at low rates. The number of servants which could be hired was scaled upwards according to rank. Very senior officers had butlers, cooks, housekeepers, gardeners and (very important) boilermen. At first this seemed a great luxury after the struggles of life on the home front. But most women had never had a full-time domestic servant and found the situation difficult to handle. Some felt they would somehow 'lose face' with the German maid if they carried out any domestic task themselves. Yet for energetic and capable women used to taking care of their own homes this could be frustrating. One woman, staying with her mother on leave in England, begged to scrub floors and do the washing: 'I just felt I wanted to really get down to being a housewife again.' She had felt she could not get down on her hands and knees in her home in Germany 'because I didn't think it was one of the things I should do, so I waited till I came home'.

Servants were not necessarily working class. One family had a bank manager's widow who spoke perfect English and lent her best silver and china when they entertained. She produced 'fantastic meals' from the basic Army rations, did dressmaking and even tailored a Harris-tweed coat. British wives were impressed by the housekeeping skills of the Germans, which nearly always included dressmaking.

For the Germans, domestic service with a British family was a much sought-after job, promising not only a steady wage but warmth and a meal. There were always perks: if not actual gifts of food from employers, used coffee grounds and tea leaves could be garnered and taken home for reuse. One woman remembered how her maid's mother would come round after dinner and take away the remains of the gravy and vegetables from the meal. Sometimes a German family which had been moved into the attic or cellar of their large house to make it available for a British family would be only too glad to provide domestic help. It was one way of looking after their property. It had been ordered that all gardens must to be cultivated. If the British residents did not want to do this, their garden must be handed over to Germans. One wife received bowlfuls of spinach nearly every day because the German owner of the garden thought she looked anaemic.

A particular addition to many households was the German nanny. There was no shortage of girls willing and able to look after small children. They were found to be extremely reliable and devoted to their charges. Some less responsible parents actually went away for weekends leaving their children in the care of the nanny. Many British infants uttered their first words in German.

The British wives, therefore, had a great deal of free time and absolutely nothing to do with it. No transport; no shops; no cafés, theatres or cinemas. Many lived in compounds. For instance, at HQ BAOR in Bad Oeynhausen the British lived and worked within the barbed-wire confines of the town centre, from which all German residents had been removed. In other areas whole streets or blocks of flats had been requisitioned. Visits to other wives' homes (with identical furnishings) hardly broke the monotony. They could meet again at clubs in the evenings, where their husbands could talk shop with colleagues with whom they had been working all day.

Of course on the surface it was gratifyingly unlike life back home. 'Entertainment was everything in Germany at that time. You entertained other people; they entertained you. You were very rarely at home really. You were either going somewhere or preparing for some party or something or other all the time.' It was just as well that there were plenty of hairdressers, where even a perm could be had for a handful of cigarettes or some coffee. But in the end sheer boredom was the overwhelming feeling, for which all too often the antidote was drink – freely available and cheap. Every family had an allocation, and in the clubs it was unrationed. (Two hundred thousand bottles of gin a month were produced for the NAAFI.) The opening of Married Families shops run by the NAAFI offered a diversion, although there was little interesting to buy. One wife remembered the aimlessness: how people would drift from the shop to a mess or club, meet others for coffee, then linger on for drinks before

going home. Some lingered all day. In such artificial circumstances marriage breakdowns were inevitable. As one woman
said, 'You had to be quite strong to keep going – to keep on an
even keel.' Some wives simply went back to England.

Life was less lonely for Army wives. There was an *esprit de corps*
within military units. Having wives and families in married
quarters was a normal aspect of service life, and the Army
looked after its own – although rank played an important part.
Thus the drawback of always meeting the same faces was light-
ened by the feeling of belonging to a regimental family. The
Control Commission wives, however, were individual civilians
without any sense of 'belonging'. Contact with the local Germans might have brought some variety into the narrowness of
their lives, but there was no question of that – at least in the
early days. One woman could remember 'this feeling we all had
out there: the feeling of being an elite, of living so much apart
from them and at a different level – they were the poor white
tribe, almost like natives'.

There was indeed in the first couple of years a system of
'apartheid' between the occupiers and 'the natives'. For some
time British and Germans travelled in separate carriages on the
Underground. British troops could attend services in German
churches – but not at the same time as Germans. German cinemas could be used for the showing of British films, but the Germans had their own separate programmes. Saddest of all,
perhaps, was that British and Germans could not sit together to
listen to music. In Hamburg, for instance, the radio orchestra
had to play every programme twice: on Sunday afternoons for
the British and on Monday evenings for the Germans. In the
early days this shared use of buildings but segregation of audiences produced a phenomenon which anyone who was out there
at the time will remember. There was a uniquely recognizable
odour in any building which was used by large numbers of Germans. It was said that this was compounded of the effects of
overcrowded living conditions and ersatz tobacco but, above all,
of starvation – which apparently generates a special effluvium

Whether the Germans themselves were aware of it one does not know.

Soundings taken among Germans in important positions under Military Government yielded valuable information on the true feelings of the occupied. 'Germans feel that the overpowering struggle of every-day life cannot be fully appreciated just through official contacts. They regret that there is little contact between British and German officials outside the office. There is very little confidence and so much stiffness.'[30] It began to be recognized at policy level that the situation whereby the British and the Germans met each other only at work and led their real lives quite separately was wholly unsatisfactory. Not only was it contrary to normal human relations, it also militated against the efficient working of the Occupation, which after all was costing the British taxpayer money. Unfortunately, it had been officially dinned into everyone coming to Germany that the Germans were a nation of pariahs and would always be so. Few of those coming out from Britain had ever met a German before, so they accepted the authorized version. The usual suspicion of 'foreigners' was reinforced when these were also an enemy who had unleashed death and destruction upon Europe. But if, as was claimed, the British were to 're-educate' the Germans in the interests of democracy, it was felt that they had better have some contact with them.

In July 1946 the office of the Deputy Military Governor issued a slightly unenthusiastic instruction to the members of the Control Commission. It was felt desirable to have more social contact with German officials, political leaders and trade unionists and to entertain German guests wherever possible – 'although we must not go to the other extreme and and make ourselves cheap by over-doing it'. The aim was the establishment of relations of confidence between British and German elements of administration which would provide a basis 'for the long-term Occupation which we contemplate'.[31] Rules were relaxed to allow dances to which Germans could be invited, but 'if Allied women are invited to such dances they will invariably be warned that Germans will also be present'.[32] Parties could be held for German children, but the food must be contributed from the rations of the hosts. And no Army equipment, such as ENSA films, was to be used. The servicemen, many of whom had children at home in Britain, found no difficulty in parting with their rations to entertain the innocents.

With the perception of the Soviet Union as a threat to the West, it became important to have the Germans 'on our side'. They must now be wooed as kindred spirits. At the Regional Commissioners' Conference presided over by the Military Governor on 18 May 1947 a new instruction was handed down: 'We should behave towards the Germans as the people of one Christian and civilized race towards another whose interests in many ways converge with our own and for whom we have no longer any ill-will.'[33]

The Control Commission called this the 'be-kind-to-the-Germans order'. Even where there was goodwill, following this order was not always easy. In Married Families' homes entertainment had to come out of personal rations. And the Germans were reluctant to accept hospitality which they could not possibly return. Rules were eventually relaxed for gatherings on official territory. Extra rations would be issued on a per-head basis, but there were strict orders that anything unused must be returned to stores. The Army favoured the official cocktail party: it was short and did not involve engaging in extended discussions. It was not a form of entertainment with which the Germans were familiar. When Vaughan Berry gave his first cocktail party as Regional Commissioner at his residence in Hamburg, some confusion was caused because his German guests had dismissed their transport on arrival, obviously expecting to settle in for the evening.

In November 1948 the Education Minister for Lower Saxony, Dr Adolf Grimme, told Lord Pakenham, Minister for German Affairs, that he did not think the problem of the relationship between the British and the Germans could be solved merely by social intercourse. The readiness of the Germans to accept

British ideas would be much increased if they felt that the officials of the Control Commission lived among them instead of
being, as at present, something of a race apart. Perhaps some
form of billeting should be considered. The Minister put the
idea to General Robertson, the Military Governor. Had the time
come, he asked, when the whole administrative plan of dividing
the life of British and Germans at its root (with complete economic separation) should be reconsidered? There were few if
any arguments from the security angle. 'The question of relationship is almost the only big topic that no particular branch of
your staff seem to have been allocated to consider.'[34]

Although the Military Governor, who was the British representative on the Allied Control Council in Berlin, also held the
rank of Commander-in-Chief of all Forces in the British Zone,
he had no power to interfere with the running of the British
Army of the Rhine. BAOR was a garrison. Its duty was to support
the Military Governor. It had no part in the administration of
the zone, which was carried out by the Control Commission.
Unlike the Commission, the Army did not work side by side
with Germans, although sometimes serving officers, such as the
Military Governor himself, were seconded to the civilian side.
Nevertheless, the Services also had a responsibility to promote
'British ideas' through friendly relations with the native population wherever they might come in contact. They had their own
way of interpreting this. A routine order by General Charles
Keightley, Commander-in-Chief of BAOR, stated in its preamble, 'Our object is to encourage the re-birth of self-respect
among the German people as this is essential to the policy of our
Government' and, further, 'to gain from the Germans respect
for our race and customs'. Political Branch at Control Commission Headquarters objected to this paragraph as implying that
the Germans had no self-respect, but it was retained and used in
subsequent routine orders.[35]

It was oddly reminiscent of the attitude of Political Warfare
Department during the war, when one of the most effective
weapons of propaganda, it was felt, was the unique superiority of

the British: 'We must preserve around ourselves some of that atmosphere of the Ultima Thule which has always surrounded us, and in projecting ourselves, avoid at all costs making ourselves seem in any way commonplace and just like anyone else.'[36]

Against exhortations from above for a change in attitude, Army prejudice stood fast. In March 1947 a revised Regulation of Relationships between CCG and Germans was drafted in the Military Governor's office. A copy was sent to the commanders of the three Services to see if it would be acceptable on the military side. Their reply was that they 'do not feel they can go so far'. They submitted their own draft. The Military Governor's office compared the two drafts. The first paragraph of the army paper read, 'The word German hereunder will be held to include all persons who, during the war, lived in Germany of their own free will.' The CCG, the office noted, 'had not thought it essential to define a German'. The Army laid down that Germans could be entertained in Married Families' homes, but there was to be no entertainment of Germans for purely social reasons in messes or clubs. Those Germans with whom units had official or semi-official dealings might be *formally* entertained with permission of the garrison commander. Where the CCG positively encouraged open association between children, the Army would have 'no objection to mutual visits arranged by their parents'. Again, regarding games and sports, the CCG encouraged participation, the Army restricted it. The CCG strongly recommended the importance of fostering and supporting German youth movements; the Services would go only so far as to lend equipment.[37]

The Army drew up its own recommendations for socializing with the Germans. These included a special safeguard for their women: *ATS should not be exposed to the risk of marrying Germans.* They should therefore confine themselves to welfare activities involving women and children. For the men, however, efforts should be made to find good-class German families to accept soldiers into their homes. Then, if they were inclined to marry a German, it might be one of the better ones. The attitude of officers, it was noted, was one of uncertainty in 'off parade' relations with Germans. There was 'no great desire evinced to associate much with Germans'.[38]

The Army would yield to no one – not even the Foreign Office, which was responsible for the Occupation – when it came to keeping the Germans in their place. About once every two months a group of specially selected civilians – local-government officers, journalists, trade unionists, educationists and so on – were sent to England on courses, under Foreign Office sponsorship. They assembled in Hanover from all parts of the zone to join the leave train to the Hook of Holland. The Army was asked to accommodate these groups overnight in the Hanover transit camp. The request was refused point-blank. The problem for the administration of finding accommodation all over the town and providing transport to the station left the Army unmoved. Control Commission Headquarters in Berlin pleaded without success. BAOR would not be budged: 'It is considered highly undesirable that Germans should be accommodated in a transit camp with Service personnel, from a disciplinary, security and morale point of view.'[39] What the underfed, unarmed civilians were going to get up to overnight to threaten the British Army stretches the imagination considerably.

The official attitude was inevitably reflected in the behaviour of the troops, most of whom were National Servicemen who had never seen any fighting. One CCG wife remembered several incidents 'when we didn't want to be thought to be British'. Sitting on the beach, for instance, when there were soldiers there 'yelling and shouting out dreadful things in English, thinking probably in their ignorance that the Germans couldn't speak any English at all'. However, individual acts of courtesy could redress the balance. A musician in the Hamburg radio orchestra still treasured, many years afterwards, the memory of an encounter on an Underground train. An officer sitting opposite him was about to put out a half-smoked cigarette. The stubs of British cigarettes were the only smokes the Germans could get. Dr S. made bold to ask if he might have it. The officer stubbed it out firmly and threw it away. He then took out his cigarette case and offered it to his German fellow passenger.

It has been said that it was the wives who lost India. Records show that it was officers' wives who were the strongest opponents of social contact with the Germans. But the Control Commission also shared their opprobrium. General Robertson was exasperated. He announced that 'although relationships between wives and CCG have improved a lot during during the past year [1948] they require constant observation'. It had been reported to him that in some places relations between wives of Service officers and those of civilian officials were not good. He wished it to be known that 'we would hold the husband responsible in any case where the wife deliberately fosters ill-feeling'.[40] The Governmental Branch of the Control Commission in Hamburg declared, 'There has to be re-education *of* the Army before you can start re-education of the Germans *by* the Army. We all know the Army attitude at many conferences where we ask for concessions to the Germans.' The Deputy Regional Commissioner wrote to Education Branch in similar vein. There needed to be a planned and thorough education of the Army before any scheme to foster relations with the Germans was launched: 'We tried in Hamburg to explain to local units the problems in Germany and the tasks of the CCG but I am sure we have not even scratched the surface. There still exists, far too generally, the view that in all spheres we can instruct the poor benighted Germans – a tendency to consider them as uncivilized Africans.'[41]

Vaughan Berry followed this up. He told Robert Birley, Educational Adviser to the Military Governor:

> I feel that what is needed is that local unit commander should take a simple and natural interest in the inhabitants of the locality in which he lives and the rest will follow . . . I feel that at Headquarters both in Berlin and in the Zone there is too little contact with the Germans whom we rule and that it is not realized there how much the Occupation is disliked.[42]

The German commander of Hamburg surrenders the city to the British Army outside the Town Hall, 3 May 1945.

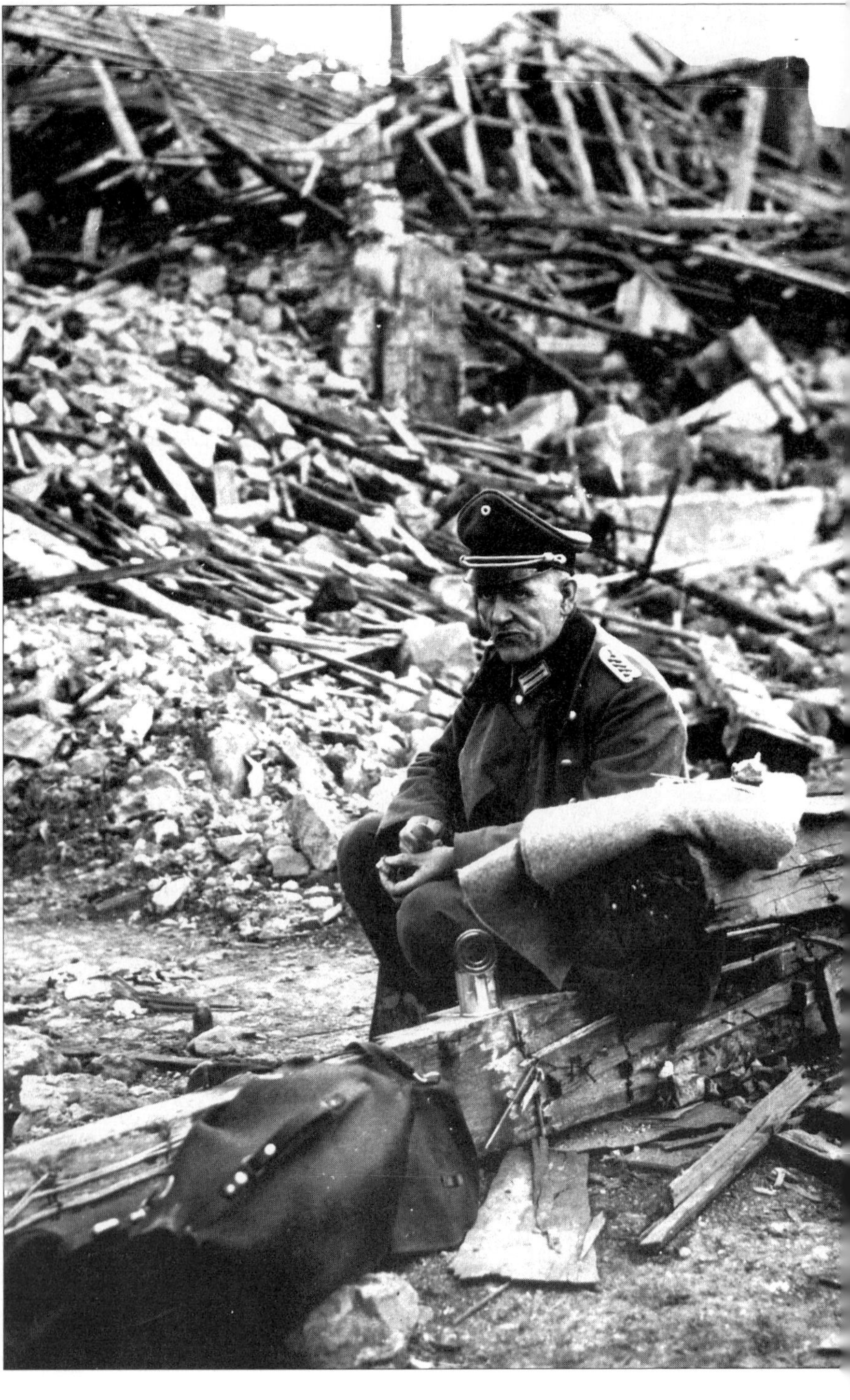

Above: Symbols of surrender in the streets of Cologne.

Left: For the second time in a generation a nation faces defeat.

Below: At the Big Three Conference in Potsdam in July 1945 the Allies agreed rules for the treatment of conquered Germany.

Tanks entering Aachen, the first important
German town to be captured by the Allies.

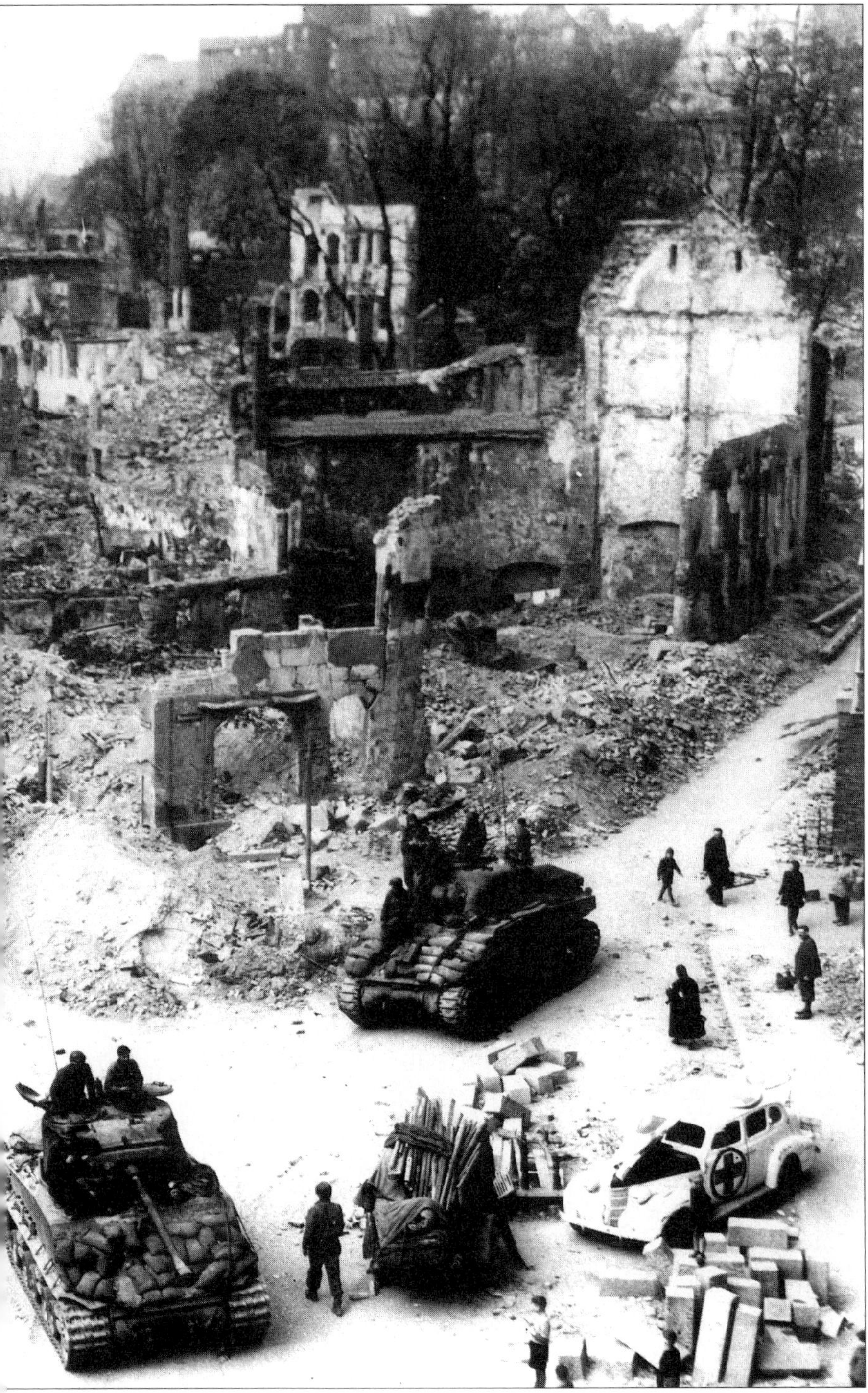

Refugees from the fighting in Aachen leave the city with what they can carry.

Refugees struggle on foot across a bridge no longer any use to trains.

German male civilians are rounded up on the streets at random and placed under arbitary arrest.

In the wreckage of the towns the homeless set up home wherever there is a roof for shelter.

In a human chain, women salvage bricks
from the rubble of the cities.

In the early days of the Occupation the edicts of Military Government were
nailed to any walls left standing.

Citizens study the regulations issued by the British Occupation authorities
which now govern their lives.

German houses are requisitioned for the accommodation of British families after the expulsion of the occupants.

German passers-by watch impassively as British officers assess bomb damage to buildings.

The first party of wives arrive from Britain to join their husbands in the British Zone of Germany in August 1946.

A well-turned-out British family stands out in the crowd on a German street.

Above: NAAFI shops provided goods and provisions unavailable to the German population.

Right: A German woman searches for food in dustbins outside a British home.

Below: Soldiers on leave trains to Britain throw out their travel rations to hungry women and children lining the tracks.

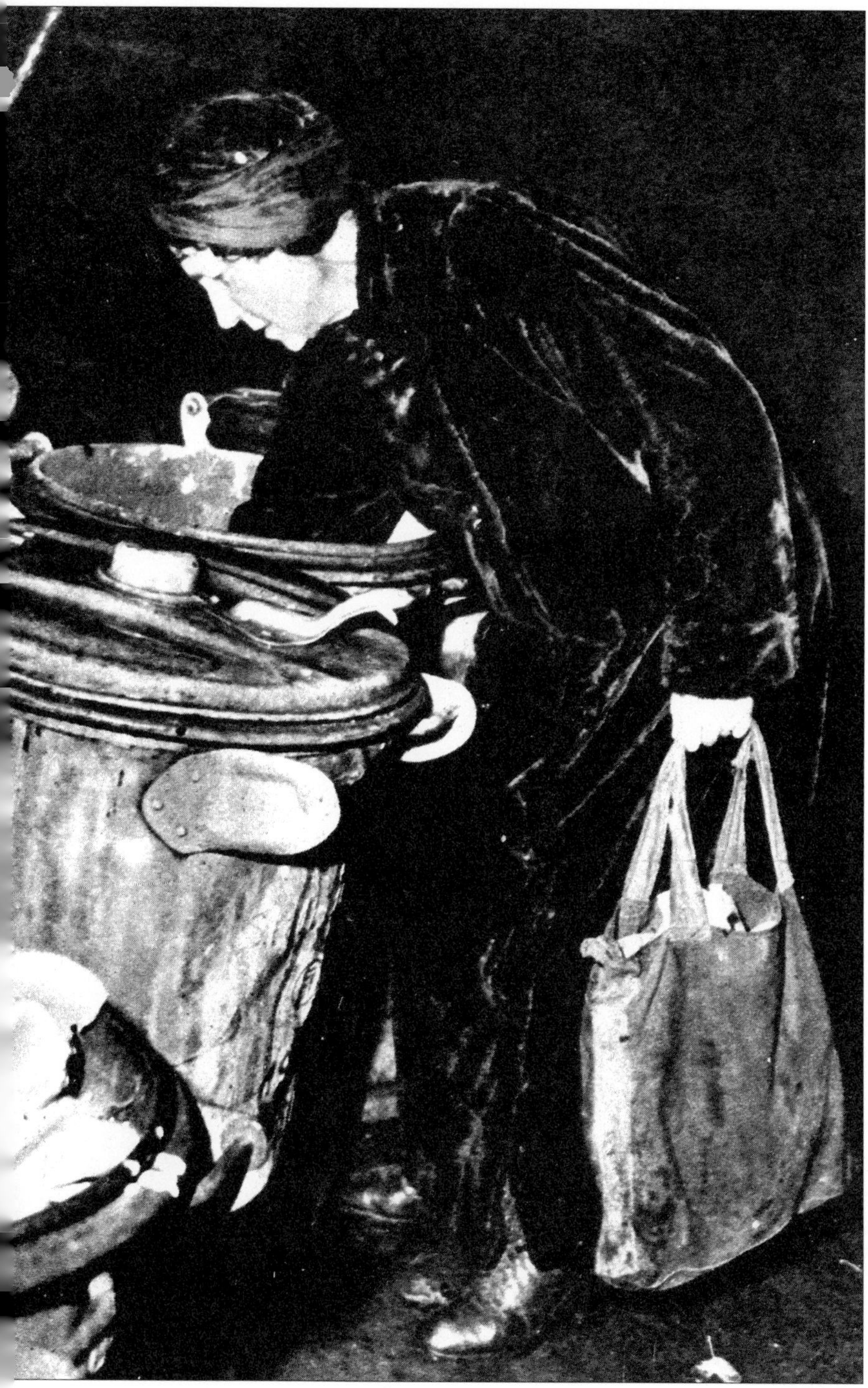

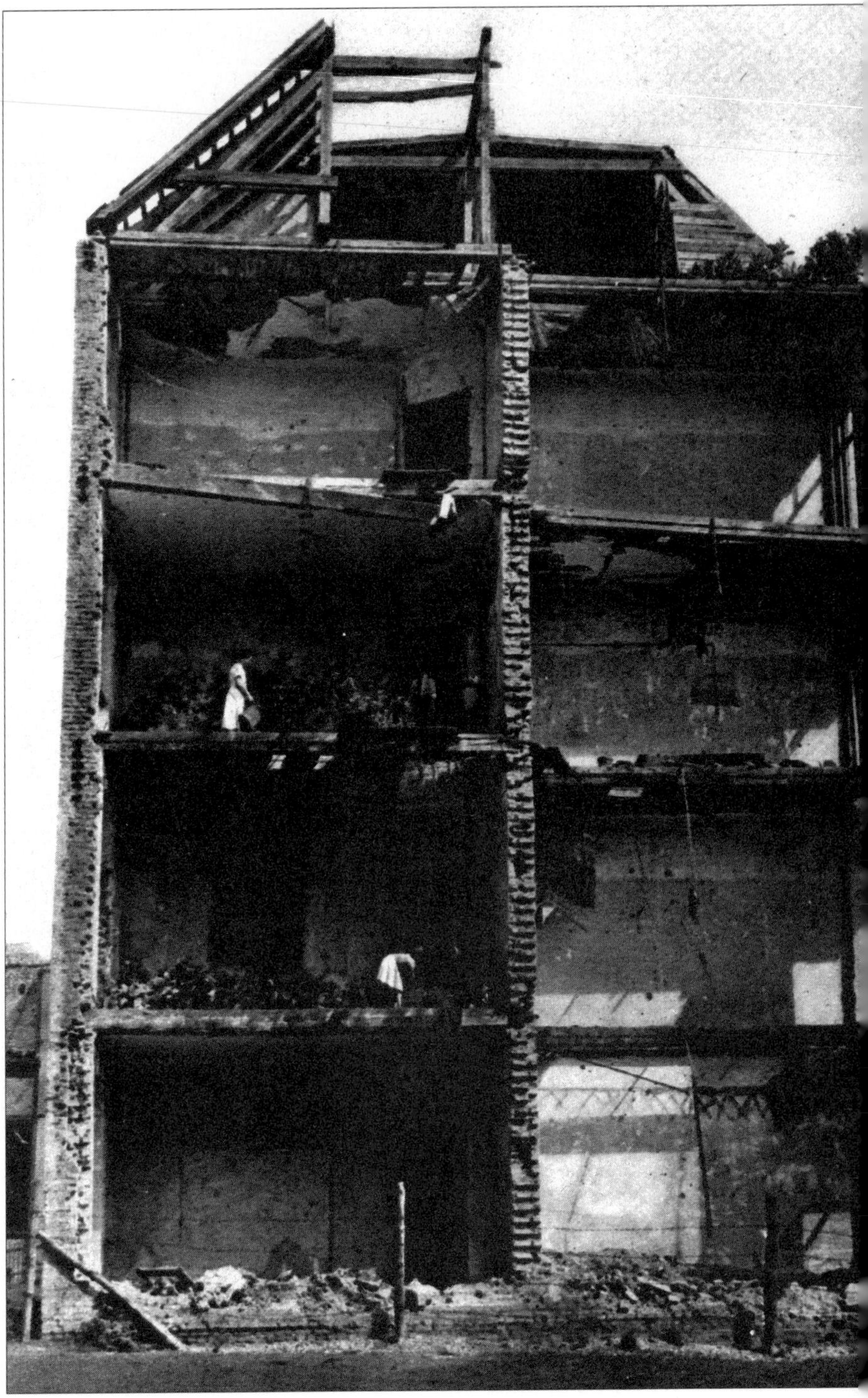

Above: Mass hunger demonstrations in the Ruhr, February 1947.

Left: Hungry people grew food wherever they could, including bombed-out buildings.

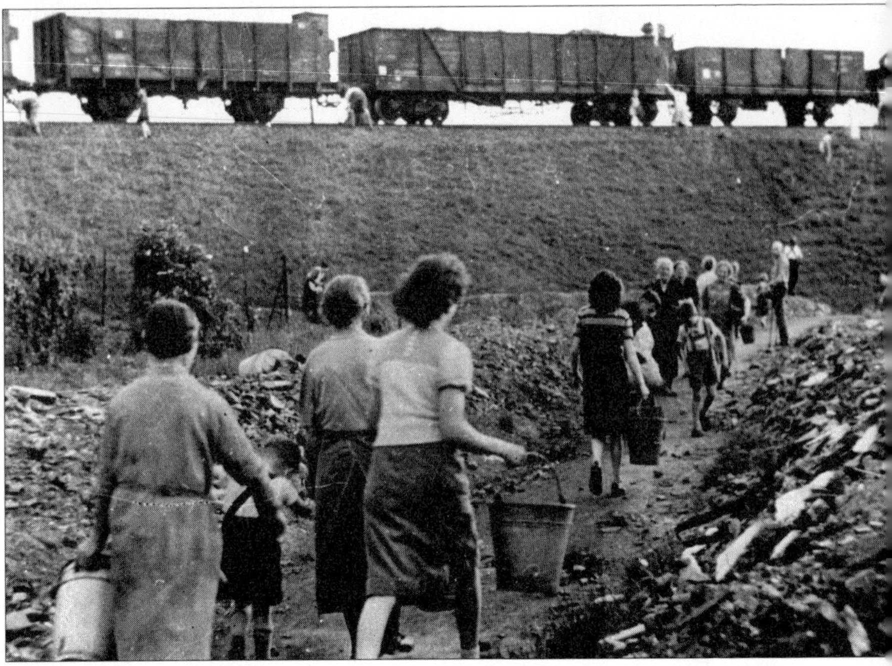

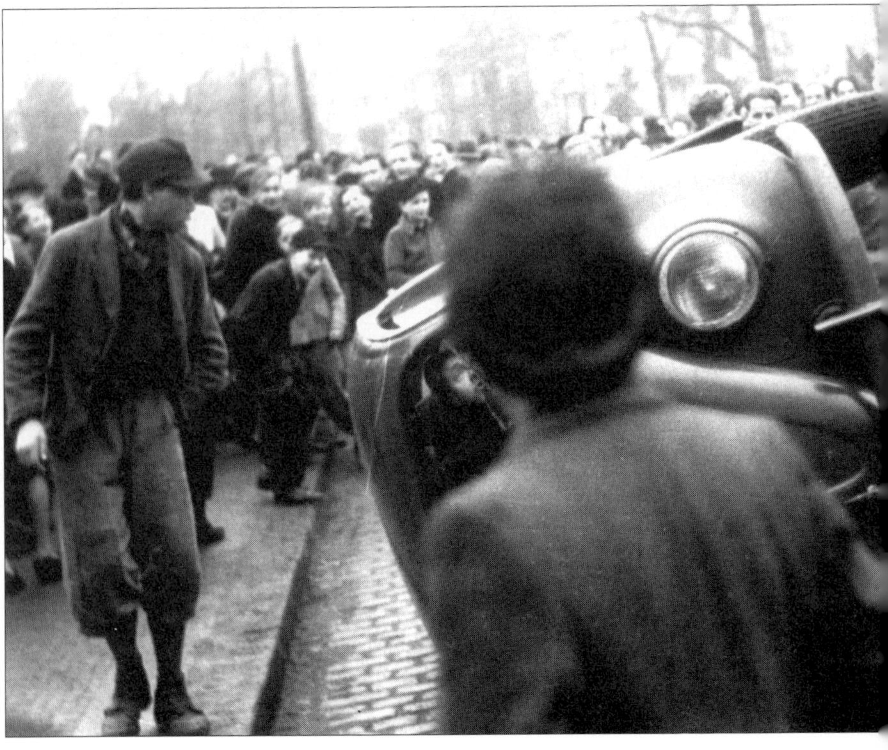

Clockwise from top left:
In the acute fuel shortage, coal
trains *en route* to power stations were
plundered by citizens for whom no
domestic supplies were available.

The Rt Hon. Ernest Bevin MP,
Foreign Secretary, ultimately
responsible for the British Zone of
Occupation.

The Military Governor, Air Marshal
Sir Sholto Douglas, visits a German
school.

A Control Commission officer's car
overturned by angry workers outside
a factory scheduled for demolition,
March 1947.

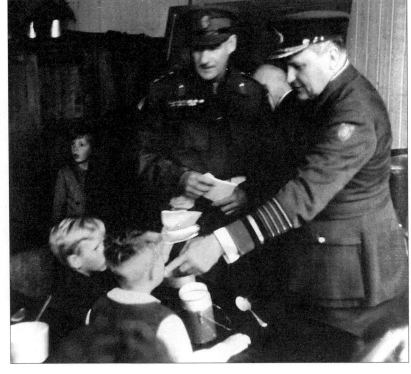

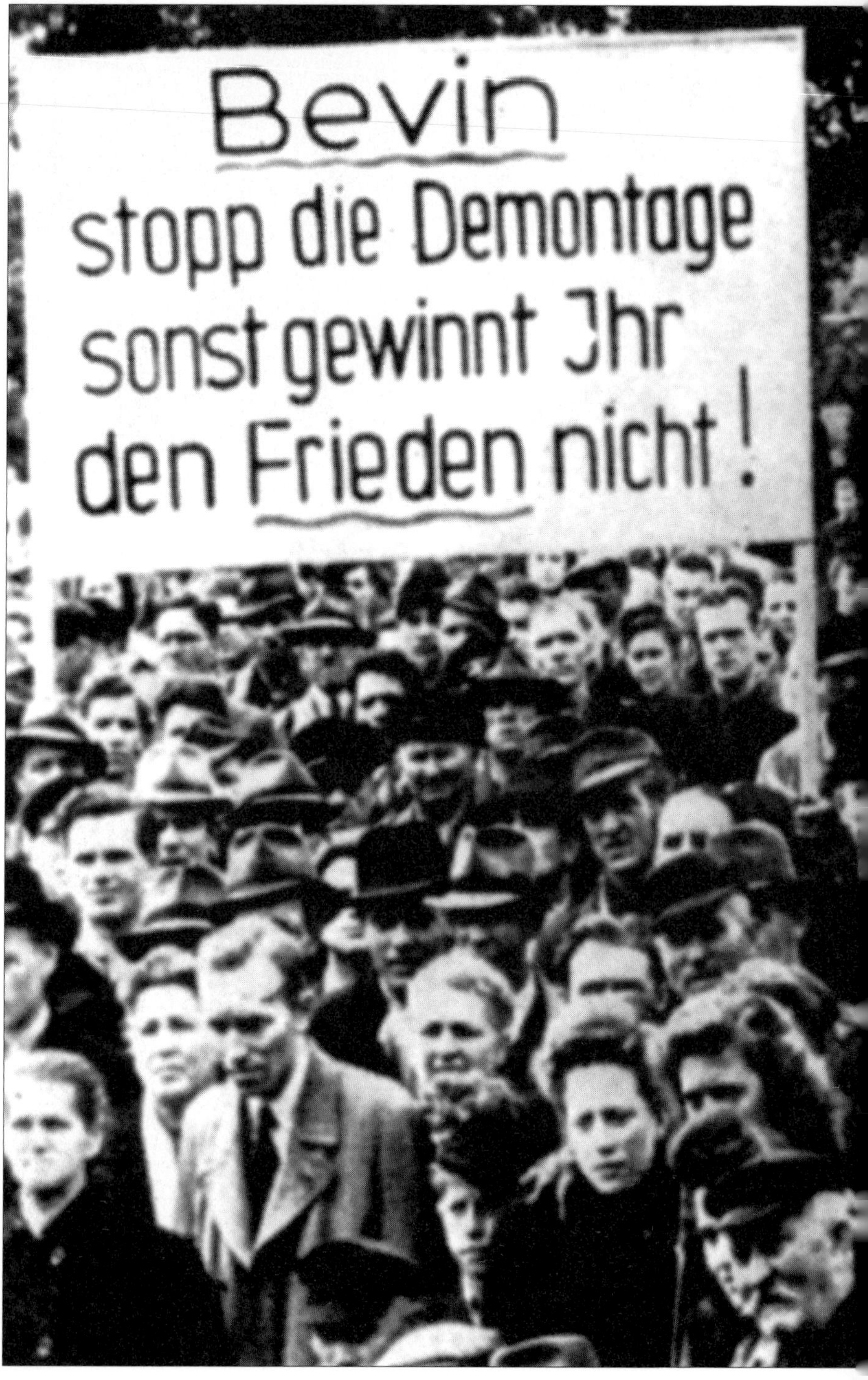
Bevin
stopp die Demontage
sonst gewinnt Jhr
den Frieden nicht!

Above: An international team visits the Krupp factory in Essen to select machinery for removal as reparations.

Left: German workers appeal directly to the British Foreign Secretary to call a halt to the dismantling of factories, June 1949.

Below: Thousands of workers protest against the dismantling of factories in the British Zone for reparations – *demontage*.

The Volkswagen factory is taken over by the British Army. The 'People's Car' now serves the needs of a foreign Occupation.

An area of the industrial Ruhr obliterated by Allied bombing.

German police guard against opposition from workers as a factory is demolished by the British authorities.

Field-Marshal Jan Smuts visits a school in Hamburg accompanied by Dr Hans Reimers from the Hamburg Board of Education.

Miss Edith Davies of Education Branch, Control Commission, inspects a girls' school in the British Zone.

British films such as Olivier's *Henry V* attracted large German audiences.

German administrators attending a 're-education' course at Wilton Park in England.

A Control Commission officer in Hanover meets representatives of the German civil administration in his office.

A Control Commission officer supervising the production of *Die Welt*, published in Hamburg by the Occupation authorities.

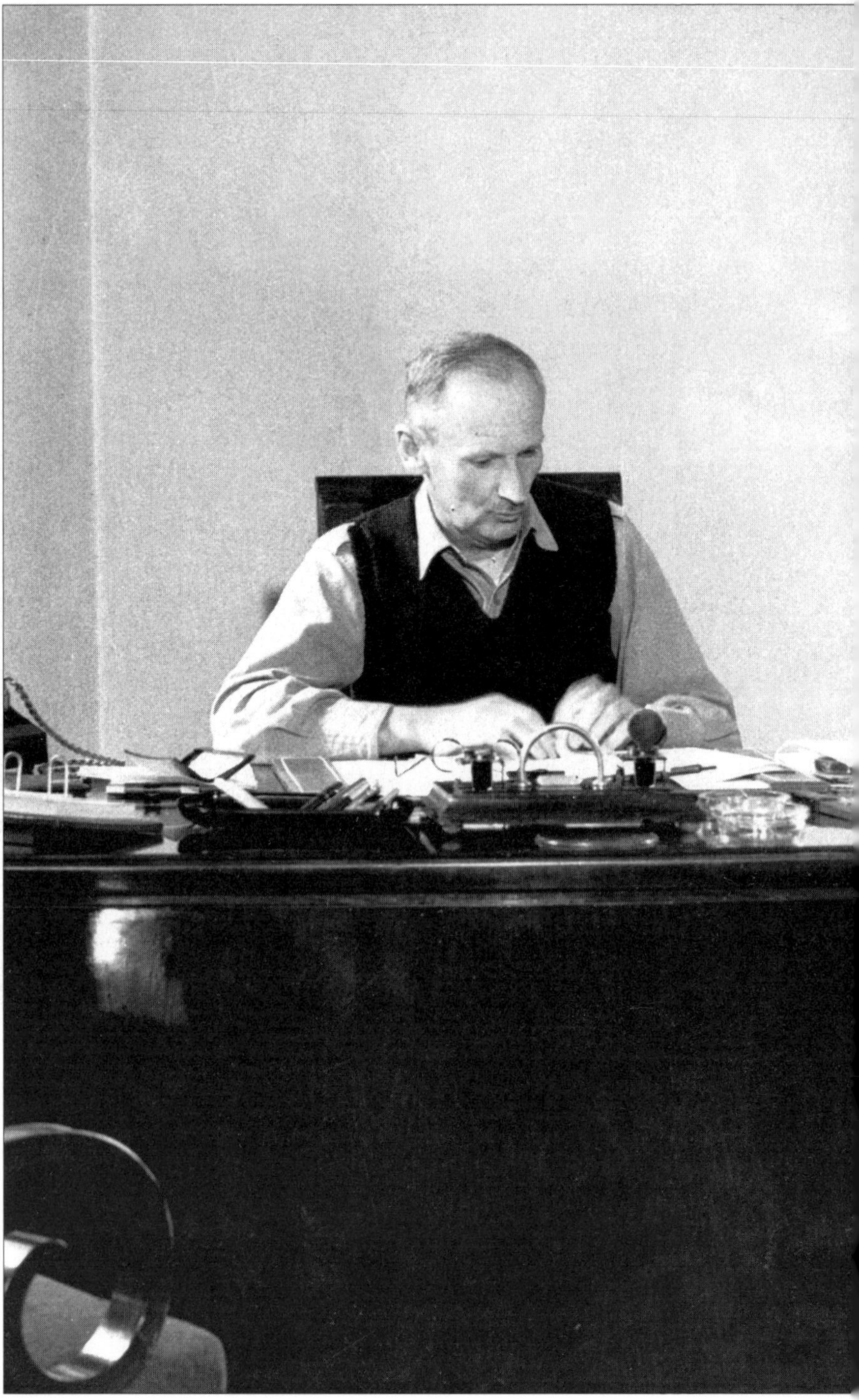

Above: Sir Vaughan Berry, Regional Commissioner, Hamburg, 1946–9.

Left: Field-Marshal Bernard Montgomery, Commander-in-Chief and Military Governor of the British Zone of Germany, 1945–6.

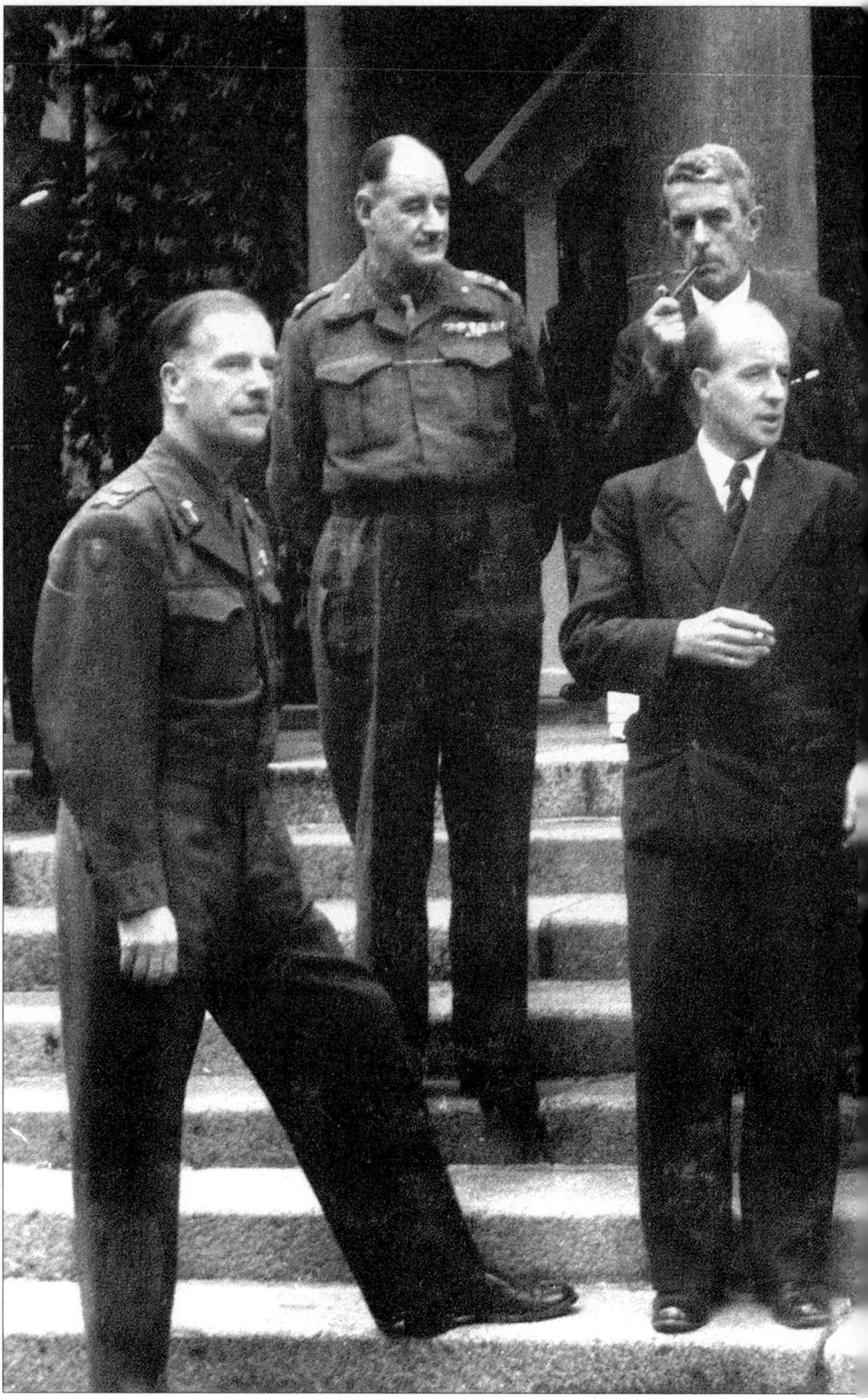

Government of the British Zone of Occupation, 1946

Front row (left to right): Major-General Sir Brian Robertson, Deputy
Military Governor; J. B. Hynd MP, Minister for German Affairs;
Marshal of the RAF Sir Sholto Douglas, Military Governor and
Commander-in-Chief; the man on the far right is unknown.

Back row (left to right): Regional Commissioners Lieutenant-General
Sir Gordon Macready (Hanover and Lower Saxony); Sir Vaughan
Berry (Hamburg); William Asbury (North Rhine-Westphalia); Air
Vice-Marshal H.V. de Crespigny (Schleswig-Holstein).

After the economic fusion of the British and US Zones of Occupation. From left to right: Major-General Sir Brian Robertson, British Military Governor; General Lucius D. Clay, US Military Governor; General Alec Bishop, British Chief of Staff.

German secretaries, doubling as interpreters, were suspected by many Germans of having undue influence with Control Commission officers.

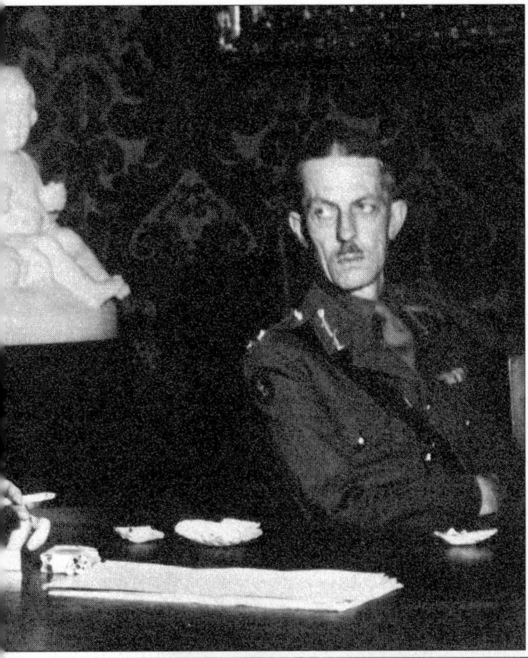

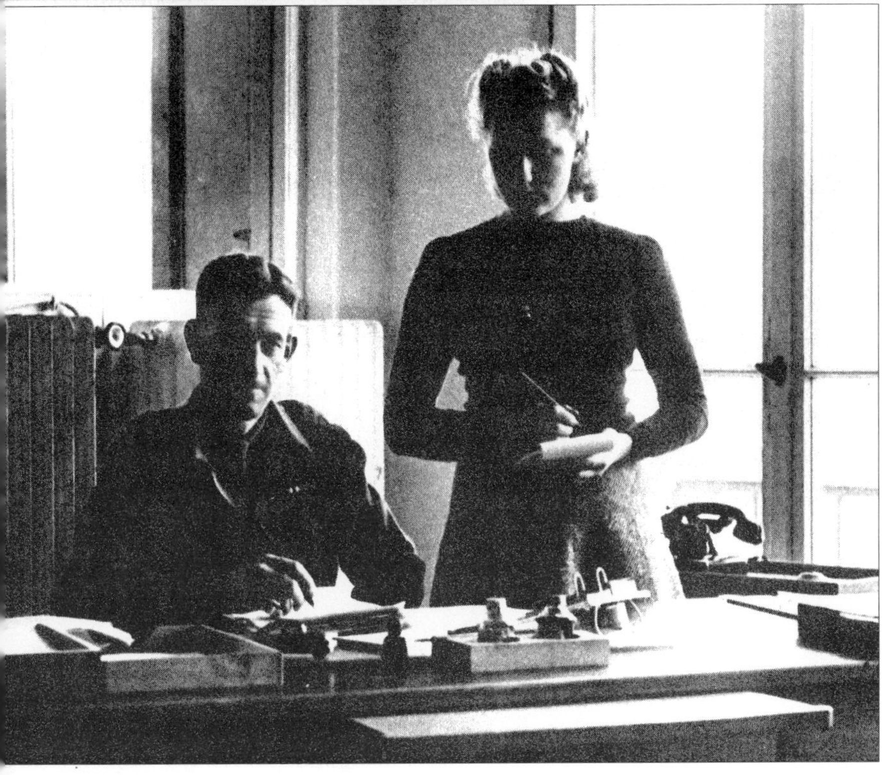

British Armed Forces Voucher.
BAFs were introduced for the use of British
personnel in British establishments in the zone.

Aware that 'the Germans whom we rule' would one day rule themselves, Berry felt it particularly important to make friends with the young. He therefore gave every practical support to the university. As an economist, he also welcomed into his house for informal discussions groups of students from the Economics Faculty. One of those students was Helmut Schmidt, who in due course was to become Chancellor of the Federal Republic.

In spite of all the difficulties generated, the establishment of British families did introduce some element of normality into the life of the Occupation forces. The ban on marriages between members of the forces and Germans was eventually relaxed, although there had to be some period of official scrutiny before permission was granted. Marriage with a British soldier could be a way of escape from the harsh reality of life in Germany, and the National Servicemen coming out to the zone were very young.

As time went by and more families came out, those who had been the pioneers had already found their initial attitudes changing. The official stereotype of the Germans faded. The common sight of people rooting through dustbins for food which they themselves had thrown away had struck home: 'Most of us soon stopped saying – and even really feeling – "Well, serves them right", because they, too, had become "people" to us.' For those living in blocks of flats, often sharing occupancy with German tenants, everyday contact began to break down barriers. Children on both sides saw only new playmates. This in turn brought the mothers into touch. As one wife recalled, 'It began with a smile and a nod and gradually grew more warm.' They fumbled with each other's languages, the Germans taking rather more quickly to English than the British to German. The British marvelled at how German women were coping: 'The women's hair was dry and uncared for, but I never saw a child whose hair was not clean, shining and neat.' Many families established friendly relations with maids and nannies and even with the owners of the homes they occupied, banished to attic or cellar to make room for themselves. Years later there were those who could testify that Anglo-German friendships forged during those extraordinary times were now extending to a third generation. And many a baby born in a British military hospital acquired a German godparent.

One dispossessed German family had become friendly with the new occupiers of their home and were looking forward to the forthcoming birth of an English baby. When the British wife arrived home with her new daughter, 'they all all came outside to greet me and I found that they had lined the stairs with flowering plants and filled the flat with flowers. I was so pleased that I turned to the mother of the family and put my baby into her arms.'

Operation Union may have started out under a cloud, but for many British and Germans it was to be a cloud with a silver lining.

8
Out of the dark

IN AUGUST 1946 Robert Birley, Educational Adviser to the Military Governor, received a letter from an officer of the French Occupation authority who had been visiting schools in the British Zone. The Frenchman had encapsulated in one sentence why Education Branch was the one truly successful aspect of British control in Germany: 'The personnel, specialists in the German language, seem to be the only ones to approach the German problem through a German window and not through the English prism.'[1]

Education Branch was indeed unique in the Control Commission. In the words of the historian Michael Balfour, 'Few people came into it unless they had both qualifications and a sense of mission, with the result that the standard of competence, integrity and idealism was above the average.'[2] British education officers had the inestimable advantage over most other officials of the Occupation of familiarity with the language, history and culture of the country. Most of them had known a different Germany. Within the context of British policy as whole, the approach by Education Branch was unorthodox. In other areas of control the Germans were either completely excluded from, or at best grudgingly consulted about, the future of the country. In education, on the other hand, they were positively included and encouraged. Education was consistently put into the hands of the Germans themselves.

With the expectation that after the defeat the victors would take over German administration as a going concern, a team of British education experts would have to be ready to take over the Education *Reichministerium*. Recruiting began, trawling the universities and schools. The British educationists would be moving into a country which had always been regarded as having one of the most advanced and sophisticated of educational systems. It had been the first country to introduce compulsory education. The experimental schools such as those of Rudolf Steiner and Kurt Hahn and the Froebel kindergartens were known worldwide. One thing was clear: control would have to be indirect.

By the end of 1944 a nucleus of officers was holed up in a mansion in Kensington surrounded by vast tomes of reference covering all aspects of Germany: education, history, culture, politics, life under Weimar, life under the Nazis, life during the war. The branch comprised sections on universities, schools, teacher training, youth work, textbooks and so on, and each section was gathering any information on its particular field which trickled back from wartime Germany. As the armies advanced into Germany, Military Government officers sent back to London any schoolbooks they could find, but these were so impregnated with Nazi principles – even the arithmetic books – that they were quite useless. Education authorities in America sent over 227 microfilms and seventy-six photostats of pre-1933 textbooks. The Board of Education Library in London supplied sixty books. All these texts had to be examined. After several months of research even these yielded only eight books considered sufficiently inoffensive for use in elementary schools; but they were hopelessly out of date.

The first members of Education Branch arrived in Germany in May 1945 to find a rather different task awaiting them from that which they had envisaged. One teacher remembered her horror, driving through the ruins of Osnabrück on her arrival in Germany, at the sight of children sitting disconsolately on the heaps of rubble. For the British education officers, coming from an education system undisrupted by the war (in spite of evacuation), it was like walking into a vacuum. The German educational system had almost ceased to exist. In Cologne, for example, 92 per cent of the buildings were unusable. In the *Land* of Schleswig-Holstein only 162 out of 1,550 primary schools were available (and the population was soon to be doubled by an influx of refugees). In Hamburg there was no schooling at all after the appalling air attacks in 1943: children from the city and the surrounding areas had been evacuated far away – to Moravia or Thuringia or the Black Forest. So, in the absence of any children, when the British Army and Military Government arrived they took over surviving empty school buildings for their own use. When the children were at last brought back home, Education Branch often had great difficulty in getting their occupying colleagues to relinquish the buildings.

Schools competed with housing for desperately scarce building materials, but a more important scarcity was teachers – teachers, that is, who were acceptable to the Occupation authorities. Elderly teachers were mostly found to be uncontaminated. There were others who had stayed at their posts to protect their pupils, where they could, from the pollution of Nazi teaching, knowing that if they left they would be replaced by dedicated Nazis. Some teachers and administrators had not worked for years, having been dismissed by the Nazi authorities in the early years of the regime. As a result they were no longer up to date with teaching methods. Many were just physically exhausted. Younger teachers trickled back from prisoner-of-war camps or were winkled out from them by Military Government at the request of the German authorities. But all had to be denazified. In the British Zone, by the time all elementary schools were officially opened, on 1 October 1945, 11,567 teachers had been arrested, dismissed or refused employment. Another 14,530 were still waiting to pass through the denazification process.[3]

Some undesirables slipped through the net. An education officer who had taught German at a girls' school in Maidstone walked into a school in Hamburg one day to find herself face to face with a young teacher who had been a German '*assistante*' at her school in 1938 and 1939. It had been discovered that she was indoctrinating the English schoolgirls during their lessons, and when she was found to have been pedalling around an airport in Kent taking photographs she was packed off back to Germany. It was a shock for the German teacher to come face to face with her past. She protested that she had had a complete change of heart and was no longer a Nazi.[4] Next day she was dismissed, in spite of the pleas of her headmaster that she was an excellent teacher – which no doubt she was. Certainly she could have been ill-spared. In the British Zone the average number of pupils in each class was seventy. In one school in Lower Saxony a master had to deal with 141 children – with only one book.

The former excellence of German education made the crime of those teachers who betrayed their pupils by embracing Nazi principles particularly grievous. Now those who had refused to poison children's minds were to have their reward. There were senior educationists, whether teachers or administrators, who had been dismissed and had spent years in menial occupations and in some cases in concentration camps. Now they emerged, as ready to cooperate with the British teachers as the latter were with them. One teacher was reminded of the prisoners in Beethoven's opera *Fidelio* coming out of their dark cells into the daylight. 'We were very fortunate in the people who rallied to us,' wrote another. 'These people were among the finest educationists one could find anywhere.'

Education officers were rarely seen back at their headquarters. The policy of the branch was that they should be dispersed as widely as possible, in order to influence German education by personal contact. This was successful because the British teachers genuinely felt for those German colleagues who had suffered the abuse and perversion of their profession. Mostly young men and women, they were willing to put up with any discomfort. Office hours meant absolutely nothing: they would work through the night if necessary.

In the British Zone there were some 3 million children waiting for them. Most had had no schooling for the previous two years. Uprooted from their homes and many of them separated, perhaps for ever, from their families, they were half-clothed, dangerously undernourished and inadequately housed. Having been cut off from the outside world all their young lives, they were now living in a maelstrom of population: expellees, refugees, former slave labourers, some speaking their own tongue, some speaking foreign languages. Not surprisingly, juvenile delinquency was widespread. It was a matter of urgency to get rootless, homeless youngsters under control.

A report by T Force provided a rather unexpectedly hopeful picture of German youth. T Force was comprised of specialists following closely behind the advancing armies and identifying targets – usually industrial – which in due course would be of particular interest to the Allies. Three British members spent six weeks in the small towns and villages around Aachen at the end of 1944. They found that young Germans were 'not as completely poisoned as one had feared. They are sick and tired of forced labour, forced training, forced living. They wanted the freedom of ordinary boys and girls.' They were thoroughly ignorant of the outside world, even of their own German history. The under-eighteens had no positive ideas about German greatness or desire to rule the world, nor any belief that Germany was better than anywhere else, nor hatred of other people. Many did not even know what Jews were. Only those in their early twenties showed Nazi characteristics.[5]

It was obvious that the three Rs would have to take a back seat to the three Fs (food, fuel and footwear) and the three Ps (pens, pencils and paper) – all of which were almost totally lacking. (The Parliamentary Select Committee on Estimates which toured Germany in 1946 noted, 'More paper is used in Britain to-day for football coupons than for the whole of German education in the British Zone.')[6] Education officers scratched around, almost literally, to make buildings at least weatherproof. There was no question of fuel for heating. Each child was supposed to bring in a piece of coal or a lump of wood for the stove. Premises which could be made available, even if only one room, had to be used in shifts – usually three a day. Sometimes lessons were held in private houses, the pupils moving from house to house, taking their coal briquettes with them. There were no writing materials: the children used slates. Teachers had to summon all their imaginative powers. A British teacher visited the Rudolf Steiner school, an experimental school which had survived the Nazis. She found the pupils learning English, French and Latin by the direct method. Invited to inspect a geometry lesson, she found herself in the gymnasium, where the children were forming themselves into circles and squares on the floor.[7] It was a slow business, but they were learning – and thoroughly enjoying themselves.

But the absence of books and writing materials opened up a new experience for teachers and pupils. They had discussions together – something previously unknown. Some Germans still remember the excitement of the classroom in those days. They felt that the teachers were relishing the ability to talk freely without fear. 'We were all good friends, the older pupils, the younger pupils and the teachers. We never had lessons like that before, because now we were involved in the talking.'[8] Teachers would abandon their traditional position in front of the class and move around the room, sometimes even sitting among the children.

The teachers who had been in the forces were particularly popular with the children. Emergency training schemes had been set up for those under thirty-five with basic qualifications. Many had been prisoners in Britain and the United States. They brought with them a breath of the outside world. The first book to which one such young teacher of English introduced his pupils was John Steinbeck's *The Moon Is Down* – the story of the Occupation of Norway. The children now learned from the other side what it was like when Germans took over other people's countries: how they treated them and how they were hated. But there were lighter moments: Jerome K. Jerome's *Three Men in a Boat*, for instance. 'We all laughed and said, "It's so nice: school can be fun" – because it hadn't been fun before.'[9]

One teacher took her pupils to her home and brought in a young actor from the Hamburg Theatre who gave them readings (in German) from dramatists from Shakespeare to Eugene O'Neill. They were to hear for the first time of Anouilh, Wilder, Giraudoux, Brecht. 'All that culture: that feeling of the Western world that we didn't know before. We longed for everything coming from abroad. They listened to the British Forces Network and were thrilled with the music of Benny Goodman, Louis Armstrong, Glenn Miller and others. And they learned English while singing songs like 'On the Sunny Side of the Street', 'Don't Fence Me In', 'Sentimental Journey'. At school they had never sung anything but nationalist anthems.[10]

Boys and girls who had been dutiful members of the Hitler Youth and the Bund Deutscher Mädel easily turned their backs on regimentation and nationalism: 'We thought we never wanted to be a nation again. We just wanted to be young people in an open world.' 'It was as if the sun came up,' one woman remembered, 'because you heard things and you learned things you never heard before.'[11]

Yet all these exciting developments emerged only gradually from the most appalling conditions. In his report on education in the Zone, Robert Birley put shoes as the number-one priority. Lack of footwear was the biggest enemy of education. Frequently there was only one pair of usable shoes in a family, and children took turns. They hobbled to school in shoes belonging to younger brothers or sisters or slopped along in shoes borrowed from parents. Some parents carried their children to school on their backs. Teachers told the British publisher Victor Gollancz that in wet weather 'shoe absenteeism' could be as high as 50 per cent.[12]

Elementary schools and school meals were 'the only barrier in large towns between young children and a life of complete barbarism', wrote Robert Birley.[13] It was Ellen Wilkinson (with the change of government in Britain now Minister of Education) who got some food into the children. When she visited the zone, she wanted to know why the schools were so slow to get going. When the problems were pointed out, she immediately took steps for the provision of rudimentary school meals, even though these might be only a form of milk soup. It was one way of making sure children attended school. Another early visitor was Field Marshal Smuts, whose interest in the well-being of the children impressed the Germans very much. However, they were rather nonplussed by Lady Astor, who visited schools in Hamburg. She urged the girls (in English) not to be afraid of men, to hold to their own opinions and never to be suppressed by anyone – not even their husbands. A later Education Minister, George Tomlinson, made a very different impression. He had a confidential way of talking to the children personally, saying he did not want the grown-ups to listen. He talked about his working-class childhood and how he had once sold ice cream for a living and so on. The children loved it.[14]

The absence of acceptable textbooks presented a great problem for the grammar schools. Robert Birley found that English was being taught by teachers who knew little or nothing of England. One teacher was copying out the chapter of *The Pickwick Papers* about the Eatanswill election, to translate to his class. The boys explained to Birley that there were now to be elections in Germany and they wanted to see how they were conducted in England.

Teachers had to fall back on their old notes. But these had first to be scrutinized by the education officers and sources had to be supplied for everything – even dictation material, songs, hymns, recitations. During the previous regime, every aspect of teaching had been impregnated with Nazi doctrine. Now new syllabuses had to be constructed in consultation with German education authorities. In biology, for instance, there had been undue emphasis on heredity. In teaching English, the British laid down that the cultural aspect of the British Empire should be stressed rather than the political.

With regard to mathematics, indoctrination had begun in the infant school. Textbooks showed drawings of toddlers on their little chairs giving the Nazi salute and waving swastika flags in response to one of their number standing before a map on a blackboard. Maps and population statistics were used for exercises in simple addition, subtraction and multiplication – a rather more political form of how many beans make five. Graphs were plotted showing the rise of membership of the Nazi Party and the decline in unemployment figures. By the time students arrived at differential calculus, they were working on the dispersion of rifle bullets, ballistic curves, the impact of hand grenades, the effect of high-explosive bombs.

But the Nazi regime went beyond the perverting of textbooks. A whole system of special colleges was established for the education of an elite. National Socialist Political Institutes – the 'Napolas' – provided specialist courses for the training of future army and government high-flyers. The pupils of the Adolf Hitler Schulen, based on the English public schools, which the Germans greatly admired, were hand-picked to be future political leaders. The schools were set in beautiful surroundings and enjoyed every possible facility. The education officer Edith Davies met seven former pupils from such a school, now aged about twenty. She entertained them at her flat, and over sticky buns they told her their stories. The school had been wonderful – there was riding, swimming, rowing, tennis, everything. They knew quite well they were being indoctrinated but did not care. It was a marvellous life, and they just wallowed in it. Now because they were ex-pupils of an Adolf Hitler Schule no one would employ them. They were youngsters of the highest mental calibre and potential: too bright, the education officer felt, to have been subjects for successful indoctrination. She kept in touch with them over the years, and they all achieved good positions in law, medicine, the universities. They were, she felt, brands plucked from the burning.

The Textbook Section had moved from London to Germany in July 1945. By December 1945 the German education authorities were sufficiently stabilized for a German Central Textbook Committee to be established, which coordinated its work fruitfully with the British Section. (It is unlikely that anyone took notice of the admonition by the Military Government commander in Hanover that 'Great care must be exercised in using such authors as Caesar and Sallust whose work it is felt may well encourage militaristic and nationalistic tendencies.')[15]

Not surprisingly, it was history books which presented the

greatest problem. A History Working Party was set up in Brunswick under a distinguished professor of history, Georg Eckert. It was decided to co-opt representatives of other nationalities: British, American, French, Polish, Italian. The difficulty of producing a history book without bias as regards attitudes in other countries seemed almost insuperable. Edith Davies was attending one of the sessions of the Working Party when the name of Copernicus cropped up. The Germans immediately claimed him as German; the Pole insisted that he was Polish; the Italians declared that Italy was his spiritual home. 'They were in each other's hair in no time about one single little point.' It seemed futile to attempt to produce history books which did not offend the traditions of other nationalities. Nevertheless Professor Eckert and his German colleagues produced a series of pamphlets on specific historical subjects (printed on scrap paper thrown away by the local newspaper) based on historical fact, and these became influential throughout the zone for the training of teachers.

Side by side with writing new texts was the problem of publishing them – and in sufficient numbers to meet the desperate need. Printing presses everywhere had been destroyed or damaged and had to be replaced. In the absence of the written word, the spoken word had become the main conduit of learning. Education Branch rose to the challenge. Early in 1947 three British history teachers were invited to visit Germany to conduct a week's course for history teachers. The teachers – hand-picked – represented three areas of British education: public school (Stowe), direct grant (a Bluecoat school) and a state school. The subject chosen for discussion was the Napoleonic Wars – when Britain and Germany had been allies. The course was held near Hamburg. Accommodation was spartan and food austere, but the Germans and the British Education Branch officers shared the same conditions. Huddled round a single stove, they forgot the cold in the excitement of totally free discussion on any subject they chose. As a profession, German teachers had suffered isolation from each other for a long time in an atmosphere of fear and distrust. Now, they told their British hosts, they felt reborn.

The universities presented different and more complex problems. Here it was a question not only of education but of changing the structure of German society which the university system had done so much to shape. In the nineteenth century German universities had been the object of admiration in the English-speaking academic world. Thomas Arnold, headmaster of Rugby, wrote of a new intellectual dawn in Germany. His son, the great educationist Matthew Arnold, declared in 1868 that the French universities had no liberty, the English universities no science, while the German universities had both. They had produced a tradition of learning, of the pursuit and extension of knowledge, renowned throughout the world. The universities were gatherings of scholars in the medieval tradition, passing on knowledge to those who were permitted to listen. Academics did not 'teach' and had little personal contact with the students who came to hear them. Conservative and authoritarian, they devoted themselves to their own research and the advancement of their reputations by academic publication. Professors had an elevated status and a respect in society not known elsewhere. But, as Robert Birley said, it was a good thing for ordinary mortals to be in awe of the great professor, but it was his mind they should reverence, not his social rank. The professors made no contribution to the society which accorded them such respect, for which they felt no reciprocal responsibility.

Although there had been individual resignations, the academics had not as a profession brought their formidable weight to bear against the Nazis' burgeoning political perversion of the state. After an address by Birley to the senate of Göttingen University, the Professor of Philosophy protested that Birley seemed to think all the professors there were Nazis. Not at all, countered Birley: the charge was that they had been ready to accept a regime whose policy was based on academic nonsense. The response, to his surprise, was 'To that charge, Mr Birley, we have no answer.'[16] A noble tradition had been degraded. One university control officer found few actual Nazis, Nazi sympathizers or even fellow-travellers among the professors. But he did find 'plenty of closed-in, ultra-conservative and nationalistic minds looking backward to what they regarded as their halcyon days pre-1933 and refusing to open their eyes and minds to a better and more democratic future'.[17] There had to be an attempt – in the words of the Parliamentary Select Committee on Estimates – 'to let sunlight into the closed temple of German thought'.

University control officers (UCOs), of which there was one appointed to each university, were mainly young, usually just out of the Services and usually with university connections either as graduates or, sometimes, as dons. (One young officer was asked by a professor what he had published.) Some came from a Foreign Office or Intelligence background. And sometimes the 'colonial' attitude which so often – and so surprisingly – manifested itself throughout the Occupation crept in. One officer wrote in 1946 of the student body for which he was responsible, 'One feels rather like an administrative officer in a backward colony . . . In fact, it is not easy to avoid having for the University the same paternal regard as a District Commissioner would feel for his native tribes, or an officer of a Gurkha regiment for his men.'[18]

This was something about which the Germans were always touchy. At a conference in Oxford long after the war the point was raised by Germans present that many of the UCOs had been serving in Africa, Burma and India, ignoring the fact that they had been there as fighting soldiers and not as colonial administrators.[19]

The UCOs needed to be young and active. Like the schools officers, they found that their initial and most pressing task was to organize premises in which teaching could take place. In Kiel four ships in the harbour were used as both living accommodation and lecture rooms. The students there were fortunate. In other parts of the zone, students were in some instances living in boarded-over bomb craters. Cologne University was without roofing, doors, windows, gas and water. The enterprising UCO managed to have men and women students taken on as council workers to clear rubble around the university and in the town, thereby earning themselves a little money and, more importantly, the entitlement to a hot meal. Everyone – staff and students alike – wore all the clothes they possessed at the same time. Students took notes on any scraps of paper – the backs of old envelopes, for example. And the notes would be taken by someone who had the only pencil and were passed around afterwards. There were of course no books.

The UCOs were confronted by a terrible scholarly vacuum. Professors had been cut off from from all outside academic thought not just during the war but for the six years before it. And they were still, even now, not allowed to correspond with colleagues abroad. So many of the classics had been destroyed by the Nazis that, as one UCO was appalled to discover, many students had not heard of Heinrich Heine or Thomas Mann. University libraries had been transported *en masse* to places of safety far away from industry and the cities. Much time and effort were needed to retrieve them, with transport begged from hard-pressed authority.

One major point of contention between the two sides was the imposition by the British authorities of the *numerus clausa* – the restriction of the number of university entrants – which remained in force until 1949. This was dictated by the hopeless inadequacies of buildings, books, equipment and teaching staff. In addition to all the men flooding out of the forces there was the influx of thousands of refugees and displaced persons from the East. In 1947–8 demand for university places was estimated at 40 per cent in excess of capacity. All students had to submit a *Fragebogen* to Public Safety Branch, but it was left to university admissions committees to make decisions, with guidance if required from the UCO. Agonizing choices had to be made. Some universities placed in the scale work done by students in rubble clearance or in helping with the retrieval of libraries from their wartime repositories and replacing books on shelves. In some universities specific periods of rubble clearing were mandatory. In Kiel a large number of naval officers presented themselves, having been quite improperly promised by the Royal Navy that minesweeping in the North Sea would be rewarded by admission to the university. But tens of thousands of students had to be turned away. One UCO declared that this had been the major nightmare of his whole time in Germany.

The British officers found the average student's ignorance appalling. He knew nothing of other countries except what Nazi propaganda had told him – and nothing, of course, of political matters or economics. His knowledge of history was warped and his general standard of learning poor. The education officer at Göttingen described the minds of the students as 'pathetically childlike'; it was as though men of twenty or more had stopped growing mentally when Hitler came to power – 'not a nation of warped minds but a nation of Peter Pans'.[20] But the older men who had been in the Services had seen something of the outside world as the *Wehrmacht* spread throughout Europe and North Africa during the war. The intellectually able among them had had some contact with other systems of political thought, whether democratic, populist or Marxist. They were therefore more independent and inclined to cause 'trouble' – in some instances by disseminating nationalistic views. The percentage of former officers was higher among the students of the British Zone than in the other zones. In November 1946 the British Control Commission authorities took the draconian step of issuing an edict excluding former regular *Wehrmacht* officers, including reserve officers, from admission to universities. But Education Branch disapproved. They argued that, as these were well-educated men who would be leading citizens in the future, it was important that they should have the experience of university education. Although professional officers might need special screening, it was unjustified to ban temporary or reserve officers. The ban was removed in February 1947.

One great and lasting benefit that the education officers imported from their own university backgrounds was the institution of halls of residence – not previously known in Germany, where student life had lacked organization and a social dimension. At a time of great hardship, Military Government, Education Branch and city authorities worked together to create such community bases. Germans themselves considered this innovation, together with the fostering of personal relations between professors and students, as the major achievement of the UCOs.

The theologian Karl Barth in his report quoted earlier declared that Germany was one vast hermetically sealed prison, a continuation of life in the Third Reich. The Germans were shut up in a terrifying way, left alone with their cares, problems, imaginings and ideas.

> In the long run it cannot be healthy for the other nations only to know Germans of to-day from a distance and in the light of the nightmare pictures of the wars of domination now at an end. It seems to me an urgent need not only of humanity but of wise policy to open at last the closed doors between Germany and the outside world.[21]

Now the doors were opened. With the help of the Foreign Office, scholars, poets and playwrights toured the zone and gave lectures to packed halls. There was no shortage of well-known names. T. S. Eliot, Stephen Spender, Bertrand Russell, Lord Beveridge, Harold Nicolson, Herbert Read and Vera Brittain were among those who came to relieve what Birley called the nation's intellectual and spiritual famine. But, more importantly, there was an outflow in the opposite direction, from Germany to Britain.

In November 1945 a former prison camp for German generals, Wilton Park in Buckinghamshire, was taken over by the War Office as a residential centre for selected prisoners of war. These men would receive an intensive course in the principles and practice of democracy in an adult-education setting. It was hoped that when they returned to their own camps they would spread the ideals of Wilton Park among their comrades and that when they were repatriated they would lead public opinion in post-war Germany towards responsible citizenship and democracy. The warden of Wilton Park was Dr Heinz Koeppler, a German who had gone to Oxford with a scholarship from Kiel University in 1933 and remained in England ever since. During the war he had worked in the Political Warfare Executive with Robert Bruce Lockhart and Richard Crossman.

The Wilton Park centre opened on 1 January 1946 with 300 students. They were drawn from all ranks, and there were no distinctions: only civilian titles were used. There were beds, not bunks, and the students were waited on at table. There was an excellent library, including even Nazi books, and all the British newspapers were available. A tutorial system was instituted with students in groups of fifteen or twenty. Work was hard but intellectually stimulating. Free discussion was encouraged, but good temper was insisted upon.

A galaxy of distinguished men and women from British public and academic life came to lecture at Wilton Park: Bertrand Russell, Lord Lindsay, Lord Beveridge, Harold Macmillan, Quintin Hogg, Kingsley Martin, A. J. P. Taylor, Jennie Lee, Barbara Ward, Herbert Read and Harold Nicolson. Politicians from opposing parties – for instance, Denis Healey and Julian Amery – would debate keenly but demonstrate that they could meet on friendly terms afterwards. Public figures from Germany were brought over: Kurt Schumacher (head of the SPD), Cardinal Frings, Bishop Lilje, Bishop Dibelius, Pastor Niemöller and the Education Ministers (much admired by Birley) Adolf Grimme and Heinrich Landahlm. The resident tutors also included German refugees.

In January 1947 the first German civilians – thirty-five in number – arrived at Wilton Park, sponsored by the Foreign Office. They included administrators, journalists, educationists and trade unionists. This was the beginning of a stream of men and women who were not only to enjoy the same intellectual facilities as the prisoners but also to have the unique opportunity to discuss their own problems in Germany. Many of them were out of work. There were seminars, classes, tutorials. They were brought into touch with intellectual and administrative life in Britain. There were visits to schools, adult-education centres, the Toynbee Hall university settlement in Whitechapel, the Royal Institute of International Affairs at Chatham House. They attended full sessions of the London County Council and visited local-government offices, the Houses of Parliament, the Law Courts and Transport House. In Fleet Street they had discussions with journalists.

Many leading members of future governments of the German Federal Republic were to attend the centre either as prisoners of war in the early days or later at conferences. Willi Brandt declared, 'Almost a whole generation of German politicians defined their concept of and attitude towards Britain and the British on the basis of impressions they received at Wilton Park.'[22]

Helmut Schmidt spoke at the twenty-fifth anniversary of its foundation. Such was the *esprit de corps* among Old Wiltonians that, when in 1956 the Foreign Office feared it could no longer sustain the expense and would have to close it, it was 'rescued' by the Germans. Even when the centre moved from Buckinghamshire to Sussex the name 'Wilton Park' was retained.

For the ordinary German, information on Britain and the British at home could be sought in the British Information Centres. These were opened up wherever premises could be found, but had to battle for accommodation against all the other priorities. The centres were given the title of *Die Brücke* – The Bridge – the function they fulfilled between the occupiers and the occupied. At first they drew people simply for the warmth they provided, but as conditions eased they expanded into well-stocked reading rooms with a regular supply of British newspapers and periodicals. By the end of 1946 about forty centres were functioning and another twenty by the middle of the following year. With the passage of time emphasis on the cultural and educational function of the centres emerged, and they were in due course absorbed by the British Council.

Almost as much as they hungered for food, the Germans hungered for news. The British were quite simply staggered by the ignorance of the outside world, past and present, which they found among all levels of the population. This was the reality of living in a society ruled for years by propaganda and censorship. All newspapers had been closed down at the time of the surrender. The occupiers now aimed to give a fair start to a free, democratic and responsible press, professionally competent and likely to survive. There were two great problems: newsprint and journalistic staff. Recruitment was difficult. Those too young to have been significantly involved in the regime were professionally inexperienced. Others who had been excluded from their profession by the Nazis were now out of touch. In between were those who had perhaps been compromised. Therefore all applications for licences to start newspapers had to be carefully scrutinized. This was a slow business.

The gap was filled in the Occupied Zones by 'overt' newspapers – that is, newspapers run by the occupiers themselves. In the British Zone, *Die Welt* was first published in March 1946. It was intended as an example of a quality newspaper, and was based to some extent on *The Times*. First published in Hamburg, it was produced by Germans under a British controller. The editor had spent ten years in a concentration camp, so was considered sound. Although intended to be an indigenous German newspaper, nevertheless it was to be a vehicle for projecting British policy and the British point of view. News alone was to be on the front page, and fact was to be separated from comment.

In the interest of the emergence of democratic politics, licences for newspapers were accorded to the main political parties in various cities. There were overseeing British controllers, but, as there was a shortage of German-speaking officers, control was not too close. And there were practical problems. General Alec Bishop, head of Press and Information Division, found that in one newspaper office there was only one electric light bulb and the British team were carrying it around to wherever happened to be the most important stage of production. By the middle of 1946 thirty-five newspapers had been set up. Newsprint was allocated on an overall circulation basis of one copy for every five persons in a specific area, and the papers themselves were restricted to sheets of four sides twice a week. Such was the demand for information that anyone lucky enough to obtain a copy could sell on pieces of it for cigarettes, the price being regulated by the topicality and in inverse proportion to the amount of advertising.

Reasoned criticism was permitted, but licensees were forbidden to bring the Allies into contempt or to interfere with the execution of policy. However, on one occasion the British controller of *Die Welt* himself resorted to subterfuge to remedy what he saw as an abuse on the part of the Army.[23] At a time when there were no shoes available at all for the Germans, and the people at home in Britain could buy them only with coupons, the Officers' Shop in Hamburg was selling German-made shoes coupon-free. With the private agreement of the Regional Commissioner, Vaughan Berry, a letter in German signed with a German signature but actually composed by the British staff appeared in the paper complaining about this unfair and 'undemocratic' practice. After publication, the sales of the shoes were stopped. This was a comparatively minor affair which nevertheless redounded to the credit of the paper among the population – and particularly among its own staff.

But there was a major crisis on the paper when one of the most brutal of Potsdam imperatives was promulgated, concerning the dismantling of industry. The long-awaited – and dreaded – list of industrial plants which were to be dismantled in the British Zone was issued and had to be defended in *Die Welt*. But the German staff demanded that the paper should carry a German editorial on a policy which was seen as an economic catastrophe. Argument continued all day, until two hours before the paper was due to go to press. The paper's controller, Major Steel McRitchie, felt this was something which had to be referred to the highest authority. Fortunately, Sir Brian Robertson, the Deputy Military Governor, was in Hamburg attending a cocktail party, and McRitchie dashed over there in his car. Robertson declared that he would never allow a German to write a leader in *Die Welt*; however, he was persuaded by Sir Cecil Weir, the Economic Adviser, who was also present at the party. McCritchie fled back to the office in time for the British leader to be set up and beneath it the German point of view signed by a prominent German economist. From then on, when major questions of policy arose, the paper presented leaders from both sides and left the reader to decide. It was sometimes attacked in the House of Commons for 'rocking the boat', but the British controllers felt they were doing the right and democratic thing. The paper gained in credibility, and at its peak had a circulation of 1 million. It was eventually sold to Axel Springer and still survives as a major European newspaper.

Another successful publication which started under licence from the British Occupation authorities is *Der Spiegel*. When a Herr Rudolf Augstein approached the British with a proposal for a satirical magazine there was some apprehension. But it was decided, in the spirit of democracy, to let him go ahead. Although the magazine did indeed prove something of a thorn in the British side, it was also a demonstration, as one of the controllers said, 'of what democracy is all about'.

Another competitor for a share in the hopelessly inadequate resources of paper was book production. The Nazi regime, the war and subsequent denazification had emptied the bookshelves. Much the same problems existed with publishers as with newspaper editors and proprietors. Some of the established publishers were compromised by their connections with the party; some of the others had been suppressed by the Nazis and were now too old and out of touch to re-establish themselves. Once again there was the slow but vital business of licensing, with all the investigations which that involved. And the limiting of editions to 5,000 hardly attracted authors. The first book published was a German–English, English–German dictionary, which naturally sold out very quickly. This was followed by something equally safe: *The Life of Jesus*, produced by the Lutheran Church.

One prestigious publisher, Ernest Rowalt, had an idea for getting round the dire shortage of printing and bookbinding capacity. He proposed to bring out translations of foreign books in tabloid newspaper format, printed on newspaper presses. Major (later Lord) Barnetson, one of the Control officials, was present at a dinner party in Hamburg where Rowalt expounded his plan to fellow publishers. One of them christened the idea 'Rowalt Rotations Romane' and another reduced this to 'Ro-Ro-Ro' – 'and we all danced round the table shouting, "Ro-Ro-Ro"!'[24] The first title was *Gone with the Wind*. Ro-Ro-Ro continued to fill the gap in book publishing for some years after the war.

As in Education Branch, the British officers – themselves with backgrounds in journalism and publishing – dealt with the publishers as one set of professionals with another. As Lord Barnetson, himself a professional, described it in later years, 'It was not the Occupation authority and a group of German publishers but a group of people, as it were, from both sides who were concerned with the future of the German mind and were determined to do something about it.'[25]

The method of communication which suffered least from shortage of raw materials was radio, although initially there was of course a dire shortage of radio receivers. The studios at Hamburg and the powerful transmitter near by were captured almost intact. BBC engineers moved in, and North-West German Radio (Nordwest Deutscher Rundfunk – NWDR) was set up with headquarters in the city, initially to serve the whole zone. In a country where listening to the BBC had carried the death penalty, British broadcasting in the zone started with remarkable credit and listener loyalty. The BBC helped greatly by making available as control officers experienced broadcasters who were also fluent German speakers.

The creation of an independent broadcasting system required someone of very special calibre. Hugh Carleton Greene, a newspaper correspondent in pre-war Germany and head of the BBC German Service from 1940 to 1946, arrived in Hamburg to take over NWDR in October 1946. His task was to establish a broadcasting organization with a director-general and a board of governors to whom control would be handed over in due course. Although the BBC would be the model, the station would have its own voice – the voice of the new Germany. It was to be a German station and not a British station in Germany. What was essential was that its charter should guarantee the sort of independence which the BBC enjoyed, free from any influence by government or political parties.

Greene maintained the relatively liberal attitude already established at NWDR. This meant that often contentious and difficult issues were presented from the German side. Quite early, some of the best-known German broadcasters – Peter von Zahn, Axel Eggebrecht, Ernst Schnabel – were allowed considerable latitude, rather to the consternation and even resentment of the other Allies. Even in the first months after the surrender there was no anti-fraternization inside the radio station. The concern of everybody was to get the news out properly and fast, but separating fact from comment. One of the great changes, as Peter von Zahn remembered, was to abandon the portentous language which had been used during the Nazi regime for even the most unimportant news. Even the weather had been described in positively Wagnerian tones. With British encouragement the German broadcasters changed to a more relaxed 'fireside' style – which confused the listeners at first. Broadcasters identified themselves by name, so that they became trusted personalities. Round-table discussions were set up with lively sessions uncensored and uncontrolled, although postmortems could sometimes call forth a stern admonition. For the broadcasters it was an exhilarating time. Outright attacks on Occupation policy were of course forbidden, but some criticism and even a little gentle fun at the expense of the occupiers was accepted. Peter von Zahn once gave a humorous talk on how to deal with conquerors which appalled the Americans, who felt the British lion was allowing its tail to be twisted.

There was one field of broadcasting in which the British were particularly successful – music. In May 1945 Sir Adrian Boult (wishing to remain anonymous) had requested his friend Lord Woolton to ask the Foreign Office about the sort of music programmes which might be broadcast by the occupying forces on German radio. These were likely to be controlled by the Americans, 'who had no-one in Europe competent to ensure that Germans got music of the high standard to which they were accustomed'. He feared that 'unless we take steps to prevent it, the Germans will be merely fed with Jazz, which will only make them despise us and may do untold harm'.[26] He need not have concerned himself.

The radio orchestra in Hamburg was one of the few surviving at the end of the war, although hardly at full strength. The support of the British controllers, who all had connections with the musical world in London, was heart-warming for the struggling musicians. The British set about resurrecting the orchestra from the standpoint of both manpower and repertoire.[27] There were no problems with denazification. The manager, Dr Friedrich Schnapp, had friends in England with whom he had managed to make contact during the war while on tour in Sweden with the Berlin Philharmonic under Wilhelm Furtwängler. The conductor Hans Schmidt-Isserstedt was picked up near Hamburg by the British and asked to conduct the newly formed orchestra. Invited to London to conduct the BBC Symphony Orchestra, Schmidt-Isserstedt took the opportunity to appeal to POW camps in Britain, some of which had small orchestras, for any strings they could spare. The German prisoners collected all the strings they could. When Schmidt-Isserstedt returned to Hamburg he handed over the parcel at a little ceremony in the studio, which was recorded by the BBC for transmission in Britain. Then the orchestra played a thank-you piece for their comrades over there. The conductor chose the last part of the overture to *Der Freischütz*, because it was an optimistic piece in C major.

The musicians suffered from the prevailing problems of hunger and inadequate clothing. There was no question of evening dress: the players wore whatever clothes they possessed, mostly old uniforms. In Hamburg the concert hall was heated, but on a visit to Cologne they were forced to play in their hats and coats. They were always hungry, and Schnapp remembered the control officer, Major H. Hartog, one evening saying that he could not keep them there any longer and telling them to go home and lie down.

But, for the orchestra, hardship was alleviated by the excitement of the repertoire: not only Mendelssohn – of course – but British composers from Elgar to Peter Racine Fricker, Benjamin Britten, Alan Rawsthorne and Michael Tippett. There was the experience of studying *The Rite of Spring* for the first time. This was done, according to one of the violinists, Ulrich Benthien, by rigging up two loudspeakers in opposite corners of the studio and simply sitting there with the score and no instruments, listening to a taped performance. The orchestral parts had been sent from London, and there was some encouragement in finding that their English colleagues had also found occasional difficulties. On Benthien's copy someone had written above one difficult passage, 'Don't look at the conductor', which he found to be sound advice.[28]

Two months after the surrender, while the orchestra was still working very hard to re-establish itself, there was a momentous event. Under the auspices of UNRRA, Yehudi Menuhin had come to play for the people – the Poles, Czechs, Russians – in the displaced-persons camps throughout the zone. Major Hartog persuaded him to come to Hamburg. On 29 July, with Schmidt-Isserstedt conducting, Menuhin played the Mendelssohn Violin Concerto with them. Afterwards they asked him to play a special piece for them and he performed a Bach chaconne. It was an unforgettable occasion of musical solidarity and great generosity.

Each concert by the NWDR Orchestra in the city was given three times: on Saturday morning for children and students, on Sunday afternoon for the British, and on Monday night for the Germans. The famous children's concerts instituted by Sir Robert Mayer in London and conducted by Malcolm Sargent were extended to Germany, and twelve concerts were given throughout the zone. Although Sargent could not come, he recommended another conductor, Trevor Jones, who spoke German and amused the children with comments and explanations in the London tradition. The German orchestras gave their services free.

The NWDR Orchestra felt it had never had a more grateful or more appreciative audience, both German and British, than during those dark days. On one occasion it had been broadcasting a performance of *La Bohème*. In the interval Hugh Greene suddenly appeared in the studio. He had been dining with friends, he said, and they had been listening to the transmission. They were so impressed by the performance that he had felt obliged to leave the table and come to the radio building to congratulate the musicians. Things were never the same, Dr Schnapp felt, after the British relinquished control: 'Nobody cared – it was like working in an empty room.'[29]

9
Make Germany pay

THE FINAL meeting of the Big Three – Britain, the United States and the Soviet Union – took place in Potsdam between 17 July and 2 August 1945. The mere two weeks assigned to the Conference would today hardly seem an adequate period for dealing with momentous decisions of worldwide significance, although the European Advisory Commission had spent some two years preparing briefs beforehand. One writer described decisions being taken 'between breakfast and lunch, or lunch and dinner, or even after dinner, hastily under the pressure of a limited stay in some foreign town, on the basis of fleeting impressions and superficial conversations . . . The results are what one might expect.'[1] The removal from the table of Roosevelt by death and of Churchill by domestic politics left Stalin in a position of seniority over the new men – Truman and Attlee. Continuity was maintained by the civil servants, working long hours to codify the results of the round-table discussions. Matters relating specifically to Germany fell into three groups: the political and economic principles governing the treatment of Germany under control; the question of reparations to be paid by Germany; and the settlement of the German–Polish frontier and 'orderly transfer of populations'.

It was decreed that the European Advisory Commission, its work now accomplished, should be dissolved and the control of Occupied Germany be the responsibility of the quadripartite Allied Control Council. A Council of Foreign Ministers representing the United Kingdom, the United States, the USSR, France and China was established 'to continue the necessary preparatory work for the peace settlements' and to deal with any other matters which the participating governments might choose to refer to it.

The Conference ended in some unseemly haste. Final drafts produced in English and Russian, prepared simultaneously but not compared word for word, were placed before the principals. Amendments were agreed 'across the table'. But there was no definitive document signed by the Big Three. They simply autographed blank sheets of paper and went home. It was left to officials to compare the two texts and deliver the final form. This task was delegated to a commission of two members from each nation. Senior Foreign Office advisers had departed with the Foreign Secretary, and the British were represented by two minor members of the War Cabinet Office. But, when the commission met, the Soviet representatives said they could not proceed as they were 'without instructions'. When the meeting reconvened the following day, the Soviet officials had been replaced by the future foreign ministers Gromyko and Vyshinsky. This was revealed some months later in an explanatory letter from the War Cabinet Office to the Foreign Office, which had suddenly discovered the absence of any original signed Potsdam Agreement. 'Nobody suggested', admitted the writer, 'that Foreign Office "regulars" should stay behind but it would have been better not to leave the WCO people alone.'[2] Given the circumstances, it was an extraordinary lapse. In the words of one historian, 'The Potsdam Agreement was an unsatisfactory document because in one or two of the most vital passages it was either ambiguous or at best open to misinterpretation . . . Anyone gifted with hindsight can discern the seeds of trouble in the very wording of the Agreement.'[3]

It had been agreed at the Yalta Conference of the Big Three in February 1945 that Germany should make reparations to all the Allied countries for the damage done to them by the war. The Potsdam Conference now put this into specific terms. To eliminate Germany's war potential, the production of all implements of war was to be prohibited and prevented. The production of items directly necessary to a war economy was to be rigidly controlled and restricted to Germany's approved postwar peacetime needs. The amount of material available for reparations would depend on a general economic plan. Germany was to be allowed a living standard not exceeding the average European standard (excluding Great Britain and the USSR). Payment of reparations should leave enough resources for the German people to subsist without external assistance. The earnings from exports were to be used to pay for imports approved by the Control Council. Allied controls should be imposed upon the German economy only to the extent necessary to ensure 'the equitable distribution of essential commodities between the several zones so as to produce a balanced economy throughout Germany and reduce the need for imports'.

The kingpin of the whole policy of reparations was the clause 'During the period of the Occupation, Germany shall be treated as a single economic unit.' The failure to implement this was the beginning of the division between East and West which finally led to the existence of two separate German states. For the British Zone this failure spelt disaster.

Although it had been accepted by the Allies that in due course there would be an alteration in Poland's western frontier, the final delineation was to be a matter for an eventual peace conference. But by the time the Big Three met at Potsdam the Soviet government had already transferred German territory in Russian-occupied areas to Polish administration and had unilaterally removed plant and materials to the Soviet Union in advance of the official allocation of zones. It was forced to admit these removals to the Conference and offered to make a reduction in its reparations claim. But the Americans maintained that such unilateral action had made overall treatment of the reparations problem impossible. Each country would have to take reparations from its own zone. As the capital plant available was located roughly 40 per cent in the Soviet Zone and 60 per cent in the Western Zones, the agreed 50 per cent share for the Russians could be made up by 10 per cent from the West. This agreement was set out in the Final Protocol of Potsdam. In an additional arrangement, the Soviet Union was to receive from the Western Zones 15 per cent of available 'usable and complete industrial capital equipment from the metallurgical, chemical and machine-manufacturing industries . . . in exchange for an equivalent value of food, coal, potash, zinc, timber, petroleum products and such other commodities as may be agreed upon'.

In November and December 1945 nineteen Allies, excluding the USSR, met in Paris. The conference determined the percentage entitlement of each member government to reparations on the basis of material damage suffered to its economy, loss of human life and the contribution the country had made to the war effort. In one respect this yardstick worked to Britain's disadvantage. Because of her great shipping losses, the United Kingdom was allocated the lion's share of the merchant marine. But, set against her reparations account, this allocation would reduce the amount of greatly desired industrial equipment which she could claim.

The committee which was set up to deal with the disposition of German shipping had 'felt bound to draw the attention of the Conference' to the possibility that any public announcement that German ships were to be divided among the Allies could result in the scuttling by their crews of ships which might be ordered to sail to Allied ports. Foreign Office minutes would seem to indicate that this caveat was the reason why the full proceedings of the Potsdam Conference – the so-called 'Secret Protocol' – were never laid before Parliament (although a shorter report was published on 2 August 1945). On the first anniversary of the Conference, Lord Beveridge put down a Parliamentary Question asking that the Potsdam Agreement 'with all relevant and consequential documents' should be produced to Parliament. The Foreign Office advised on the reply: 'We have never published the whole of the Potsdam Protocol or said publicly that there are parts of it unpublished.' The 'really important' omission from the published report concerned the disposal of the German navy and merchant marine. A brief paragraph had stated that agreement had been reached in principle and that a further joint statement would be made in due course. In fact no such statement had been forthcoming.[4]

The Paris Agreement came into force on 24 January 1946, and the Inter-Allied Reparation Agency (IARA) was set up to allocate reparations to the various claimants. Its deliberations were to be based on the principle of Germany as an economic whole. But a challenge to this concept had arisen immediately after the conclusion of Potsdam.

The Conference had agreed that, although for the time being no central German government should be established, certain essential central administrative departments should be set up to work under the direction of the Allied Control Council. Concrete proposals for these were submitted to the Council in October 1945. But France was completely opposed to any proposal which smacked of centralization. Not having been invited to take part in the Potsdam Conference, France behaved with the balefulness of the wicked fairy who had not been invited to the royal christening. The Allied Control Council, of which France *was* a member, could only act unanimously. France's opposition therefore brought to a halt plans for the administrative structures necessary for implementing economic unity. The French were even opposed to the establishment of a Transport and Communications Department for the whole of Germany. Railways constituted war potential, they argued. The Central Directorate of the Reichsbahn was potentially as dangerous as the German General Staff. The latter had been suppressed, so why not the former?[5]

The Potsdam Conference had laid down that the amount of reparations to be removed from Germany must be determined within six months of the conclusion of the Conference. The physical removal of industrial capital equipment must be completed within the following two years. In September 1945 a committee began work on creating a formula to comply with the order to set the German standard of living at a European average. It was decided that this should be set at 74 per cent of the average of the years from 1930 to 1938. This formula was based on the pre-surrender preoccupation with reducing Germany's power. The payment of reparations should leave the German people sufficient resources 'to subsist without external assistance'. But by 1945 Germany, devastated by war and incapable of feeding, clothing or housing her population, simply had no standard of living at all. The immediate need was to prevent the country from collapsing altogether.

In March 1946 the four Commanders-in-Chief published a 'Level of Industry Plan' establishing the norm for Germany's postulated 'peacetime needs'. Plant surplus to these requirements was to be declared available as reparations or – if not so required – was to be dismantled. Industry was divided into three groups: (1) prohibited (of military importance); (2) allowed but restricted (capable of military use but essential for civilian purposes); (3) without any military significance. Fourteen industries were prohibited and twelve limited. A decision was reached to retain in Germany industrial capacity equivalent to 75 per cent of German production in 1936, taken as an average of the years 1930–38, 1932 being the slump. A crucial point, much argued about, was steel production. The British pressed for a higher production figure but had to agree to a capacity of 7.5 million tons being left in Germany, output in any one year not to be allowed to rise above 5.8 million tons.[6]

In setting the level of industry, realistic consideration of the actual state of Germany was sacrificed to speed and, ostensibly at least, to achieving agreement among the Allies. In January 1946 a Foreign Office minute deplored the haste. The writer presciently warned, 'There is every indication that Level of Industry decisions are being rushed through without sufficient knowledge of the facts and consideration of them . . . Much of what is being decided and done at present in Berlin will in a very few years' time, if not before, be regarded as highly irresponsible and will probably require revision, if not scrapping.'[7]

The British press was also condemnatory. *The Economist* declared the plan to be 'anachronistic and dangerous, negative, restrictive and basically unworkable'. The *Manchester Guardian*

wrote that the assertion that a low standard of living and production would guarantee against a revival of nationalism was
naïve: 'If anything but political catastrophe comes out of this it
will be a miracle.' The *Observer* warned that de-industrialization
plans were designed to drive western industrial Germany to
unemployment, to desperation and into the arms of the Communist East.

The Germans themselves were doubtful whether, with the
resources which would be left to them, they could even reach the
level of industry permitted. The reduction of the machine-tool
industry was a considerable anxiety. As a member of the German
Zonal Advisory Council declared, 'I cannot see how we can arrive
at any economic development if even the possibility of carrying
out repairs on what we have left is taken away from us.'[8]

The Parliamentary Select Committee on Estimates had
doubts about the whole policy of dismantling. The security problem was different from that envisaged at Potsdam. Would not
some form of security be assured by the destruction of Category-
I war plants – those scheduled by Potsdam as having been
employed exclusively on war production? For the rest, even if it
was practicable to carry out the necessary dismantling, packing
and transporting of plant to the receiving countries, it was estimated that when re-erected its productivity would be only about
20 per cent of what it had been *in situ*.[9] Further, there was the
waste of scarce resources diverted into packing and shipping.
German industrial recovery was affected by such non-productive
consumption of materials such as timber, paper and so on,
already in short supply, and by the use of skilled and unskilled
labour on non-productive work.[10]

The Russians, in their zone, had no such problems. Plant
which was allocated to them as reparations from their own zone
was left in place, the ownership being transferred to Russians
and production exported to the Soviet Union. Even plants allocated from the Western Zones, such as the Kügel-Fishcher ball-
bearing factory, were re-erected in the Soviet Zone. In January
1947 dismantling in the Soviet Zone was suspended. It was a

clear indication that Germany would never be treated as an economic whole.

In April 1946 the Foreign Ministers met in Paris. James F. Byrnes, the American Secretary of State, pressed for urgent consideration of several points, among them that resources left in Germany should be used on behalf of the country as a whole and particularly for exports; that procedures for effecting economic unity should be agreed within ninety days; and that zonal boundaries should simply delineate Occupation areas and should not be treated as economic barriers. Foreign Secretary Molotov refused any such proposals. The Russians did not even deny that eastward reparations removals from their zone included both materials and manufactured goods. Had Germany been treated as an economic unit these items would have earned money as exports or reduced the quantity of imports, thus saving money for the American and British taxpayers who had to pay for them. At the Allied Control Council in Berlin the American Military Governor, General Lucius Clay, made a stand. He announced that, as the Level of Industry Plan had been based on a balanced import–export programme which obviously did not exist, the Plan had no validity. In order to safeguard the economy of the US Zone, he was suspending all reparations deliveries.

Foreign Secretary Bevin explained to Secretary of State Byrnes that the British would not be openly following the American lead: they did not want to give the Russians the chance to accuse the Western Allies of ganging up against them. To withhold allocations would, it was feared, cause an open breach of Potsdam, which the British were loyally endeavouring to support. However, in a note for the Foreign Office, Bevin expressed his view that action should be taken to show support for the United States' move and demonstrate that Britain took a serious view of Russia's actions. The two Allies should tell the Russians that there must be a review of the industrial capacity required in the West and that, although dismantling would continue, plants would be allocated only down to a certain level.

Dismantling would be restricted to those factories allocated to the Western powers. Care must be taken, however, warned Bevin, that the stopping of future dismantling did not interfere with Britain obtaining its immediate requirements of special plant and machinery.[11]

In the Foreign Office an idea was floated for a possible concession to the Russians. Why not substitute people for products? 'Germans are virtually the only items of which there is a surplus. Carefully used, I believe that a concession in the field of reparation labour might have considerable propaganda advantages assuming, as I think one safely can, that the Russians would take full advantage of any concession to them in this field.' However, a dissenting voice pointed out that any scheme to use labour as reparations must take account of world opinion. 'We could not face the political implications of slave labour . . .'[12]

On 11 July 1946 Secretary of State Byrnes took a major step. He offered to merge the US Zone, for economic purposes, with that of any other power which was willing to do so. The offer was promptly taken up by the United Kingdom government, alone.

The following day Byrnes made a crucial speech in Stuttgart expounding the justification for the fusion. The United States was prepared to carry out the Potsdam Agreement on demilitarization and reparations. However, if Germany was not to be administered as an economic unit there should be changes in the agreed Level of Industry Plan. He reiterated the American readiness to unite the US Zone economically with any of the other zones. Germany must be given a chance to develop a balance of trade sufficient to make her economy self-sustaining. Recovery in Europe and particularly in the states adjoining Germany would be slow indeed, Byrnes warned, 'if Germany with her great resources of iron and steel is turned into a poorhouse'. Where so many vital questions were concerned, the Control Council was neither governing Germany nor allowing Germany to govern itself. The purpose of the Occupation did not contemplate the prolonged alien dictatorship of Germany's peacetime economy, nor of Germany's internal political life. It was the view of the American government that the Germans throughout Germany, under proper safeguards, should now be given the primary responsibility for the running of their own affairs. 'The United States government favours the early establishment of a provisional German government, not hand-picked by other governments.'[13]

In the House of Commons, Bevin endorsed Byrnes's speech. Britain had a major interest, he said, in seeing that Germany did not become a permanent distressed area in the centre of Europe. Such a distressed area could only result in bringing down the standard of life all over Europe, including Britain's own and indeed that of the world.[14]

No financial arrangements had been entered into when the Bizonia Agreements between the British and the Americans were signed on 5 September 1946. In fact Britain was in dire financial straits. By the Lend-Lease Agreement of March 1941, America had supplied food and materials to Britain against credit or repayment in kind. In August 1945 the Agreement was abruptly cancelled: now payment had to be in cash on the nail. Britain was facing a dollar crisis. The obligations which unconditional surrender imposed called for the feeding of Germany, which could not feed itself. In peacetime most of Germany's food had been produced in the eastern region of the country, although 20 per cent had still had to be imported. Russia now controlled the whole of that food-producing area. The 1945 harvest had been between 10 and 15 per cent below expectations. As a result of the influx of refugees and expelled Germans from the Eastern territories, the population of the British Zone had swollen by millions. Dollars which were needed at home had to be diverted to send food to Germany. One million tons of food had to be imported into the zone between 1 June 1945 and 15 April 1946.

At the beginning of 1946 the Chancellor of the Exchequer, Hugh Dalton, had written to the Foreign Secretary that he was 'very much disturbed by the large sums which I am having to find for the Germans and the very poor prospect of getting anything out of them in return'. He had been asking his officials for a proper balance sheet, but they were unable to provide one: 'Control Commission had to take over a pretty bad muddle from the War Office.'[15] The Chancellor defined the escalating burden in no uncertain terms in the House of Commons and in a speech at the Mansion House on 16 October 1946: 'We cannot continue to carry this mounting burden any longer. Morally it is wrong that the British taxpayer should pay what amounts to reparations to the Germans on this appalling scale. Economically it is wrong that our reserves of foreign exchange should be diverted from feeding our own people to feeding and supplying Germans.'[16]

But it was not quite so simple as that, as Sir William Strang, Political Adviser to the Commander-in-Chief, pointed out:

> The cost of the British Zone should not be regarded as reparations to Germany. It is not for their sakes we are paying. It would not be practical politics to leave our soldiers and civilians in Germany among a starving population. We must therefore either pay to feed them for a necessary period or get out. And getting out now would be letting the Russians in.[17]

The Parliamentary Select Committee monitoring expenditure in the zone at that time declared in its eventual report that, in view of the 'magnitude' of the figures involved, 'your Committee were astonished to discover that there was no branch of the Commission in Germany which was responsible for checking expenditure in that country'. This should be remedied immediately. Surprisingly, the Chancellor himself showed no inclination to check conditions in Germany for himself. He told Sir Vaughan Berry, on a visit from Hamburg to Control Commission Headquarters, that he 'regretted that he had been unable up to the present to take more than an occasional interest in German affairs but that next year he expected to have more time'. Berry urged him to visit the zone. Dalton said 'he might'. At least, his Private Secretary consoled Berry afterwards, it was the first time the Chancellor had not actually turned this suggestion down flat.[18]

The Chancellor of the Exchequer put his concern about German costs in a memorandum to the Cabinet. A large part of these costs to the taxpayer would have to found in dollars for food for Germany. The fusion of the more agricultural US Zone with the heavily industrial British Zone seemed to offer the hope of some relaxation of the burden. It was therefore decided that, when the negotiations to decide the division of financial responsibility for the Bizone began in Washington in November 1946, the Americans should be told that there was 'no question of our splitting in equal shares the cost of the Bizone'. The ratio suggested was that used for UNRRA: 4 to 1. Bevin duly pressed the Americans on the question. He reported to Attlee that he had been able to have a conversation with his opposite number, Byrnes. He had pleaded that the British could not afford to shoulder a half-share of the costs of the Bizone. Byrnes's response was that Congress would accept nothing less. The only funds it would be possible to get Congress to vote would be for 'distress and unrest imports' – food, fuel and fertilizers. Bevin then intimated that Britain might have to withdraw from the zone altogether. Byrnes riposted that if Britain's zone was too costly for her they should swap zones and the Americans would run it: 'They were satisfied that with their industrial experience, organization and the potentiality of the zone, they could make a success of it in a very short time.' In such a case they would consider a 60–40 or even 65–35 split in favour of the British.[19]

The American Military Governor, General Clay, who was present at the meeting, thought Byrnes was 'half serious'.[20] Bevin thought him wholly so. The head of the Foreign Office, Sir Orme Sargent, prepared a brief on all aspects of financing Germany. An exchange of zones would be 'a public confession of failure'. With regard to withdrawal, as the Americans would probably not take over *both* zones but return home, the whole of Germany would eventually be run by France and the USSR. The whole of north-west Europe would pass under Soviet control, and

Britain would probably end up finding more money for increased defence expenditure than it would cost to remain in Germany. Bevin agreed that an exchange of zones was politically impossible. He told the Cabinet, 'Control of German policy would pass into American hands and it would jeopardize our own plans for socialization of German coal and steel industries, to which I attach great importance.' The Americans might also pour in capital and create a competitive position with Great Britain which would be very serious.[21]

Bevin's apprehension about the fate of his plans for nationalization in Germany was well founded. At a press conference some months later General Clay declared that 'present difficulties are so great that experiments such as socialization cannot be attempted before there is an improvement in the situation'. When the United States was paying so much money out of its own pocket, it had the right to reserve for itself decisions of economic questions.[22]

The fusion agreement between the two zones was signed on 2 December 1946 without agreement having been reached on costs. The argument continued. A Foreign Office paper to the Prime Minister philosophized, 'The economic effects of modern war are bound to be disastrous for victors and vanquished alike.'[23] In almost identical words, the Select Committee on Estimates recorded in its report that 'The burden of supporting the German in peace is proving as irksome as the burden of defeating him in war.'[24]

In April 1947, while Bevin was attending the Council of Foreign Ministers' meeting in Moscow, the Chancellor of the Exchequer sent him a paper on the dollar situation, asking him if he could persuade the Americans to take on a larger share of the financial burden of Germany. Bevin replied in a personal note that he would tell them that the burden 'is proving almost more than we can bear'. But he did not feel it was the best moment to do so. General George Marshall (who had taken over from Byrnes) had many preoccupations and was far from Congress. Bevin would consider how best to pursue the matter when

back in London: 'We will shortly have to discuss our whole financial position quite frankly with the Americans.' However, he told
the Chancellor, he was severely handicapped in his arguments
because he had no complete figure on how Britain had benefited
from Germany through the use of patents and of the value of
POW labour in the United Kingdom and the Middle East, 'all of
which saved you dollar purchases'.[25] In the end, Britain had to
settle for a fifty–fifty division of financial responsibility and
tighten her belt at home.

In his Stuttgart speech on the future of Germany, Byrnes had
indicated that, if Germany was not to be administered as an economic whole, there would have to be a revision of the Level of
Industry Plan. Bevin took this up in a Memorandum on Germany for the Cabinet on 17 October 1946. Britain must insist on
Russian implementation of Potsdam. Failing this, there must be
a substantial upward adjustment of the Level of Industry Plan,
especially in regard to steel. Various remedies should be put in
hand. There should be an increase in food rations as soon as
possible. The drive to increase coal production should be given
the same priority as an operation of war. There should be a
reduction in coal exports sufficient to rehabilitate the basic
industries. Substantial quantities of raw materials should be
imported. There should be an early relaxation of restrictions on
German trade: Germans should be allowed to correspond with
the outside world and travel abroad to rehabilitate commercial
connections. Finally, as regards the revision of the Level of
Industry Plan, Bevin suggested that the British and the Americans should not try for a reassessment of a 'reasonable standard
of living' but simply cut restrictions on production by 50 per
cent.[26]

The following month Bevin was in New York for a meeting of
Foreign Ministers. (Sir Brian Robertson once said that 'all the
meetings of the Council of Foreign Ministers that have been
held since the signing of the Potsdam Agreement have not
amounted to one further agreement that was worthwhile.'[27]) In
a 'Top Secret and Personal' telegram to his Foreign Secretary,

Attlee stressed his anxiety about the general situation regarding Germany:

> There is evidence that quite apart from the food and coal factors, the economic machine is running down. Reparation demands cause uncertainty and hopelessness as to the future . . . Pressure here is increasing. Some of our colleagues are much disturbed. I am myself apprehensive as to the future if we continue to be tied by the Potsdam decisions and the Quadripartite Commission much longer.[28]

In August 1947 the Allied Control Council published the new Level of Industry Plan, now relating solely to the Bizone. The previous version had stipulated the retention of 75 per cent of 1936 production over the whole of Germany. The revised Plan now allowed for 100 per cent of the 1936 figure to be retained in the Bizone. Levels in restricted industries were materially increased. Steel production, which had been fixed at a figure not exceeding 5.8 million tons annually for the whole of Germany, was now fixed at 10.7 millions annually. The overall effect of the latest revision was to reduce the number of plants to be dismantled from 1,636 to 682, of which 302 were definitely classed as military in character. The balance of 380 plants was selected on the principle of reducing in any particular industry the equivalent capacity built up during the Hitler years leading up to the war.

But the Economic Adviser Sir Cecil Weir had reservations about the new Plan, as he wrote to the Minister for German Affairs, J. B. Hynd. With the prospect of an inflated population of 42–44 million in the Bizone, compared with a figure of 34 million in that area before the war, the result would be a per-capita production figure of only 74–78 per cent of the 1936 level – a standard of living drastically lower than in 1936. 'We cannot remove factories with a worldwide reputation without damage to the balance of payments.' The Ministry of Supply wanted to keep restrictions on heavy engineering on so-called 'security grounds'. In Weir's opinion there was much confused thinking about security. The greatest menace to security, he warned, would be a Germany in poverty and despair, a prey to Communism and chaos. Furthermore, 'limitation of industry to an extent . . . which could be represented as motivated by ulterior considerations would defeat our security objective'.[29]

The 'ulterior considerations' about which Weir hinted in his letter to Hynd had already been formulated before the war ended. In April 1945 Lord Cherwell, Paymaster-General, had submitted a paper to the Cabinet on the subject of reparations from Germany. These were to be the spoils of war. The main advantage which Britain could secure from reparations, he wrote, would be the capture of Germany's pre-war export trade:

> We shall soon be occupying the most important industrial area in Germany, devastated by the ravages of war. I trust we shall do nothing to encourage the rebuilding of German industry. It should be possible to reach an agreement with the Russians by which they would take existing German machinery, raw materials and forced labour, while we should take Germany's export markets.[30]

A. V. Alexander, the First Lord of the Admiralty, thought his colleague's conclusions 'realistic and irrefutable'. The Foreign Office, however, was scathing about this buccaneering attitude: 'That we should take German export markets is ridiculous.' It had been claimed that, if Germany was not allowed to export, Europeans would instead have to buy from Britain in gold or hard currency. But this ignored the question of their ability to pay. Furthermore, would the Americans accept this? And would the USA be able to prevent American exporters and those of third countries moving into a market vacated by Germany? Lord Cherwell's solution for the resulting unemployment, concluded the Foreign Office memorandum, was to set the workers to building houses – in spite of the fact that 'we are to take the maximum amount of timber from Germany and prevent the rebuilding of industries'.[31] But no such pragmatic considerations guided the counsels of the Cabinet when they met to consider Cherwell's proposals. While agreeing with them, ministers nevertheless thought 'it would be inexpedient to relate our reparations policy to this objective, still more to avow it as an object of our policy'. Public opinion might not stand for it. Furthermore, it was pointed out 'that such a policy was already being criticised in the United States as both immoral and unpractical. It was agreed by Cabinet that British reparations policy should not be explicitly related to the destruction of Germany's pre-war export trade.'[32]

But the discussions were not confined merely to the restriction of competition. What was being envisaged was nothing less than the complete destruction of one competitive industry for generations to come. The political and economic principles of the Potsdam Agreement were explicitly related to 'the initial period of the Occupation'. The British were taking a longer view: 'We have drawn up a plan for the total elimination of major shipyards, the equipment of which is to be allocated to reparations or destroyed.'[33]

In July 1944 a working party of representatives of the Admiralty, the Ministries of War, Transport, Economic Warfare and Labour and the Board of Trade had met to prepare a brief for the Armistice and Post-War Committee. They had in their sights the German shipbuilding industry. It was agreed that 'the volume of orders which British industry can expect to receive will obviously be higher if the competitive industry in Germany has been destroyed'. The First Lord of the Admiralty 'felt bound to ask nothing less than total elimination of the German ship-building industry at the earliest possible moment after the German collapse'.[34]

At the Cabinet meeting on reparations the following April, the First Lord reminded his colleagues of his earlier demand for the total elimination of German shipbuilding and shipping. The Admiralty view was that the pressure by the economic planners for less drastic terms over a short period of years 'has every disadvantage and should be rejected'. The Foreign Office view was that Germany was bound some day to have a merchant fleet: 'It is ridiculous to set out in a peace treaty that she will not have one. The Admiralty would only feel safe if *no* foreign country had a merchant fleet.' The Minister of Food thought German fishermen should be prevented from fishing in the North Sea. They should be restricted to the Baltic. He managed to rationalize the proposal with a security twist: 'This would reduce the number of Germans with knowledge of seamanship and in consequence limit the German potential for manning submarines.'[35]

Planning and Intelligence Branch also voted for elimination:

> We should adopt restrictive measures of the utmost severity and then endeavour to overcome the resulting economic disadvantages (food, balance of trade, unemployment). These measures must be maintained for a generation to be effective. It means the complete dispersal of German marine engineers and skilled workers. Seafaring tradition will take at least a generation to eradicate.[36]

At Control Commission Headquarters the director of Shipbuilding Branch and the director of Commercial Branch reviewed the possibilities. As not only the shipbuilding industry was involved but the merchant navy as well, the whole German economic system would be substantially weakened. But Commercial Branch agreed with the Admiralty. It was assumed that measures for security would be taking priority over economic rehabilitation and the extraction of reparations: 'Therefore our expectations of receiving reparations from Germany will be reduced to a minimum or abandoned.'[37]

The policy on shipbuilding was confirmed at a meeting of the Armistice and Post-War Committee in May 1945. Prohibition for less than a generation would be insufficient. The Admiralty and the Ministry of War Transport considered that Germany should be prohibited *indefinitely* from owning, operating or building merchant shipping. The consequences to the German economy and balance of payments would have to be accepted. Other departments dissented, however. Direct control after the period of Occupation would be difficult to enforce – especially as the United Nations would probably not regard the prohibition as reasonable and could not be expected to support it as a measure designed to eliminate German competition with British shipping.[38]

Nevertheless, in the brief prepared for the delegates at the Potsdam Conference, intentions were clearly defined. If these measures were *not* carried out, Germany 'would be in a position to re-plan in ten years' time her shipyards and construction facilities on completely modern lines untrammelled by old assets and equipment'.[39] The brief aimed at the suppression of a competitor, not a measure of security against a potential enemy.

At Potsdam the British government succeeded in agreeing the adoption of an amendment to the section on economic principles which added 'sea-going ships' to 'arms, ammunition and implements of war' whose production was to be prohibited or prevented.[40] The British-inspired Proclamation No. 2 – the 'Additional Requirements' – issued a month after the Potsdam Agreement, was more specific: 'The German authorities will place at the unrestricted disposal of the Allied representatives the entire German ship, ship-building and ship repair industries and all matters and facilities directly or indirectly relative or ancillary thereto. The requirements of the Allied representatives will from time to time be communicated to the German authorities.'[41]

This demand had been part of the original draft terms of surrender drawn up by the British in 1943 but rejected for their length by the European Advisory Commission. When the clause was redrafted for inclusion in Proclamation No. 2, the British had been a little unhappy about the use of the collective phrase 'Allied representatives'. This 'might hamper any action we may want to take in our Zone. This was of special importance in connection with German merchant shipping in respect of which we might be obliged to take unilateral action.'[42]

Neither the Level of Industry Plan of 1946 nor its revision in 1947 had alleviated any sanctions against the shipbuilding industry. But in April 1948 there was a sudden change of policy. In a paper to the Overseas Reconstruction Committee the Foreign Secretary announced that the government 'had for some time doubted the practicability and desirability' of the prohibition on shipbuilding: 'I have come to the conclusion that the Potsdam policy of complete prohibition of any German ocean-going ship-building would now be politically impossible to implement as well as economically undesirable and should be abandoned as unrealistic. The problem has changed.'[43] 'The problem' was no longer Germany.

The attitude of the US government to reparations had begun to diverge from that of the British. Considerable concern was growing in the US administration that there was a danger of transferring as reparations to the USSR plants 'which might possibly be used for war purposes against us. While these plants are in Germany they are at least under our control.' The greater numbers of plants for dismantling were in the British Zone. Now that the United States was contributing so largely to the maintenance of the zone through the fusion agreement, Congress began to demand more strongly that nothing should be done that would prejudice Germany's economic recovery and the relief of the US taxpayer.[44] The Marshall Plan, passed by Congress in March 1948, offered aid to foreign countries damaged by the war. It contained a provision that agreement should be obtained from the countries concerned that capital equipment scheduled for removal as reparations from the three Western zones should in fact be left there if such retention would most effectively serve the European Recovery Programme. Towards the end of 1948 an advisory committee of leading American industrialists under Senator Hubert Humphrey studied the German economy in relation to the European Recovery Programme and the reparations policy. The following spring the committee recommended that 167 of the plants listed in the revised Level of Industry Plan should be retained in Germany.

This was endorsed by the governments of the three Western occupying powers.

In November 1949 the British, American and French military governors (by this time redesignated High Commissioners) met the Chancellor of the new German Federal Republic, Konrad Adenauer, at Petersberg on the Rhine. Among other matters concerning the new status of the Occupation, a reduction in reparations and dismantling was negotiated. As a result the list of plants was further modified. The IARA received a schedule of 667 plants, which was declared to be final. By April 1950 descriptions of these plants were in the hands of the IARA, and by September 1950 the last allocation had been made.

In a talk on Anglo-German relations at a private gathering of leading Germans in Düsseldorf in December 1949, the British High Commissioner, Sir Ivone Kirkpatrick, did not hesitate to utter an assurance which was quite the opposite of government policy:

> It is difficult to persuade any German that British policy today is not actuated by a resolve to eliminate Germany as a commercial competitor . . . I have had rigid instructions from the British government to pay regard only to considerations of security and to attach no weight whatever to any argument which might be based on fear of German competition.[45]

Did his audience believe him? In a survey of public opinion carried out by Public Relations Branch the question was put to the Germans: What was the main objective of the British Occupation? The answer received was: The ruin of the German economy.[46]

10
Spoils of war

In a speech on 22 July 1945 when the four national flags were raised outside the Allied Control Council Headquarters in Berlin, President Truman declared that the United States did not seek any material advantage from victory. The State Department issued a statement of policy: the United States did not seek to protect American markets from German goods, to aid American exports, 'or for any other selfish advantage' by eliminating or weakening German industries of a peaceful character which had been effective in world markets. It was equally opposed to any other country using the industrial disarmament of Germany laid down at Potsdam for its own commercial ends.[1]

Britain had a different agenda. Herbert Morrison, Lord President of the Council, advised the Prime Minister, 'It is most important at this formative stage to start shaping the German economy in the way which will best assist our own economic plans and will run the least risk of it developing into an unnecessarily awkward competitor.'[2] Morrison recommended to the Cabinet, 'Let us see that Germany exports to us the things we need and to others, the things which we do not mind their getting from Germany.'[3] The removal of capital equipment would help *permanently* to capture certain export markets previously supplied by Germany. Throughout the choppings and changings of dismantling policy, Britain kept its eye on the ball.

Acquisitive Allied eyes had been turned on German industry while the war was still being fought. 'T Force' had been set up to target locations of industrial and scientific intelligence in the wake of the advancing armies. With the end of hostilities the Combined Intelligence Objectives Sub-Committee – CIOS – was created to follow up the information gathered. This later split and the British had their own sub-committee – BIOS.

With the zones of control not yet delineated, Germany was a free-for-all. Later, at the Potsdam Conference, Stalin circulated lists, city by city, of equipment, property and personnel removed by Americans and British from areas which were eventually due to be occupied by the Russians.[4] When in due course Bevin asked the Foreign Office about these removals he was informed, 'There have been certain removals of prototype machinery for the benefit of UK industry alone. A detailed list of such removals could no doubt be obtained but this would represent a considerable labour . . .'[5]

The Potsdam Agreement stipulated that any material constituting reparations which had been unilaterally removed by any power before the establishment of the Inter-Allied Reparation Agency (IARA) would be debited against that power's reparations 'account'. The claim of 'booty' became a way round this ruling. Booty had been defined as material captured by an army on the field of battle: arms, munitions and implements of war and research and development facilities relative thereto, and scrap resulting from the destruction of war materials. But, as the Foreign Office noted, 'The definition of booty . . . is fairly wide and of our own unilateral manufacture.'[6] On 7 August 1945 a Special Technical Mission to Germany led by Sir Roy Fedder of the Ministry of Aircraft Production reported that jet-engine-powered 600 m.p.h. fighter planes were in being in prototype form and within a few weeks of flying. The Foreign Secretary expressed his anxiety to acquire the experimental rocket stations and the wind tunnel for development of the jet engine, in order that they should not become available to the Russians as reparations. The Foreign Office was able to reassure him. The material had already been removed as booty.[7]

One target area was marked out at an early stage. In a 'Review of Scientific and Technical Research in Germany since May, 1945' the Foreign Office recorded that it had been realized that one of the most valuable forms of reparation was the acquisition of the fruits of German research and development in military, scientific and industrial fields.[8] The Potsdam Agreement had laid down that the Allies would control 'all German public or private scientific bodies, research and experimental institutions, laboratories &c., connected with economic activities'. But Proclamation No. 2 – Additional Requirements Imposed on Germany – expanded this phrase. The element of economic 'control' by the victors was replaced by the actual handing over of the results of research. Many hundreds of investigators were dispatched to interrogate German scientists and technicians and bring back details of new techniques and processes, and drawings and prototypes of new equipment. The Control Commission standpoint was that in the matter of industrial designs and formulas it was essential to attempt to gain knowledge of all secret processes which the Germans might possess. 'That is one of the objects of our Occupation.'[9]

On 3 August 1945 Stafford Cripps, President of the Board of Trade, wrote to Herbert Morrison of the necessity for efficient machinery to obtain from Germany the maximum amount of technical information and assistance for the benefit of British industry. He at least did not consider security paramount: 'The *economic* significance of such information is vastly more important than its *military* significance.' But there were to be no public advertisements for recruiting the necessary personnel, because of 'present uncertainty regarding the legal ownership of the information (particularly patented processes) which British industries and individual firms may claim'. The President of the Board of Trade proposed that no application should be accepted by the Patent Office for any patent governing an invention made in Germany since 1938.[10] This decision meant that no German inventor would be able to receive any royalty payments from British industry.

But the fruits of research and of secret processes were not available solely on paper. The Western Allies compiled lists of those whom, in the Foreign Office phrase, 'it is considered desirable to deny to a potentially hostile power'. In January 1947 the British set up 'Operation Matchbox'. Its objectives were:

(a) to remove from Russian influence and control scientists and technicians eminent in certain warlike subjects re war material, contributing to Russian war potential; (b) to prevent or damage Russian sponsored scientific and technical enterprises of a war potential nature by the removal of key personnel; (c) to obtain intelligence coverage of Russian sponsored research and development in the Russian Zone and if possible in Russia; (d) to assist in restricting the migration from the British Zone to the Soviet Zone of scientists and technicians eminent in certain warlike subjects.[11]

There was no compulsion. Scientists were persuaded by offers of food, improved accommodation and the opportunity to work in their own sphere. 'Evacuation' from the Soviet Zone was usually organized by various intelligence agencies in Berlin and by means of an address in the British Zone to which a 'candidate' for Matchbox could proceed under his own arrangements. He and his family were then accommodated in a transit hotel pending their future disposition. Where possible, teams were kept together. Early in 1947 it was reported that a team in Dresden was working on a unique design and manufacture of turbines for marine underwater propulsion. The Russians were on the point of moving the team to the Soviet Union. In February 1947 it was reported to London that the team leader and seventeen of the key designers and constructionists 'had been successfully removed from Dresden'.[12]

The implementation of Matchbox was, however, hampered by bungling and bureaucracy. The transit accommodation proved inadequate. Research Branch reported a bottleneck: it could not receive any more scientists as it had simply nowhere to put them. There were squabbles with other departments and with the Army for any derequisitioned premises which became available. In September 1947 the Chief of Intelligence reported that the latest 'evacuations' had not been as successful as hoped: 'We had to keep the subjects waiting too long and thus lost touch in some cases and therefore failed to extract all the persons we wanted.'[13]

There was a surprising lack of interest on the part of British industry itself. The Foreign Office, anxious to find employment for these displaced scientists, recorded in July 1947 that it had circularized fifty firms through the Ministry of Supply and had received only six replies. In the zone attitudes were ambivalent. To some, the scientists were 'enemy prisoners' and could be disposed of as such. There was a reluctance to give assurances about work, or arrangements for families, both inside Germany and abroad. Entry into the United Kingdom was mired in bureaucracy. The French in their zone, on the other hand, operating with support at the highest administrative level in Paris, were able to settle all questions and contracts for fifty scientists and technicians and their families in three days. British scientists 'in the field' had established a good relationship with their German opposite numbers on 'Operation Backfire' – the investigation of German techniques for launching long-range rockets. Yet it was the Americans who made off with 115 of the German experts.[14]

But with a change in the international political climate the question of the German scientists became an urgent one. In June 1948, after the Berlin blockade had begun, the Military Governor, Sir Brian Robertson, wrote to the Foreign Secretary, 'Under the emergency plans if war comes, what we have built up might be of considerable value to the Russians if they were to succeed in over-running Western Germany without any great degree of destruction.' New plans had to be made 'in the light of this new threat'. If peace was maintained 'for at least three years', consideration might be given to transferring to the Commonwealth a relatively large number of high-grade German scientists 'who might otherwise provide the leadership of German scientific effort in the service of the Eastern Powers'. But the scientists would have to be wooed: 'We should make it clear to the Germans that – unless they were politically unacceptable – they are regarded more as colleagues requiring and deserving help than ex-enemies to be treated strictly.'[15] Such comradely attitudes were not to be extended to German industry, however.

At a meeting of the Overseas Reconstruction Committee in January 1947 reference was made to the earlier Cabinet decision 'that we should pursue a draconian policy over a selected field of industry, a policy which is assumed to be still in place'. Ministers were quite ruthless in their proposals. For example, the Minister of Supply, John Wilmot, recommended that watch-manufacturing capacity 'should be entirely eliminated' and production prohibited. Optical and photographic production should be restricted to German domestic needs only. Exports should be prohibited.[16] In the manipulating of markets, steel was a major factor for the British. The German steel industry had not been mortally damaged by the bombing: it was buildings rather than plant which had suffered. With an imposed limit on production, surplus capacity would be available for removal as reparations. Although the United Kingdom could not absorb all this capacity, the government was loath to see it go elsewhere. It was therefore proposed that the Ministry of Supply should increase British demands in order to avoid the allocation of this plant to other claimant countries. In the Foreign Office there were mixed feelings: 'I think we should certainly try to take all the plant of which we can make proper use but it hardly seems legitimate to take more for the purely restrictive purpose of preventing other people getting it.'[17]

By the time the war ended, the Ministry of Supply already had in its sights the important Salzgitter Steelworks in Lower Saxony.[18] It was identified to the Foreign Office as 'a completely modern unit which goes all the way from ore production plants and blast furnaces to a variety of rolling mills, including one said to be the best in the world'. It was likely to become available for reparations after the fixing of the Level of Industry Plan. The Ministry of Supply was determined to have it, but there were conflicting views about its removal from Germany.

Bevin sent his parliamentary private secretary, Jack Jones MP, a steelworker for thirty-four years and an official of the Steel Workers' Union, to visit Salzgitter and assess the situation. Jones held a public meeting, chaired by the local KRO, Lieutenant-Colonel Fawnes, and attended by representatives of the plant, the local administration and the Control Commission. Fawnes spoke warmly of the Germans and made it clear that he appreciated their difficulties.

On his return to London, Jones reported to Bevin and the Minister for German Affairs, Lord Pakenham. He confirmed that Salzgitter was the most efficient and important steelworks in Germany. The plant was in an ideal situation: it was the main source of indigenous ore for the whole of the German steel industry. Power for many thousands of mines was generated there. The economy of the whole area was dependent on the works. It had not been badly damaged and was sited in an agricultural area where living conditions for the workers were healthy. Jones felt it was a technical impossibility to tear down the equipment and remove it to England. Steel furnaces, blast furnaces and coke ovens were in a desperate condition, having been forced to stand idle for two years. Even the Russians, who had recently inspected the plant, had considered that it was not fit for reparations. The removal of the plant would be a catastrophe for the people of the area, for whom it had been the main source of employment. Sixty per cent were living on public assistance. The human condition of the population was appalling. (The Foreign Office objected to the introduction of a 'social element' into the argument.) Jones claimed that his trip to Germany had revealed 'a penetration of vested steel interests into Germany'. In his opinion the best plants should be left in Germany to expedite industrial recovery for all the nations of Europe.

Bevin considered it of the highest importance that the matter should be settled once and for all and as soon as possible. If the plant was left in Germany, there would be no need to import ore from Sweden: 'We must give up all idea of moving it here.' He believed that it would be to British advantage in the end to get the German steel industry working properly. It was infinitely preferable that it should be producing billets of steel rather than standing idle, as it had been for so long, with the machin-

ery becoming derelict while a decision on its future was awaited.
The Germans themselves raised objections to the dismantling
on two counts. On the economic side, it militated against the
Marshall Plan. It was better to leave the plant in production in
Germany and let it work for European reconstruction. The sec-
ond argument was political. The main purpose of dismantling
was clearly to eliminate German competition in world markets.
This was a blow to democratic and well-meaning circles in Ger-
many and strengthened nationalist and Communist elements.
But no arguments prevailed.

Early in February 1949 the Regional Commissioner for
Hanover reported that the arrival of a British Royal Engineers
officer at the plant had caused spontaneous protest. A few weeks
later, 600 workers forcibly removed explosive charges from
plant, wrecked a forty-five-ton derrick and manhandled dismantling staff, including two Control Commission officials. One
hundred and fifty German police were present but had been
'passive and ineffective'. Five companies of infantry and one
squadron of armoured cars were stationed there on 7 March.
The trade-union leader Hans Böckler came to the plant to
reason with the workers that the law was the law and they had no
hope of prevailing against it. The British authorities reported to
the Foreign Office that the demonstrations were 'primitive and
emotional' – no doubt a fair description of starving workers
watching the disappearance of their only hope of future employment.

When the Military Governor announced that dismantling
would definitely begin on 2 June 1950, Konrad Adenauer, now
Chancellor of the new Federal Republic, entered the lists. At the
meeting at Petersberg in the previous November, discussions
about dismantling had resulted in eleven steel plants being
removed from the reparations list. Now Adenauer claimed that
Salzgitter had been one of them. Sir Brian Robertson – now
High Commissioner – disputed this, and letters were sharply
exchanged. Adenauer appealed for at least a blast furnace to be
spared, without which conversion to peaceful industrial activity

would not be possible.[19] But Robertson declared that there was no chance of a reprieve and the sooner the dismantling was complete the better.

Years later the diplomat Sir Frank Roberts remembered how, when stationed at the High Commission at Bonn, he had visited the plant as the dismantling of the last of the furnaces was being carried out. He noticed that a new furnace was being built by the same British firm which was carrying out the dismantling of the old.[20]

The chemical industry, too, had its predators. The facilities for producing synthetic rubber and related high polymer at the synthetic-rubber plant at Leverkusen were considered the best in the world. Founded in 1920, the plant had become part of the I. G. Farben complex in 1937. In 1947 the President of the Board of Trade, Sir Stafford Cripps, wrote to the Foreign Secretary that acquisition of the plant with its technical and research scientists 'would give us 2/3 years lead over the rest of the world in this field'. But Leverkusen was listed for reparations. Britain had no claim to unilateral removal. The Board of Trade thought it wisest to make an application at a low level in the Control administration so as not to attract attention. Consultation with other powers should be avoided. Bevin warned Cripps that I. G. Farben assets were held by the Allied Control Council. Fusion with the US Zone made it necessary to consult the Americans, who would be unlikely to agree. 'Surely it may not be impossible', wrote Bevin, 'to devise some colour of justification for the removal.'

But the Economic Adviser, Sir Cecil Weir, was colour blind. He wrote, 'Under existing quadripartite agreement it is practically impossible to advance any real justification for the removal of this establishment unilaterally to the United Kingdom.' The Foreign Office was equally stern:

> The Minister may decide that the value of this plant to the UK is so great as to make it worthwhile to take it at the price of damage to our relations with our Allies. But before they

make that decision, it is of the first importance that they should understand clearly what they are doing. This is not a small thing, one more little piece of cheating in a game in which everybody else is cheating in a small way, too. It is a large item. It will be a breach of the rules of a new game; and it would be quite flagrant.

The Military Governor, Sir Brian Robertson, was concerned that ministers in London should appreciate the effect of the proposed action. He cabled from Berlin, 'While we may, on purely legalistic interpretation of the rules, produce specious justifications for removal, I am under no illusion as to what would happen and do not wish you to be.'

Meanwhile, a team from the Board of Trade and the Ministry of Supply visited the Leverkusen site in mid-July to count its chickens. A report of the unofficial visit was made to the CCG Director of Research by two of his officers who were present at the plant. They had been told by the visitors from London that this inspection of the plant was at the request of the Foreign Secretary with the object of reducing British requirements to a minimum. However, the inspection was 'rather rapid' and the team 'seemed to know in advance' what it wanted. It was proposed to remove the whole laboratory including furniture and fittings. This had apparently been agreed by the President of the Board of Trade and all other interested ministries. The Ministry of Supply representative, the report continued, had declared that the plant represented a dangerous war potential and the only alternative to its removal would be to blow it up. The CCG representatives had queried this. Was not some of the plant usable for general purposes applicable to other research? But the team had wanted the whole laboratory 'as it stood'. The officer from Chemical Branch had begged that equipment should be left to run the tyre-manufacturing sector. The shortage of rubber was desperate. Requirements for rubber in the zone were not being met. Natural rubber was not coming into the country, and no one knew when it ever would. It was 'economi-

cally unsound to stop synthetic rubber production in the immediate future'.

This was the view of the Americans when perforce they were
consulted. On the instructions of the US government, General
Clay lodged a formal protest against unilateral removal to
Britain. In a letter to Sir Brian Robertson he gave his personal
opinion: 'I have difficulty in viewing this laboratory as a security
threat. Germany must have the opportunity for research along
peaceful lines for her economy to become self-sufficient.'

By the end of July 1947 the matter was finally resolved. The
British were not to be allowed to dispose of Leverkusen for
themselves. Normal reparations procedure was to be adhered
to, and dismantling was scheduled to take place in October
1949.

A *cause célèbre*, because of both the industry involved and the
sophistication of the opposition mounted by the Germans, was
the famous soap plant of Henkel & Co.[22] The plant had been
pinpointed as early as October 1944, when directives for an
eventual armistice were being drafted. It had been suggested,
in the course of preparing a Directive on Soap and Washing
Materials, that, for safety, 'all suspect personnel should be
replaced as the relationship between confessed Nazis and soap-
making is not clear'.

The appearance of Henkel on the dismantling list when the
revised Level of Industry Plan was published in August 1947
triggered an uproar in the press both at home and abroad. Even
Bevin himself queried the inclusion of a soap factory on the list.
He was told by his advisers that soap factories came under the
heading of 'Miscellaneous Chemicals' subject to restriction
under the Level of Industry Plan. But in Germany suspicion fell
heavily upon Unilever – both firms made Persil. Unilever vehemently denied any involvement. But a member of the Dutch
division of Unilever headed a team inspecting soap factories
located in the French Zone.

Henkel's management threw itself into a frenzy of public
relations. It was an emotive cause, and the company lobbied

intensively abroad. A pamphlet entitled *Death by Dirt* contained extracts from protests in the domestic and foreign press. An elaborate presentation – in colour – used all manner of graphics to highlight the results, in terms of health and mortality, of further reducing the already minuscule amount of rationed cleaning material. The German Zonal Advisory Committee (ZAC) protested that normal peacetime consumption had been 900 grams per head per month. In wartime that had been reduced to 530 grams. Now the ration was 275 grams.[23]

In November 1947 the Regional Commissioner for North Rhine–Westphalia, announced that Henkel had been selected because its soap-making was associated with one of the main glycerine-production units in Germany and glycerine was an important raw material for the manufacture of explosives. Henkel countered this statement in a letter to the Commissioner, Asbury: 'Glycerine arises from the processing of oil seeds whose fats contain a certain quantity of it. It is not used for the manufacture of soap powder – not used, not even wanted. The process is not to *obtain* glycerine but to remove it.' In any case the question did not arise, since for years it had been impossible to obtain oil seed.

The German authorities stressed deep concern about the likelihood of epidemics and the spread of vermin given the appallingly overcrowded living conditions. They instanced the already increased figures for tuberculosis and infant mortality. But the Brigadier at the head of Public Health Branch accused Henkel of lying and demanded that the company be prosecuted for 'causing a hostile attitude towards the authorities by the German people'. But prosecution was not an option – it would cause too much public disturbance; above all 'it would not be in our interest to ventilate all the facts concerning the health of the German population in open court'.

In reply to parliamentary questions from Members who had been lobbied by Henkel, Lord Pakenham and his Minister of State, Hector McNeil, held to the 'glycerine/explosive' line: 'Restriction of the German soap industry in general and of the

Henkel factory in particular is therefore fully justified as a restriction on German war production.'

The cornering of markets was a game of ping-pong, nationally and internationally. For instance, the British Aluminium Company (BAC) had a strong commercial interest in the fate of the aluminium industry in Germany, since this might affect the prospects not only of the company's own plant in Britain but also of certain Norwegian plants in which it had a financial stake. The Ministry of Aircraft Production (MAP) complained that 'BAC have recently represented to us that the German aluminium extraction industry should be wholly eliminated.' But the MAP opposed this. It hoped that cheap German aluminium would be a useful weapon to keep down the price of Canadian and US aluminium. Some time later it was found that the Americans had put in a bid for an aluminium-foil works in the French Zone. According to the Foreign Office, the plant was useless to the Americans but they were going to try to get it to keep the French from having it. If they succeeded, they were going to dump it into the sea (well, according to Sir Desmond Morton). Britain wanted the machines, which would increase British production of foil by about 50 per cent. The British would therefore support the US bid if it could be privately agreed that, after allocation to them, the Americans would cede the machinery to Britain.[24]

Eighty-six per cent of the heavy industry of Germany lay within the provinces of North Rhine and Westphalia. And the largest firm concerned was Krupps. In November 1945 a Controller was appointed for Krupps. He was a former chartered accountant from Harrow. Dismantling was scheduled for 1947. It took two years to list everything in the company, down to the last telephone and typewriter. The Americans, French and Russians took reparations. The only item which went to the United States was the biggest hammer in the world, which went to Chicago. But the British were after more than just plant.

Intelligence Branch produced a report which stated that British policy was 'to render the enormous works at Essen incapable of any future activity'. But the report stressed that virtually half the population of Essen – the workers, their dependants and pensioners – relied entirely on Krupps. The town was also served by many small private businesses linked to the existence of the major enterprise. The destruction of the war element of Krupps aroused neither surprise nor opposition among the workers. But it was assumed that some form of heavy industry would be resurrected in Essen because of the mines and the communications which existed there and because of the desperate need everywhere for the products of such industry. There was no resentment of British control, concluded the report, but there would be if it was discovered that there was to be only destruction.[25]

This report was echoed by the man on the spot, Douglas Fowles, the Controller. In February 1946 he addressed a lengthy appeal to Control Commission Headquarters for something to be done about reactivating industry in Essen, particularly for railways and bridge-building – so desperately needed throughout the zone. 'The special circumstances of Essen . . . should be taken into consideration as widespread disaffection will result from the removal of all possibility of employment.' His appeal was dismissed out of hand. Fowles was obviously 'pestered perpetually by burgomeisters, priests, politicians, etc.'[26] According to General Sir Alec Bishop's recollection after the war, 'The order came down from Berlin that the whole of this group of factories was to be destroyed so that not one stone stood upon another.'[27]

And yet Krupps had always been the producer of more than just armaments, and its potential was vital to the devastated country. At a meeting of the ZAC on 13 June 1947 the question of Essen was the main item on the agenda. The chairman, General Bishop, was forced into loyally defending a policy which to him – as the recently appointed Regional Commissioner for his area – was indefensible. Even the smallest repairs to locomotives of any description, the Germans stressed, could not be continued at the present rate without the delivery of products from the Krupps works. The intensification of agriculture required machines for which Krupp products were essential. There was also great anxiety at the intention to dismantle by blasting. This would probably destroy the Krupps waterworks and power station, on which the town had to rely in emergencies. Mountains of rubble would be created and would have to be removed. 'This present British scheme', declared one committee member, 'would carry destruction to such lengths that all human activity, work and recreation would be impossible for an indefinite period over the whole of this huge area.'

A question mark hanging over the dismantling arose because the Council of Foreign Ministers had fixed a time limit of 30 June 1948 for the liquidation of Category-I war plants. The question was whether, in order to meet the deadline, the demolition should be carried out in such haste as to lose any value from it. The best General Bishop could do in response to the concerns expressed by the ZAC was to promise faithfully that all available information would be laid before the Commander-in-Chief. He would supplement this by explaining personally to Sir Brian Robertson 'how keenly, how very keenly, you gentlemen feel on this subject'.

The Germans were now becoming convinced that what was taking place was the implementation of the notorious 'Morgenthau Plan'. In 1944 President Roosevelt had appointed a Cabinet committee to consider the treatment of post-war Germany. The Secretary of the Treasury, Henry Morgenthau, laid before the committee an extraordinary document. Its terms suggested that not only Germany but also Europe was a faraway place of which the author knew little. Among many strange recommendations, the most bizarre concerned the future of the Ruhr. This area, upon whose industries the whole reconstruction of Europe would depend, was to be stripped of those same industries in such a way that it could never again be resurrected. Within six months of the end of the war all industrial plants and equipment should be destroyed or dismantled and removed from the country. Anything still remaining after the expiry of a set period of time was to be completely destroyed or reduced to scrap which would be allocated to the United Nations. To ensure this industrial desert, all inhabitants of the area having special skills or technical training would be 'encouraged' to 'emigrate permanently' to other areas and should be dispersed as widely as possible.[28]

When Morgenthau's programme was proposed to Churchill at the Quebec Conference in September 1944 the Prime Minister rejected it. But Lord Cherwell, his special adviser, who was of much the same mind as Morgenthau, intervened. Churchill substituted a brief statement confined to the future disposition of the Ruhr, avoiding the worst excesses of the original. But the sting was in the tail: 'This programme for eliminating the war-making industries in the Ruhr and in the Saar is looking forward to converting Germany into a country primarily agricultural and pastoral in its character.' The Prime Minister and the President initialled their agreement.[29] Neither the British Foreign Office nor the American State Department had been consulted. The agreement was quietly shelved and was never a serious item of policy. But it leaked out to the American press and the Germans got to hear of it. The shadow of pastoralization lay over the dismantling policy. The way in which the policy was being executed seemed to the Germans the logical preparation for their future in the fields.

One of the main complaints against the dismantling of industry voiced by Germans giving evidence to the Parliamentary Select Committee on Estimates had been that there was no coherence in the dismantling programme – no recognition that closing one factory or mine had a knock-on effect on others. There was substantial support for this complaint on the British side. The economist Alec Cairncross, in a letter to the Economic Advisory Panel, condemned the designation of plants as surplus without consideration of their relationship to each other. Fierce criticism of the sheer incoherence of the dismantling programme came from Harry Collins and his American co-chairman of the UK/US Coal Control for Bizonia. The Economic Division of Bipartite Control Office had issued a statement that the dismantling list was not interfering with supplies to the mining industry. The two Controllers were furious. They charged that the statement had been issued in Berlin with no reference whatever to conditions in the Ruhr – which the investigators had obviously not visited. Nor had those firms on the dismantling list which they themselves had specified as essential to the industry been investigated: 'We deplore the manner in which our request has been treated. We wish to place on record that the policy recommended can only have the effect of starving not only German industry but other European coal-producing countries of essential equipment.'

Headquarters in Berlin commented dismissively to the Foreign Office that they 'recognise the feelings of UK/US Coal Control, who are anxious to make assurance of mining supplies doubly sure and are not concerned with reparations'. They put forward as a defence that 'it is not possible to have a reparations policy without disrupting necessary industrial connections' – a proposition with which they seemed quite at ease.[30] But the representative of the Ministry of Fuel and Power who had attended the European Coal Division meeting in Geneva at that time reported the deep concern in Europe. At a discussion on dismantling, the Dutch, French and Belgians strongly objected to the dismantling of German plants which were producing equipment of major importance to their mines.[31]

The dismantling programme reached its peak in 1949. Protests and strikes proliferated throughout the zone. Workers refusing to carry out dismantling were sent to prison. Cologne City Council passed a resolution that 'morale is collapsing, people despair of any improvement, all confidence in the young democracy and in the Occupying Power threatens to disappear and the best possible conditions are being created for dark political forces to conduct destructive agitations'.[32]

For the senior British administrators on the ground – such as General Alec Bishop, now Regional Commissioner for North Rhine–Westphalia – it was a nightmare. They were executing policy which they saw as calamitous. Bishop reported in June

1949 that resistance to dismantling was supported by people, press, administrations and politicians up to *Land* level. He himself did his best to minimize the possibility of violence. On one occasion two synthetic-oil plants at Dortmund and Bergkamen, the main source of employment for miles around, were scheduled for dismantling. The workers seized whatever weapons they could – crowbars, hammers, lumps of coal – to deny the dismantlers entry to the plant. Bishop was very worried: he feared that force would have to be used if the situation continued. He took over the radio station at Cologne and broadcast in German an appeal to the workers. He understood their feelings, but this was an Allied decision and if they persisted they would almost certainly get hurt. If they would give up, he promised he would do everything he could to secure alternative employment for them. The policy would have to be carried through, but 'I trust and pray that you will not force me to use drastic measures to accomplish this end.' The workers responded and the resistance was called off.[33] Bishop felt so strongly about the dismantling policy that he went to London to see the Foreign Office. He was told that it was Allied policy and nothing could be done – and if he did not want to carry it out they would find somebody who would.[34]

Fortunately the hard-pressed Regional Commissioner had sources of support and cooperation available to him in Germany. He had the greatest admiration for the Minister-President of North Rhine–Westphalia, Karl Arnold – 'a really splendid man'. They would meet in one another's offices or at the Commissioner's house, when the Englishman would endeavour to explain official policy without criticizing it and the Minister would suggest ways to obviate its worst effects. Hans Böckler, the redoubtable leader of the trade-union movement, was another tower of strength. One day a general strike was planned, to demonstrate to the world the near-starvation in which the people were living. But on the chosen date the United States Congress was debating an extension of the Marshall Plan. General Clay warned that news of a general strike would probably wreck any chance of Congress agreeing to the extension. Bishop called Böckler to his house and explained the danger. Böckler agreed to try to get the strike called off. If the workers would not listen to him it would be the end of his career, but he would do his best. His prestige was so great that the workers did listen and the strike was called off.

Thirty years later Sir Alec Bishop could still denounce the policy of dismantling as 'a complete nonsense and one of the greatest difficulties thrown at us in addition to the other problems we were facing. It didn't seem to the Germans or honestly to us to make sense.' The political leaders, the trade-union leaders, the Church leaders, the educationists – 'everybody came to us and said, "Do you realize what you are doing – how you are nullifying all your other admirable efforts by this?"'[35]

Further north, meanwhile, the undeclared policy of wiping out the German shipbuilding industry was being implemented with a will. Of all Germany's ports, Hamburg was the most important. And in Hamburg the most important shipbuilder was Blöhm & Voss. Founded in 1877, the firm had developed into the foremost builder of ocean-going passenger liners. Hamburg, unlike Kiel, had never been a naval base, and Blöhm & Voss was not a naval yard. One battleship and one cruiser had been built there in the inter-war years. No submarines had been built until after the outbreak of war. It was not listed as a Category-I war plant. Even the Navy conceded that Blöhm & Voss was not of interest to the Services. But it was targeted from the very first days after the surrender, when the Army moved in and shut it down.

Burgomaster Petersen protested to the local commander, Brigadier Armytage. There were some 3,000 wrecks littering the harbour basin and the river, but the huge shipyard cranes were being destroyed. There were twenty-seven fully operational mobile electric cranes which could be used on the 43 million cubic metres of rubbish. The blowing up of gantries had buried valuable and much needed salvageable material under debris.

Dismantled material from Blöhm & Voss had been allocated to the Soviet Union. In February 1947 a Russian delegation came to inspect their prize. The British conducting officer described what they found. A huge mass of valuable machinery was lying in the open, ruined by exposure to the weather. Gantries and cranes had been blown up and had fallen across submarines on the slipway. A large charge had been exploded in the engine room of each submarine. 'The resulting shambles was inspected with great interest by the Soviet officers.'[36]

Petersen drew the attention of the British authorities to the fact that the Americans at Bremen were removing from submarines all useful living equipment – furniture, engines, refrigeration units and so on – before destroying them. The Royal Navy insisted on destroying submarines completely, salvaging nothing.[37] Questions were asked in the House. R. S. Hudson protested that the Navy was blowing up a great amount of accommodation which could be available for civilians. 'It is in fact only with the greatest difficulty that they are stopped.' Richard Stokes joined in with customary gusto: 'Will my Hon. Friend take some steps to prevent the Navy going completely mad and going around Germany blowing everything up? Does he not agree that steps are necessary to stop them behaving in this dastardly manner?'[38]

But not only the Germans were unhappy. The Control Commission – particularly Public Utilities and Railway Control – protested vehemently at the destruction. Only Blöhm & Voss had the facilities to cope with building and repairing desperately needed locomotives. The huge turbines needed to maintain Hamburg's electricity supply, worn out after wartime years without proper maintenance, would have to be transported all the way to the Ruhr for repair, to the only other plant capable of handling the work. A plant in Bremen which might have helped was itself due for dismantling. Brigadier Armytage suggested removing the crucial sixteen machines from Blöhm & Voss to another Hamburg yard where the work could be carried on. This helpful and eminently sensible suggestion was shot down by Trade and Industry Division and Reparations, Disarmament and Restitution Division. As so often, much of the trouble with the beleaguered German economy came from the stultifying infighting among elements inside the Control Commission.

The destruction of shipyards and dockyard installations in June–July 1946 was a catastrophe for Hamburg. The trade unions addressed an appeal to the Military Governor, Sir Sholto Douglas, at least to dismantle rather than blow up, thus saving machinery and cranes from purposeless destruction. They were 'observing with great sorrow' the bitterness which this forced destruction was already having on the population, which threatened the cooperation of the democratic parties in the establishment of the economy. Armytage held a meeting with representatives of the SPD and the unions at which he told them they would 'have to persuade the population that there were other means of existence apart from shipbuilding'.[39] Burgomaster Petersen resigned. In May 1947 the Economic Inspectorate on Morale in Shipyards issued a sombre report: 'The appalling conditions in which the majority of workers are existing and the hopelessness of any future in Germany for many years to come has had the most telling effect on the morale of the people and on such industry as is allowed to function.' As a result of the dismantling and removal of machinery and the uncertainty of the fate of the shipyards, a large section of the population firmly believed that the policy of the British government was to grind the people slowly down. It was difficult to convince them otherwise. 'Unless a stop is put to the plundering of what little resources are left in Germany, trouble is going to come in a big way.'[40]

The Hamburg newspaper *Hafen-Nachrichten* hit the nail precisely on the head: 'British animosity against German shipbuilding is very far-reaching – from powerful personalities in London to the small ship-owners in Belfast . . . The result of this destructive hostility, which has nothing to do with war potential but has a great deal to do with economic interest, is seen in our empty workshops, unemployed workmen and unused technical assets.'[41]

Having earlier assured the private gathering in Düsseldorf

(see p. 205) that nothing was further from the mind of the British government than fear of German competition, Sir Ivone Kirkpatrick went public with an even bigger whopper. In August 1950, in a High Commission press release, he referred to remarks by Max Brauer, the new burgomaster of Hamburg, in which he had 'detected . . . a belief that the British Government in its policy has been influenced by fear of German competition in the field of shipbuilding'.

> I should like to say at once that there is no foundation for this belief, nor for the belief often entertained in Germany that in the matter of dismantling or of restrictions on German industry England has been influenced by the desire to throttle German competition . . . There is no danger that petty considerations such as fear of German competition will influence our policy.[42]

German morale and British prestige plummeted side by side as the policy of dismantling was pursued. The *Manchester Guardian* correspondent reported on 17 August 1946:

> A year ago the British held an asset in the embarrassing goodwill of a large proportion of the inhabitants, their anxious readiness to help and to believe in our good intentions. To-day it has, to all appearances, vanished. The state of feeling now is unmistakable and the British are hated. As hunger is prolonged, sickness spreads, factories continue to stand idle, and skilled artisans can find nothing better to do than fill wheelbarrows with rubble from the ruins.

The Select Committee on Estimates was reporting to Parliament in the same vein:

> The citizen of Hamburg, where employment is centred on the port, sees gantries being blown up and docks dismantled: the inhabitants of Essen, where employment is centred

on Krupps, witness rolling mills being dismantled and the manufacture of railway engines for which the whole of Europe is crying out, prohibited.[43]

The Political Adviser to the Military Governor produced his own sombre assessment. The conviction was steadily spreading that, instead of a well-worked out policy for the re-education, reconstruction and rehabilitation of Germany and for a system of reparations that would profit the victor while enabling the vanquished to live, 'the British government have no policy at all but only haphazard directives aimed at the wholesale destruction of the German economy and the continual misery of the German people'. The Foreign Office commented that, failing a constructive programme, 'forces on which we rely for the emergence of democratic Germany – the SPD, the Trades Unions, the co-operatives and the Western-minded – will be completely discredited and alternative forces could come out in opposition to Military Government'.[44] In the House of Commons, Churchill declared himself 'chilled' by the policy which had 'draggled and straggled' on for four years. He brushed aside Potsdam (of which he had himself been an architect) as 'some agreement which now no longer has any validity or application to current affairs':

> I am sure that the munitions which could be made by these factories which still remain to be dismantled would never do half the harm to the cause of peace, or to any future victory of the Allies against aggression, that is done by the great setting back and discouragement, out of all proportion, of the German movement towards Western civilization and Western ideas.[45]

Side by side with official dismantling, a considerable amount of private enterprise was going on – or, to use T Force's description, 'trade piracy'. The carpetbaggers arrived – businessmen from Britain out to acquire information or plant from Germany for their own private profit. In February 1948 the President of the Chamber of Commerce of the cities of Essen, Mülheim-Ruhr and Oberhausen wrote to Lord Pakenham about the proposed dismantling of Chemische Fabrik Holten, in business since 1910. It was difficult, he said, to avoid the impression that certain private interests were at play:

> I personally am certain that it is intended to cripple and if possible completely shut down a very important field of modern German chemistry – Ethylene chemistry, developed over 40 years – in order to secure this field for the industry of another country which, so far, has played no role in it. This is the only explanation for the action of the representatives of British Military Government whom we have to deal with. Nearly all of them were, and will probably be again, employees of the Imperial Chemical Industry, British Celanese and other chemical firms.[46]

In evidence to the Select Committee on Estimates, the chairman of the German Economic Advisory Board, Dr Victor Agartz, declared that he was repeatedly receiving reports that British firms were attempting to induce officials of the Occupation 'to detrimental actions against their German competitors'.[47] Agartz was referring to the buccaneering activities of representatives of private companies who were coercing German manufacturers to divulge details of secret processes or technological advances. Some of these officials, and the men who came out from the United Kingdom, were known personally to staff of German firms from commercial contacts before the war. The Germans were afraid to give evidence against British personnel which would put them in bad odour with the occupying administration, resulting in the refusal of permits to work, buy or sell. The Control Office commented, 'While we do not want to encourage tale-bearing by the Germans, in cases of fraud or attempted fraud by British officials we must take their evidence, otherwise they would remember democracy as being as corrupt as the Nazi regime.'[48]

One CCG whistle-blower reported a flagrant example to his

Member of Parliament. It concerned the textile firm L. P. Bemberg. The commander of the Düsseldorf Area carried out an investigation. Bemberg had developed a new spinning machine (the Dureta spool-spinner) embodying certain revolutionary techniques. Completed at the end of the war, it had never been operated. This machine was seen by certain named members of Trade and Industry Division, who showed great interest. On their oral instructions, the machine was put into operation. Although no official permit to operate had been issued, power had been supplied by the Wuppertal power station and 872 tons of hard coal had been supplied to the company. Records showed that these sources of power had been supplied on the orders of various Control Commission officers. Interest in the new Dureta machine appeared to have been taken by officers of Courtaulds. Public Safety Branch confirmed to the Deputy Inspector General, CID, that for several months there had been a rumour that 'Messrs. Courtaulds, England, has had business connections with silk firms in Germany, Courtaulds having arranged for their representatives to take positions in the CCG in the firm's interest.'[49]

One of the most blatant examples of 'trade piracy' concerned the world-famous '4711' eau-de-Cologne.[50] In March 1946 a team was sponsored by the Toilet and Perfumery Manufacturers Federation. Of the six members, five were representatives of perfumery and cosmetic firms: Pears Soap (Unilever), Max Factor, Potter and Moore, Yardley and Grossmith. The sixth member was the proprietor of a manufacturing chemists whose father before the war had known the Mühlens family – the owners and manufacturers of '4711' eau-de-Cologne.

Without authorization, three of the men presented themselves at the Mühlens factory, wearing khaki uniform with CCG flashes. The joint general managers, Hubert Schutte and Hans Verres, had met one of the visitors (or intruders) before – the chemist who had known the family. The British party were escorted round the factory. When they reached the laboratory they demanded the formula for '4711', claiming that they were authorized to obtain it. They were told that it was a family secret and only Frau Maria Mühlens possessed it. The British replied that they had orders from Military Government to take the formula back with them, and if they did not obtain it the factory might be closed. The whole Mülhens family together with their chief employees might be taken to England and a new company would take over the business in Germany and abroad.

The team was then driven to Frau Mühlens's home at Röttgen, near Cologne. After an amicable meeting over tea, the atmosphere abruptly changed. Demands for the formula were renewed. Frau Mühlens explained that she had been instructed by her late husband that she should hand it over only to her heir, in accordance with family practice. Her son had been killed in the war, and her heir was her seven-year old grandson. Fearful lest the formula should come into the hands of the Americans, who had taken over the area in the closing stages of the war, she had committed it to memory and destroyed the document on which it was written. According to Frau Mühlens's subsequent evidence, she was then browbeaten and threatened with imprisonment. At this point the old lady became unwell and retired to her room. Her guests warned that it might be necessary to call a prison van to take her to the prison hospital. The team then left, saying they would telephone at noon the next day to see if she had changed her mind. But the next day the answer was the same.

The story of the harassing of the widow Mühlens spread through Cologne. (The team were even said to have been carrying revolvers.) A correspondent of the BBC German Service, David Graham, heard British officials talking openly about a 'scandalous state of affairs' about which it was difficult to take preventive action. Dr Adenauer, lord mayor of Cologne, had given him details of cases which had gravely shaken his faith in British integrity. One of these was the '4711' affair. In a BBC broadcast entitled *Why Recovery Lags*, Graham set out the events in a series of questions each beginning 'Is it true . . . ?' On 8 November two left-wing weeklies – the *New Statesman and Nation* and *Tribune*, which probably had their information from trade-union leaders and members of the SPD – printed the same facts as Graham but without equivocation. The *Tribune* article was reproduced in the European edition of the *New York Herald Tribune* under the heading 'German Patent Racket Laid to British Firms'. The paper stressed the purely commercial aspect of these activities, unconnected with any former war factories.

On 6 January 1947 Sir Gilmour Jenkins, Permanent Secretary at the Foreign Office, wrote to Sir John Woods, at the Board of Trade, that 'our people in Germany' had made a careful investigation and it seemed clear that a certain team behaved most irregularly. Members concerned attempted to secure the '4711' formula for private profit. The Board of Trade was dismissive of the investigations. As to the team's motives, because its members were known as pre-war competitors the Germans concerned 'would quite naturally jump to the conclusion that they were out to get something for their own firms'. But, even if this were true, there were no legal sanctions which could be invoked against them. Sir Gilmour agreed: 'In the circumstances we cannot press any charges against those men, though I have little doubt that their behaviour at the interview with Frau Mühlens was irregular . . . it seems to me that the proper course is to let this affair die a natural death.'

The eau-de-Cologne affair had drama, a household name and a glamorous product. Another case which had none of these elements nevertheless went right up to the House of Commons itself.

At the end of May 1946 a small comb factory in Westphalia, Kuster-Kolibriwerk, was inspected by a three-man team, although it had not been selected for dismantling or reparations.[51] One member of the team was the owner of a comb factory in England. He selected certain machines for dismantling, making it obvious to the Germans that he was in the same line of business. On the T Force form 'Application for Allocation of Enemy Equipment' he listed thirteen items, described as 'prototypes' for the purpose of research and development in the

United Kingdom. The consignment was designated for his own firm in Northamptonshire.

However, when the application reached the Board of Trade only one item of the thirteen was approved as a prototype. Furthermore, that the name of the 'investigator' was also the name of the consignee indicated exploitation for individual private interests. And the remaining twelve machines were required for essential production in Germany. The Foreign Office, which had to approve removals, returned the application with twelve items deleted. Nobody noticed. The evacuation of the thirteen machines went ahead. When the mistake was realized, Trade and Industry Division solved the problem by simply reversing the earlier decision: the machines were *not* necessary for the German economy.

Kuster appealed to the KRO, to the *Land* President and to the Regional Commissioner. He also wrote to Tom Driberg MP and to the Minister, Lord Pakenham. The bureaucrats now justified themselves by accusing Kuster of being obstructionist and even of having been a leading member of the Nazi Party. The firm vigorously denied the accusations. Kuster himself said of the so-called prototype which had been used as a pretext for the wholesale removal of machinery that it was a simple electric heating cylinder which he had made himself: the design was so simple that he was sure other manufacturers had invented similar machines.

The Regional Headquarters, North Rhine–Westphalia, found the effects of the publicity 'most damaging to our prestige . . . A particularly unsavoury factor is the connection with the comb industry in the UK.' The Bipartite Control Office declared that 'it was one of the worst types of interference by British private industry under the guise of a Government charter'. Headquarters in Berlin reported to the Foreign Office that the British industrialist concerned appeared to be building up a large plant in England out of all proportion to former capacity and that there was an enormous demand for combs inside Germany and for export. The three comb factories in the zone would have difficulty meeting demand. Nevertheless, incredibly, it was decided by Headquarters that 'it would be regarded as a sign of weakness to stop the evacuation'. The machines reached England in August 1947.

Sir Brian Robertson wrote to the Foreign Office that he felt 'bound to condemn strongly the action which has been taken'. It would be difficult to fix responsibility without a full court of inquiry, but he did not propose to hold one:

> for the same reason that I do not propose to ask for the return of the twelve machines which in my opinion were improperly removed.
>
> This reason is that I am sorry to say that what has happened in the case of Kuster Kolibriwerk is evidently only one instance among many. If these machines were returned, claims would come forward from a large number of other German firms. This would stir up a volume of criticism which is undesirable.

But by now the affair had reached the House of Commons. Under pressure from MPs, the Foreign Office gave in. The inquiry, which began in January 1948 ('Inquiry officers should not take any steps which might bring further undesirable publicity'), criticized the inefficiency and carelessness of the British officials: 'The whole situation could have been saved without loss of face.' The inquiry could not understand how officials could have gone ahead with the evacuation 'knowing the Foreign Office were finding it difficult to justify to Members of Parliament the removal of the equipment'.

But heads did not roll – nor even wobble. According to the Foreign Secretary, as the officials responsible had had no criminal intent and had not stood to gain personally no one was to blame. Apparently inefficiency and dereliction of duty did not matter. Sir Cecil Weir's comment on the inquiry report was: 'Mr K. may have a legitimate grievance but the Germans as a whole do not.'[52] Nevertheless, after five months lying idle in a Ministry of Supply depot, the machines sailed from Hull for home in January 1948.

There was one plum, legitimately available for the picking, which British industry spectacularly missed. In 1938 Hitler had laid the foundation stone of the factory at Wolfsburg which was to manufacture the 'People's Car' – the Volkswagen – but only 210 cars had been built before it was turned over to war production

The end of the war found the factory virtually in ruins. Thousands – former slave labourers, displaced persons and refugees from the Soviet Zone just five miles away – were crowded into wooden barracks. The British Army took over the derelict buildings as a REME repair shop for former *Wehrmacht* and British Army vehicles. A few German workers still holding on in the plant retrieved hidden machinery, set it up and, virtually without the British noticing, produced two cars. But the officers running the REME unit knew about cars and recognized a good thing. Some employment was desperately needed for the thousands of rootless people in the area, and it was decided to start the plant operating again – at least temporarily. The officers sprayed a car khaki and took it to HQ BAOR. The British Zone was starved of transport: Headquarters ordered 10,000. Working conditions were appalling, but German workers and British management pulled together. Both sides believed in the product.

The next three years were extraordinary. The British staff – car enthusiasts to a man – fought for the Volkswagen . The factory went on turning out the black 'Beetle', as it was nicknamed. It was the wheels of the British Occupation. In October 1946 there was an Anglo-German celebration at the plant on the production of the ten-thousandth Volkswagen.[53] But in the dire conditions of 1947 production began to fall. Lack of food slowed down the workforce. Materials were ever more difficult to come by.

The technical liaison officer, Wing Commander Richard Berryman, approached the car manufacturer Sir William Rootes.

Volkswagen was a gold mine waiting to be exploited, he said, and could probably be got for a low figure as reparations. A British commission of motor manufacturers led by Sir William went to Wolfsburg to inspect the factory. They were not impressed. They predicted that the enterprise would collapse of its own inertia within two years. To build the car commercially would be completely uneconomic. Volkswagen would present no undue competition on the world market against British products. Berryman tried time and again to interest British firms, but the car industry was not ready for Porsche's revolutionary design with its rear-mounted, air-cooled engine. Pressed Steel Ltd at Oxford declared it 'could not learn anything from it'. A report by the Motor Trade Association stated that a study of the engine indicated that the unit was, in certain details, most inefficient: 'We do not consider the design represents any special brilliance and it is suggested that it is not to be regarded as an example of first-class modern design to be copied by British industry.'[54]

Having been the property of the Nazi organization Deutsche Arbeitsfront, abolished by Allied decree, Volkswagen had no owner. Unable to give it away, the British handed it back to the Germans. The rest, as they say, is history.

II
'Let Germany live!'

As THE war receded, so distress in Germany advanced. The year 1946 had been bad; 1947 was to be worse. The winter of 1946–7 was the most bitter for almost a hundred years. The great artery of the Rhine was clogged for fifty-five days by ice: normally, shipping was never interrupted for more than ten days a year. The bridge at Düsseldorf was damaged by ice and drifted away. The Main had seventy-eight days of ice against a normal average of twenty-eight days. The Necker was frozen for sixty-eight days against an average of twenty-one days. The Weser was frozen for ninety days against an average of twenty-eight days. The Elbe was frozen for a hundred days against an average of twenty-two days. The great network of canals in the British Zone was ice-bound for ninety days. The Elbe–Lübeck canal was frozen for 111 days. The Kiel Canal was frozen from the Baltic to the North Sea. Refugees from the Soviet Zone walked across the frozen Baltic at night, knocking on doors in the icy dawn at the summer resorts of Travemünde and Scharbeutz. Transport from the ports was limited to about 45 per cent of the essential minimum. The state of the railways was desperate. Engines were put out of service through frost damage, but the workshops were only partially repaired and it was impossible to heat them.

The effect of the appalling weather on the distribution of food and fuel was catastrophic. By economic standards, wrote Regional Commissioner Vaughan Berry in his monthly report for January 1947, conditions were unparalleled since the Napoleonic occupation. He translated the awesome statistics into life in Hamburg. With icy winds sweeping from the east, the temperature was never above freezing. There were 26 degrees of frost at night. Ice on the Alster – the lagoon in the centre of the city – was 20 inches thick; cars were driving across it. Consumption of coal at the electricity works had been reduced from 2,600 to 1,100 tons per day. Electricity supply was cut so drastically that two-thirds of the inhabitants were sitting in their homes for hours in darkness. The trams stopped at 8 p.m. The city was barely alive. Restriction to two hours of gas consumption each day caused serious overheating of plant during those hours, with danger of burning out and breakdown, so the plan was revised to one day in three all day for each of three different areas of the city in rotation. Blizzards halted supplies, and coal reserves fell dangerously: consumption was cut to barely one-fifth of normal. Only essential services – water, sewage, food – functioned. 'This great city is totally without light from seven o'clock in the morning until ten o'clock at night. Much of the day it is without heat. It is a desperate situation.' A total of 111 factories were closed and 9,000 workers were idle. Offices connected to the same heating grid went out of action early in February. Berry allowed no concessions to the British administrators. Ink froze in inkwells. An officer's cup of tea froze on his desk.[1] Everywhere in the zone factories closed down. Thousands of workers sat in idleness in cold dark homes on a food ration hardly adequate to sustain life.

Arrests for stealing from coal trains rose dramatically, from 1,000 in December 1946 to 17,000 by March 1947. The head of Public Safety Branch reported to the Regional Commissioner in Hamburg that the severe weather was drawing people of all classes, not just the poor, to the coal yards. More than 10,000 were to be found there daily. At the marshalling yards crowds waited for the coal trains to arrive. Six hundred tons were taken from one train. The crowds consisted mainly of women and children, so clashes with police had to be avoided.[2] Hynd, the Minister for German Affairs, was 'surprised' to learn in March that no domestic fuel had been issued since the previous October.[3] But the theft of coal, however desperately needed in individual terms, robbed the community as a whole by impairing the public services.

It was in these circumstances that a memorable clash took place between the Regional Commissioner for North Rhine–Westphalia, William Asbury, and Cardinal Frings of Cologne. Outside Germany, myth still surrounds the affair. On 31 December 1946 the Cardinal delivered his New Year sermon in the cathedral. British Intelligence – short on either German or theology or both – reported to the Regional Commissioner that Frings had told the Germans that they were entitled to take what they lacked: in other words, to steal. But in his sermon the Cardinal had in fact instructed his listeners to consider whether 'in these terrible times' they had faithfully obeyed the Commandments. On the Seventh Commandment – 'Thou shalt not steal' – he said that there had to be a just balance between those who had lost everything and those who had a little:

> We live in an era in which at a pinch the individual may even be allowed to take that which is necessary for his life and his health, if he cannot obtain it by other means, by his work or by appeals. But it is my belief that in many cases people have gone far beyond this. And there is only one way open: to return without delay unlawfully acquired property, otherwise God will not forgive us.

The Regional Commissioner considered that the Cardinal 'seemed to give his blessing to people helping themselves, particularly to coal'. His Religious Affairs Adviser assured him that the Cardinal had been enunciating a fundamental principle of the Christian Church: that in extreme necessity man is entitled to the minimum essential to preserve life. But the former town councillor from Middle England was not receptive to theological niceties. Although it was late on Saturday night, he insisted that the officer depart at once to Cologne to demand an explanation, by return. This the Cardinal, who had already gone to bed, declined to provide, but he wrote the following day that the passage had been taken out of context. In a few days' time he would be addressing a group of teachers. He would take the opportunity to elucidate, and he would ensure that his words received adequate publicity.[4]

The *Kölnische Rundschau* was of the opinion that the Cardinal's sermon had been quite clear; nevertheless, his words 'seem to have been misunderstood here and there'. The paper therefore reported the gist of his address to the teachers. The Cardinal had referred to traditional Catholic moral theology: the Creator had bestowed the earth's natural wealth on the whole of mankind to provide the essentials for life. In a case of the greatest need, the individual would have the right to take for himself what was needed to preserve life if it could not be obtained by other means. But there were stipulations. It must be a matter of direct need: immediate danger of death, serious bodily injury or threatened loss of freedom. Any other person involved must not thereby be reduced to the same distressed condition. The duty of compensation remained whenever this became possible. No one could infer from his words, concluded the newspaper, that the Cardinal justified organized raids on coal trains. On the contrary, he had declared that 'rather are these to be condemned in the sharpest terms as a great danger to the community'.[5] But the legend that the Cardinal told the Germans they could steal lives on.

The four-month blanket of snow and ice descended upon a people already on their knees from lack of food – one might say, 'literally'. Sir Brian Robertson gave evidence to the Select Committee on Estimates that 'signalmen have fainted on duty and men in the shop have dropped at their machines'. Basic industries were barely being maintained, while the rest of industry was achieving about 10 per cent of the pre-war level. The Select Committee noted the 'vicious inter-action' between lack of food and lack of productive capacity. Many people now complained that they spent most of their time thinking about food and were unable to concentrate on their work.[6] When the Committee met informally with the leaders of the Miners' Union in Essen they expected to hear about organization, status and policy, instead of which they were confronted with 'a pitiful and primitive local plan for the exchange of coal for potatoes'. A Control Commission brief for the Committee stated that to retain an industrial population in health and working efficiency a daily ration of at least 2,550 calories was required. The first requisite of economic recovery in western Germany was an adequate food supply to rebuild the morale and working capacity of the people.[7]

The food problem had two aspects: production and distribution. The Soviet Zone had been the breadbasket of Germany. Under the reparations agreement the USSR was obliged, in return for 15 per cent additional reparations from the Western Zones, to supply an equivalent value of commodities – particularly food – lacking in the other zones. But this was never done. Discharged servicemen had been mobilized under 'Operation Barleycorn' to work on the 1945 harvest, but this had been 10–15 per cent below expectations. The area covered by the British Zone could provide only 400 calories per day out of indigenous resources.[8] Between the beginning of June 1945 and the middle of April 1946 a million tons of food needed to be imported into the zone.

One of the most pernicious consequences of the black market was its effect on the availability of food through normal channels. Farmers withheld their produce from the open market, refusing to part with it except for valuables. This was a criminal offence, and police made many raids on farms. But, as one farmer wrote to General Bishop, agricultural prices had not changed in seventy-five years. In 1870 one ton of wheat cost 222 marks; in 1948 it cost 200 marks. Before the war the proceeds of ten litres of milk would have paid for a milk pail; now 100 litres were required.[9]

But with the continual eroding of the official ration – which registered entitlement but did not deliver – hungry people sought extra food wherever they could find it. This foraging, on which the whole population was engaged, was known as 'hamstering'. People streamed out into the countryside on foot or sometimes on bicycles but mostly by train. A train ticket was one of the items which could be purchased with otherwise useless currency. Hynd's successor, Lord Pakenham, suggested a 'drastic increase in railway fares to counter hamstering'. (This was three years after the end of the war.) The Military Governor replied that, if barred from transport, 'people who now take a day off work would take a week'.[10] People carried with them whatever possessions might be exchanged with the farmers for food. Or they picked over the land itself. During the harvest in the Ruhr in 1946, the correspondent of *The Times* reported that precautions taken against the operation of gleaners proved unnecessary: 'In perfect order, hundreds of women and children, joined by miners coming straight from the pithead, waited until the last stooks had been gathered and then asserted their rights by streaming on to the stubble.'[11]

Sometimes painfully acquired produce was confiscated on the way home during police raids on trains. A proposal inside the Control Commission that 'the little man with a few potatoes for his starving family' should not be prosecuted was vigorously rejected by the bureaucrats of Food and Agriculture Division. It would be impossible to get food distribution right: small things added up to very large proportions. It was admitted that it was 'extremely unpleasant to take food from people striving to keep themselves alive'. And the conclusion of the memorandum was chillingly pragmatic: 'No-one can deny that if nine-and-a-half million normal consumers in the Zone had obeyed all the regulations and eaten no more than their legal 1,050 calories since March, most of them would have been dead by now.'[12]

Sir Jack Drummond summed up the conclusions of a nutritional survey, of which he was chairman, carried out in the summer of 1946. For the previous six months the ration had been augmented by the panic distribution by the local authorities of municipal food stocks just before the surrender. These reserves were now nearly exhausted. The official ration of 1,550 calories per day (little more than half the ration in the United Kingdom) would lead to a grave nutritional disaster. The effects of the low ration were becoming alarming, and there were increasing signs of hunger oedema. Children were showing signs of arrested or retarded growth. It had been discovered that the inmates of asylums – not recognized as hospitals and therefore not on the special hospital ration – were starving to death. Ruhr miners were showing loss of weight for the first time.

Having regard to the probability that grain stocks would be virtually exhausted within a month, a catastrophe might follow if further drastic cuts of ration levels were to be made, concluded Drummond: 'The greater part of the population of the large German towns appears to be facing nutritional disaster the magnitude of which and the consequences of which the Committee fears may seriously retard the recovery of Western Europe and probably disturb its political development.'[13]

The British set up a nutrition laboratory in the Berlin suburb of Dahlem to experiment with ersatz foods for the Germans. The *Illustrated London News* ran a feature on this. Berliners were instructed about various wild foods which could be collected from the woods and parks surrounding the ruins – such as stinging nettles, dandelions, berries of mountain ash, acorns, horse chestnuts, leaves of brambles, and various roots. The photographs show pine needles being cut up for brewing as a substitute for tea; the bitter element being removed from horse chestnuts to create a 'valuable food containing starch and fat'; nettle soup simmering in a boiler. An illustration of the official daily ration for a family of four displayed on a plate suggests that a root-and-branch supplement might have been almost welcome.[14]

In January 1947 Herbert Morrison MP, Lord President of the Council, went to Washington to discuss the procurement of food for Germany. Half a million tons of food intended for domestic consumption had already been diverted to Germany, and it was agreed to reduce UK stocks by a further 200,000 tons. Against a background of world food shortage and a dollar crisis, Britain introduced bread rationing at home in July 1946.

The creation of the Bizone had held out the hope of an increased ration in Germany. But there were problems of American shipping strikes and grain failures. By the spring of 1947 the ration in many large industrial communities was only 800–900 calories per day. The arrival – or not – of grain ships from the United States was a constant anxiety. Vaughan Berry complained to Headquarters of the effects of conflicting information. Early in April 1947 the Regional Food Team had told him that the stock of bread grains was 26,120 tons (a fourteen-day supply) and no further supplies were in sight. Berry tried to get information about the possible arrival of grain ships into Hamburg without success. Then on 11 April came a message from Sir Cecil Weir that stocks were not, after all, 26,000 tons but 42,000. But in the meantime a cut in the bread ration had already been announced. Accurate information on the real position and prospects was essential, insisted Berry, if Regional Commissioners were to exert any sensible influence: 'Nobody, on the British or German side, has accurate knowledge of the arrival of imports, i.e. of the procession of ships across the Atlantic: where they are, what they contain and where they will dock.' 'We live', said one official, 'from ship to ship.'[15] At a monthly meeting of the ZAC a German member asserted that they had the impression that 'everything was considered quite all right so long as we were able to keep going from one day to the next'.[16]

The Nutrition Committee recommended a daily ration of 1,500 calories, to avoid serious malnutrition and actual starvation. In his report for May 1947 Berry recorded that for the previous four weeks the average daily ration had been 1,000 calories. For the first half of that period the figure had been 850. If the situation deteriorated further, it might be that food stealing – like coal stealing during the winter just past – would cease to be regarded by the citizens as a criminal offence. In order to avoid sporadic demonstrations being planned by the Communist Party – the KPD – the trade unions in Hamburg proposed to take the lead and arrange mass protests which they would control. The details were discussed with the Regional Commissioner and the burgomaster. On 9 May 120,000 people assembled 'in orderly and peaceful fashion'.[17]

In June, Berry's monthly report recorded the daily ration still at 1,000 calories and a steady rise in hunger oedema: 'The ration for one individual for one week can be comfortably contained on an ordinary dinner plate.' There was little food even on the black market. He put in a special plea for Hamburg: 'There is not the slightest doubt that at least half-a-million people – more than the entire population of Düsseldorf or Köln – are at their wits' end to know how to feed themselves and their children, and the number may be one million.'[18] A report by Public Safety Branch echoed that of the Commissioner. An outstanding quantity of meat, fish, cereals and potatoes had not been available for a long time, and fats and sugar were unobtainable even on the black market. The discernible effect of lack of food was not only physical: 'The dearth of rumours is attributed to apathy, resignation, fear and exhaustion in which humour and rumour will no longer play their part as a means of relief.'[19]

At the final ZAC meeting of 1947 Hans Schlange-Shöningen, Director of Food Administration, warned that if food shipments came to a halt because of strikes in the United States people might become so desperate that a situation might develop against which no bayonets would prevail. In December 1946 an Instruction for the Defence of Hamburg had been issued. Armed CCG volunteers were to be organized to defend office buildings and British families: 'A shortage of food or accommodation or a variety of reasons may cause civilian unrest in Hamburg.' A state of emergency would be declared by posters, which would threaten shooting on sight or the death sentence through the courts. This instruction – all twenty-four paragraphs of it – was now updated in June.[20]

In December 1947 a delegation of three observers from the Medical Research Council spent a scant two weeks touring the British Zone. They produced a report which flew in the face of the experience of the men on the spot, both British and German. While acknowledging that in the past eighteen months it had not always been possible to honour the ration, they complained that the Germans 'harped on' about the need for more protein for muscular work and for more fat to preserve health and resist infection. 'This is supported by very little evidence.' They had been told by German doctors that the nutritional state was worse than in the same period a year ago: 'No satisfactory evidence for this gloomy point of view was forthcoming.' There was a tendency to exaggerate the number of cases of TB. Certainly milk supplies for children had fallen to a very low level, and children's rations were 'far from being ideal but would have been regarded as satisfactory in England not so very long ago'. The delegation had been 'impressed by the satisfactory appearance of the majority of Germans we have seen: men, women and children on the streets are for the most part alert and active. It is evident that most people are getting enough food to keep them in reasonable shape.' Some did, however, 'exhibit a pallor which may perhaps be associated with unfavourable nutritional conditions'. A shortage of vegetables might be acute in the spring of 1948, and the young might suffer serious consequence of vitamin-D deficiency. There was little doubt that if gross signs of deficiency appeared 'the Occupying Powers will get the blame. But if the Germans evade responsibility for collecting food, little can be done.' Food and Agriculture Branch reacted angrily to the superficiality of the report. The observers, they complained, had not examined the actual ration issued as distinct from the 'official ration', which was so often not implemented.[21]

As part of the devolvement of responsibility to the Germans, the collection of indigenous food and its distribution had been handed over to them. German officials, however, protested that they lacked the facilities which the Occupation authorities had at their command – for example, the deployment of troops, if necessary, against black-marketeers and farmers, and the use of army vehicles for the transport of food supplies. The *Land* administration in the Ruhr had asked BAOR for 2,000 of its surplus lorries – even broken-down vehicles, which the Germans were ready to repair. None were received. In fact the situation with regard to the availability of vehicles for essential purposes provided an all too typical example of slackness and inefficiency in the Occupation bureaucracy.

In the summer of 1947 the Society of Friends Relief Service complained to Control Commission Headquarters about the tens of thousands of surplus lorries standing idle in army dumps. So serious was the content of the report that the Permanent Secretary of the Ministry of Supply, Sir Archibald Rowlands, came out from London to investigate. He called a meeting of heads of divisions with Sir Cecil Weir. It was asserted that the vehicles had been offered for sale to neighbouring countries without success – because they were priced in dollars. It was claimed that it had been the impression that the Ministry of Supply had forbidden the use of surplus vehicles in the German economy. The Permanent Secretary stated that this was not in fact true. It had never occurred to anyone on the ground to check this 'impression'. Highways Division declared that there was no use in taking over the dumps as it already had 54,000 lorries out of commission for lack of tyres. The Permanent Secretary pointed out that the lorries in the army dumps actually *had* tyres. And, furthermore, there must be small garages all over the country capable of carrying out repairs. It was further revealed that there were 6,000 Lend-Lease vehicles standing idle because they were not allowed to be sold outside Germany; nor could they be used inside Germany without permission from the US Occupation authorities. Sir Cecil solved that one by simply picking up the telephone then and there and obtaining instant permission from the relevant American authority.[22]

In a letter to *The Times*, Schlange-Shöningen rebutted criticisms of the way in which the Germans were discharging their responsibility for food distribution. The British had devolved authority only at the lowest level. The drought of 1947 had been the worst since 1808. The soil was exhausted. There was a lack of both manpower and draught animals. Production had declined to 30 per cent of the pre-war average. There had been no change in agriculture prices for years.[23]

At a meeting of the ZAC one of the members present underlined the sort of difficulties with which German officials could be confronted. A cargo of soya beans had arrived in Hamburg designated for Austria. The British authorities cancelled this allocation: the beans were to be used for the school feeding programme. Then that instruction was cancelled in turn: they were to be distributed throughout the British and American Zones. This was changed again and the soya beans were to remain in the British Zone. Again, a cargo of vegetables and fruit arrived. This was to be used for the schoolchildren in the British Zone; then it was to be used for general consumption; then it was to be distributed among the *Länder*. The ship was almost completely unloaded when it was instructed that 2,000 tons were to be reserved for the children after all. Where was the executive power for the Germans themselves in all this, he asked?

There was an echo of this question in the contribution to the parliamentary debate on Germany in October 1947 by the former Minister for German Affairs, J. B. Hynd. Referring to the 'stagnation' of the German economy, he pointed out that 'All this is taking place in a country possessing tremendous resources, largely concentrated in the British Zone; a country which possesses people of great genius thwarted, starved and deprived of necessary authority.'[24]

In his letter to *The Times* Schlange-Shöningen had written that there was 'a high degree of willingness on the part of Military Government to understand our misery but between this and actual understanding there is often a gap'.[25] But at the ZAC meeting referred to above, chaired by General Bishop, opinion was more forcibly expressed. The physical and moral powers of resistance of the nation were already crumbling, declared one council member. The young democracy could not be expected to take upon itself the responsibility for this economic decline. This rested entirely with Military Government: 'Military government demanded our unconditional surrender; it took over the entire administration; it took over the administration of industry; it has complete control of coal; it has deprived us of all possibility of buying anything abroad ourselves. In such circumstances it is the responsibility of Military Government alone if Germany starves to death.'

The first month of 1948 was one of crisis. Manpower Division reported general unrest in the Ruhr owing to serious shortage in the supply of essential foods – particularly fat, meat and potatoes. The ration was 1,100 calories per day, but consumers in industrial areas were receiving only 800. There had been no meat or fat for four weeks, and no potatoes since the previous autumn. The extra ration for heavy workers was not being honoured. Undernourished workers meant an inflated labour force to keep some kind of production going. The miners, at the end of their tether, threatened to withhold 205,000 tons of coal and iron unless the rest of the Bizone delivered their official quotas of food. The collection system was bedevilled by the tendency of the more agricultural *Länder* in the Bizone to retain produce for themselves. A meeting of representatives from the *Länder*, alarmed by the threat from the Ruhr, agreed to renounce the fat ration in their areas for one ration period in order to make up the lack in the Ruhr.[26]

An inquiry into labour unrest in January 1948 reported that mass demonstrations taking place were 'orderly and restrained in view of the provocation'. Strikes were controlled by the trade unions. Announcements were made that work would stop at a given hour. The workers would hold a protest meeting and then disperse quietly, resuming work again at a given hour. The maintenance of all essential services was ensured. The Germans wanted the British authorities to take back responsibility for food administration, because they had facilities for collection denied to the Germans. They also had the authority to put pressure on farmers and on those *Länder* (particularly Bavaria) which retained produce for themselves instead of delivering their quotas for distribution to the whole of the Bizone. And they could import food from abroad, also forbidden to the Germans.[27]

The local trade-union committees in the Ruhr met on 31 January in Bochum and put forward several demands. Foreign currency earned by German exports must be used to buy food abroad; Germany should be permitted a whaling fleet and a share in the herring-fishing industry; and synthetic-fat plants should be reactivated.[28] The trade-union leader Hans Böckler maintained that cattle in Denmark and fish in Holland were available for immediate exchange for coal, although the authorities denied this. The American Military Governor, General Clay, insisted that only dollars were acceptable in payment for German exports. This made trading difficult for neighbouring countries which had no dollars to spare. Holland had a surplus of agricultural produce but could not trade it for German goods. The Dutch complained that half their industrial equipment had come from Germany; now they could not get parts for their machines or sacks for reinforcing dykes. Their factories were forced to run at half-time or less.

In Germany itself a new sort of commerce was establishing itself in the marketplace. The Chief of Food and Agriculture Branch reported that barter (or 'compensation trade') was becoming the usual method of trading between manufacturers and producers. He cited the situation in the fishing industry, quoting a letter from a fish firm to a brush factory: 'We could supply a barrel of herrings for your employees . . . in exchange for brooms, brushes and scrubbing brushes.' Another firm in the same industry, trying to rebuild its premises, could not get goods or services without bartering herring. Another firm offered preferential supplies of marine engines for even the smallest quantity of fish – particularly herring. The owner of an important shoe factory offered five pairs of shoes, to specification, for every ton of fish.[29]

The British were also concerned that the impression was growing of a deliberate policy of starvation. It was proposed to compose and publish an article explaining the difficulties and problems of the food situation. This major public-relations exercise – 'Operation Stress' – was launched in March 1948. Officials of Information Services Division were invited to contribute their ideas. The head of the Hamburg office wrote to Headquarters in Berlin that he felt there was indeed much to explain. The question the Germans always asked was: Why were they forbidden to attempt to increase their rations from other than indigenous sources? Even the Allies admitted that 'the efficient collection of indigenous food production would provide barely 50% of a starvation diet'. There was good reason for Germans to doubt that there was absolutely no more food available. Extra bonus rations could be found for the miners. Substantial supplies of vegetables from Holland and other countries were refused because they were considered 'too expensive in relation to their food value'. Germany was exporting at the rate of $150 million per year but was still denied the opportunity to buy food abroad. And why should Germany not be allowed to send out a whaling fleet to increase fat and oil supply? Foreign currency was being used to buy and transport whale oil to Germany. The answer was always a reference to the tonnage limits imposed at Potsdam (at British insistence). Food administration had been handed over to the Germans at a time when supplies had reached an all-time low. They complained that they had been given responsibility without authority, as Military Government interfered at every level. Unless all these points were properly and completely answered, concluded the writer, 'the proposed article will do nothing to clear the air'.[30]

A few days later a new development caused the same official to raise a further point with Headquarters. General Clay had announced that he would ask Congress for additional funds sufficient to raise the German ration to 1,800 calories per day. The obvious conclusion would be that 'in spite of everything we have said, there is additional food available if additional funds are forthcoming. Hitherto we have maintained that lack of funds has never been the reason for lack of food.' The statement by Clay now indicated that this was not true.[31] A handwritten note at Headquarters summed up: 'The short answer is that Germany lost the war.' So much for public relations.

The Allied authorities were becoming seriously alarmed about the physical state of the population, their attitude towards the Occupation and the stagnation of industry. A formal communication was received from the burgomaster and Senate of Hamburg: 'The fulfilment of the expectations and hopes for a commencement of the resurgence from the miseries of the war has been removed to such a far-off distance that in many fields initiatives for reconstruction are in danger of disappearing altogether.'[32]

In January 1948, in preparation for the six-power conference on Germany to be held in London, Bevin urgently requested a briefing about improving the collection and distribution of indigenous food supplies. Were the Germans allowed real authority and power to enable them to perform duties in food matters which the British had placed upon them? The Military Governor prepared a report for Lord Pakenham. One of the causes of the current food crisis, wrote Robertson, was the inefficiency of collections between and within the *Länder* – the responsibility of the German administration. However, the overriding cause, he stressed, was that there was not enough food – indigenous and imported – available. There were 40 million people forced to live more or less on the black market. No ration system, he declared, had ever worked unless there was enough to go round at a reasonable level. The steps needed to put the situation right were a substantial increase in imports, financial reform, and the establishment of an elected and responsible government recognized abroad.[33]

In forwarding the Military Governor's recommendations to the Foreign Secretary, Lord Pakenham added his own. It was impossible to start another year with the German fat ration at less than 25 per cent of the British level, even in theory. To start as low as that would end with a complete absence of fat for many weeks. The whole emergence of a democratic and harmonious Europe depended on Germany, which depended on food. Germany would be the critical battleground during the coming year in the struggle between economic stagnation and Communism on the one hand and economic recovery and civilization on the other. The whole world, concluded the Minister, was waiting on the recovery of Germany.[34]

Two years earlier Churchill had warned the House of Commons:

We cannot afford, nor can the United States, to let chaos and misery continue indefinitely in our Zones of Germany. The idea of keeping millions of people hanging about in a sub-human state between earth and hell, until they are worn down to a slave condition or embrace Communism, will only breed at least a moral pestilence and probably an actual war . . . Let Germany live![35]

12
Separation and sovereignty

A YEAR after the surrender, Sir William Strang, then head of the German Section of the Foreign Office, had reported to the Foreign Secretary, Ernest Bevin, after a tour of the British Zone:

> The German people still give the impression of great and unbroken inner strength . . . They are outwardly docile, patient, enduring but above all they wait and have a grim and unshaken faith in the future of Germany. The walls are in ruins but the men are still there.
>
> This spirit will probably survive the testing ordeals which face the Germans in the coming year. Whether, if it does, it will be so used as to build up decent political institutions is one of the great questions of our time . . . [1]

There were to be two years of 'testing ordeals' before, in the summer of 1948, the first glimmer of recovery came. On 18 June the three Western Allies introduced the new currency – the Deutschmark – into their zones. On that one day each German was allowed to exchange at the bank just forty Reichsmarks for forty new Deutschmarks; otherwise the old marks were now worthless – mere waste paper. This was real cash in hand. The effect was dramatic. Shelves were stacked overnight with goods which had been held back by shopkeepers until they could be sold for real money. Now the cigarette would no longer be a unit of currency but simply a coveted luxury. It was the beginning of the return to normality.

A writer who was working in the British Zone at the time described vividly the atmosphere of the first day of currency reform – the magic air of expectation, the scarcely-daring-to-

touch. The breathless excitement was like that of children who, after endless waiting, are allowed in to see the Christmas tree. Western Germany celebrated its return to a sound currency not with champagne but with ice-cream. 'The population were trailing along the shopping streets, licking ice-cream and gazing ecstatically at such normally unexciting objects as zinc baths and leather suitcases, bath towels and window curtains.' A nearby repair shop, which hitherto had hardly been able to find parts to fix a broken pram, now housed a stock of sixty new bicycles. 'No-one had seen them arrive. It was impossible to suppose that they had been stored among so much discarded junk. Their appearance was part of the *legerdemain* associated with that day.'[2]

A great deal of uneconomic activity which had been directed towards securing the necessities of life ceased. Trains no longer overflowed with 'hamsterers' off to scour the countryside. Miners were putting in a full day's work. There was a substantial registration of labour, hitherto hidden, now that there were real wages to be earned. One *Land* minister declared that the most important element in any recovery was the restoration of the working capacity of German labour, which hunger had extinguished. What did still exist, however, was the moral will to work, and this should be utilized for the reconstruction of Germany and the world.

For the Berliners, the issuing of the new currency brought harsher conditions. Russian pressure on West Berlin had begun in April, when the Soviet Military Governor, Marshal Vassily Sokolovsky, had stormed out of the Allied Control Council. On 16 June the Russians withdrew from the Allied *Kommandatura* which jointly administered Berlin. A week later, on 23 June, the Allies introduced the Deutschmark into the Western sectors of Berlin. The Presidium of the German People's Council denounced the 'separate' currency reform in the West as 'a decisive act in the division of Germany' and the 'rape of the German nation'.[3] The Russians introduced their own new Ostmark into the Soviet Sector and the Soviet Zone, also on 23 June, and cut all access to Berlin from the West by land and water. The response by the Western Allies to this blockade was the Berlin Airlift. The Berlin blockade began on 24 June 1948 and lasted until 12 May 1949. It was against this background, with East and West now irrevocably divided, that the independent West German state began to emerge from the Occupation.

The Potsdam Agreement had stipulated that the administration of Germany should be directed towards the decentralization of the political structure and the development of local responsibility. Local self-government should be restored on democratic principles through elective councils as quickly as military security permitted. Democratic political parties with rights of assembly should be allowed and encouraged throughout Germany.[4]

The British, more than the Americans, were cautious in their approach to the emergence of political parties. Initially, permission for meetings had to be obtained from Military Government; numbers were limited to six persons, and agendas had to be submitted for approval in advance. The idea was that political life should advance slowly. But the Americans and the Russians were moving more quickly, and the British had to follow suit. By the end of 1945, Military Government Ordinance No. 12 announced permission for the formation of political parties. Lord Annan (then an officer in Political Division of Military Government) later vividly recalled the effect of the announcement: 'I remember one old Social Democrat, who had one of those emaciated faces which you saw then – yellow, trembling hands, suffering of course from starvation – said to me, "This news is better to us than white bread."'[5]

In Germany, historically, power had emanated from above and filtered down. In licensing political parties, the British stood on the basic principle that parties should develop from below. Local government began with the establishment of councils whose members were nominated by Military Government. The British wanted to establish the separation of powers, with the executive function reposing in a *Stadtdirektor* or town clerk, as adviser and servant of the council. The responsibility for policy-making would rest with the elected council. Schools in local government were set up, initially supervised by the British authorities. According to one of those who took part, they were conducted in a relaxed atmosphere with a few lectures but much informal discussion.[6] Committee work brought together Germans from different parties who might otherwise never have talked to each other. For several weeks in the summer, visitors came out from Britain: from town clerks of major cities to parish councillors. Germans and British lived and ate together. Excellent understanding was built up through valuable direct contact locally provided by the KROs.

The British Zone again lagged behind the American (and the Soviet) Zone on the question of elections. It was felt that the local councils should have time to find their feet. In July 1946 the British Zone was reshaped by the combining of the two provinces of North Rhine and Westphalia into a single *Land*. The states of Hanover, Oldenburg, Brunswick and Schaumberg-Lippe were joined to form the *Land* of Niedersachsen (Lower Saxony). The two Hanseatic cities, Hamburg and Bremen, retained their separate identities. In September and October – some months later than in the US Zone – the first elections were held at local-government level. A voting system was agreed with the Germans which combined proportional representation with the majority system. One German claimed that the British were so anxious to teach the Germans democracy that they even prescribed the length of string to be attached to the pencil in the voting booth.

In December 1946 Ordinance No. 57 defined both the powers of the *Länder* and the powers reserved by the Occupation authorities which would ultimately be transferred to a federal central government.[7] The prime minister or minister-president of the *Land* presided over a cabinet which reported to the provincial parliament, the *Landtag*, instead of to the occupying authorities. In February 1947 the state of Prussia was abolished by Control Council Law No. 46 and its territories were given *Land* status or absorbed into other *Länder*.[8] In April elections were held at *Land* level.

But there was an element in German society which some felt was being overlooked. It took women in Britain to call attention to it. In August 1946 women's organizations, including the Townswomen's Guild and the National Federation of Women's Institutes, noted that the number of women in Germany exceeded the number of men by 70 per cent. Many of them – women of ability – were being treated like schoolgirls, although women's groups were doing good work. The Women's Affairs Branch of the Control Commission asserted that women offered the best bridge towards a democratic way of life. They were less hampered than the men by political and party considerations. They were intensely interested in the outside world, and yearned for social intercourse. But to participate in anything beyond the daily struggle for existence involved sacrifice of time, which was precious, of strength, which had to be preserved, and of energy, which was failing. Totalitarianism, women felt, had deprived them of status, professions, free speech, even their children, but had at least provided them with the basis of existence.[9]

In November 1947 the Council of Foreign Ministers met in London to discuss Germany. Six British women's organizations – including the National Federation of Business and Professional Women's Clubs, the National Council of Women of Great Britain and the YWCA – wrote to the British Foreign Secretary requesting that the women of Germany should be consulted before a peace treaty was framed. With women outnumbering men, upon them would fall the heaviest task of reconstruction. Their political influence would be enormous. Some had been to Britain to study democratic organizations and were working to educate their fellow countrymen. It was essential that their voice should be heard at the conference table. The letter to Bevin concluded with a request that the Council should receive a deputation of representative women from the British Zone. The Frauenring der Britische Zone was non-party. However, the Foreign Office made short shrift of the idea: 'Women of Germany can best serve the interests of themselves and their country by working through normal constitutional machinery which is now taking shape.'[10]

At the end of 1946 the head of Manpower Division declared that the largest body of organized and representative opinion in the zone – exceeding that of all political parties put together – was the trade-union movement. Manpower Division itself was, with the possible exception of Education Branch, the most efficient of all the divisions of the Control Commission. Its officers were experienced civil servants, seconded from the Ministry of Labour, and included outstanding personalities such as R. W. Luce, Frank Kenny and E. M. Cullingford. Their opposite numbers in the German trade-union movement were also first-class men. Frank Kenny, who had known many of them before the war, was able to re-establish contact at once when he went to Germany in 1945. The men at the top of the British Occupation on whom the heaviest responsibilities devolved and who were working positively for the recovery of Germany found a tower of strength in the trade-union leader Hans Böckler. He had the support of a membership which by the end of 1946 was nearly 2.5 million. His control over a desperate workforce in the face of food shortages and dismantling has already been described. Greatly respected for his integrity, he has been described by those British who knew him as a very great man and even of deserving a high place in the history of post-war Europe.

Some of the British – mostly those not actually working 'in the field' – were hostile to the trade unions. In spite of their history of suppression under the Nazi regime, they were not *personae gratae* in some circles. Sir Walter Citrine, General Secretary of the Trades Union Congress, made the astonishing statement at a conference of the International Labour Organization in May 1944 that 'German workers had worked and voted for Hitler and must be punished.'[11] At a meeting of the Armistice and Post-War Committee which drafted post-surrender policy the Foreign Office representative, Troutbeck, warned, 'If the Trades Unions do become a force in Germany – and they very well may one day – it will be as part of a left-wing government no less dictatorial that Hitler's or Stalin's. And the owners will be hanged.' When the Ministry of Labour representative asked for great patience and tolerance towards the unions in the early days, Troutbeck objected strongly. The War Office backed him.[12] Speaking in the House of Commons, a former member of the Control Commission declared that Germany was being controlled 'by people who vie with one another in distrust of the German Trades Unions and of a few British Trades Unionists who were trying to give them a fair deal. At every turn they were treated with suspicion and hostility yet many of them had come out of years in concentration camps.'[13] The *Daily Mail* wrote snidely of the rebirth of the Miners' Union, 'There is no doubt we shall hear lots more about these old trade unionists with fiery glints in their eyes who have never been anything but anti-Nazis and have never lost faith with their own ideals.'[14]

Before the war the trade-union movement had been divided into three groups of unions partly based on political or religious affiliation and to some extent antagonistic to one another. These groups themselves then split up. The Nazis then set up their own *Arbeitsfront* which the disunited trade-union movement was unable to withstand. Böckler, who had spent the war underground, had had time to reflect on the errors of those years. He was ready with plans for a movement of just sixteen industrial unions. Cullingford of Manpower Division, an expert on post-war German trade unionism, considered it 'superbly organized'. In later years he vigorously discounted what he called 'the legend' that British trade unionists had created German trades unionism after the war: 'It was a purely German movement created by Germans, exceptionally gifted trades unionists, with the support and help of the Manpower Division . . . Our trades unionists did nothing to impede and in a vague distant sort of way their presence on occasional visits may have helped. But every bit of positive thinking and organization the Germans did.'[15]

An important and fruitful contribution by the German trade unions to industrial recovery was the relationship with North

German Iron and Steel Control. The Potsdam Agreement had decreed that the excessive concentrations of economic power represented by the big industrial complexes – the cartels – should be broken down. Most of these were built around the steel industry, and nearly all of them were in the British Zone. It was the task of the Controller, William Harris-Burland, to restructure these complexes into separate companies for eventual transfer to public ownership. Harris-Burland was approached by Böckler, who proposed that in forming the companies the principle of worker participation (*Mitbestimmung*) should be incorporated. It did not seem possible to the Controller to carry out the deconcentration of economic power without the cooperation of the unions, at that time almost the only organized bodies in the country. So he agreed. 'In a few meetings after that we hammered out all the details and within eighteen months we had formed twenty-five companies, each one operating a major steel-producing works in which this principle of co-determination was given full effect.'[16]

On 7 June 1948 the members of the London Conference on Germany – the United Kingdom, the United States, France and the Benelux countries (Belgium, the Netherlands and Luxembourg) – issued a communiqué. The Germans in the Western zones were to be given the political organization and institutions, with the minimum requirements of Occupation and control, which would enable them to assume full governmental responsibility. The conclusions of the Conference were conveyed by the three Western Military Governors to the Ministers-President of the *Länder*. A Constituent Assembly was to be held not later than 1 September which was to draft 'a democratic constitution which will establish for the participating states a governmental structure of Federal type which is best adapted to the eventual re-establishment of German unity at present disrupted'. If the Allied Military Governors approved the constitution they would authorize its submission for ratification by the people of the respective *Länder*. Because of its special circumstances, Berlin was not to be accorded the status of *Land* and was to be allowed only an observer's role at the deliberations. The Germans did not wish to produce a 'constitution', however, as this would assume an acceptance of a permanent separation of the two parts of Germany. The document which the Constituent Assembly drafted was therefore known as the Basic Law; the Assembly itself became the Parliamentary Council.

But the establishment of constitutional government called for the defining of the relationship between such government and the Allied authorities. It was laid down that legislative, judicial and executive power would be granted to the German government, but the Military Governors would reserve to themselves such powers as were necessary to ensure the fulfilment of the basic purpose of the Occupation. These powers mainly covered German foreign relations, foreign trade, reparations, the level of industry, decartelization, disarmament and demilitarization. The Military Governors would resume the exercise of their full powers in any emergency threatening security.

The terms of the relationship were embodied in the Occupation Statute. Military Governors would have a new title: High Commissioners; Regional Commissioners would become *Land* Commissioners and KROs British Residents. The function of the Resident was to ensure good relations with Germans in his area and to observe and report on local politics. He should be at pains to distance himself from former Military Government attitudes. From now on Control Commission officers would no longer give orders to Germans.[17]

The Basic Law was passed on 8 May 1949 and was submitted to the Military Governors. The text stated, 'This Basic Law shall, on the accession of another part of Germany, be put into force for that part by Federal Law. The Basic Law becomes invalid on the day a Constitution is adopted.' The new parliament was housed in Bonn in a concrete building which looked almost purposely temporary.

On 12 May, at a meeting of the Military Governors, the Ministers-President and representatives of the Parliamentary Council, a letter was handed to Konrad Adenauer, President of the

Parliamentary Council, approving the Basic Law: 'In our opinion it happily combines German democratic tradition with the concepts of representative government and a rule of law which the world has come to recognise as requisite to the life of a free people.' Adenauer responded:

> Gentlemen, you will appreciate that this hour deeply moves us on the German side. After sixteen years – that is, sixteen years after 1933 – we are finally able to arrange political and governmental matters in at least one part of Germany according to democratic principles. What that means to us can only really be appreciated by those who have lived through those years as we have done.[18]

The blockade of Berlin ended the same day. A month later the German Democratic Republic was established in the East. Stalin sent it a message of congratulation and support.

In November 1949 Adenauer – now Chancellor of the new Federal Republic – and his ministers met the Allied high commissioners at Petersberg on the Rhine.[19] Agreement was reached on some major reductions in the dismantling list and on the maintenance of Germany's demilitarization. Finally Germany was to be integrated into Western Europe in all possible ways. On the Allied side this was seen as entailing some surrender of Germany's independence. But did the Germans feel apprehension on that account?

Two years earlier, after lecturing at six universities in Germany, the leading Liberal politician Lady Violet Bonham-Carter had reported 'intense interest everywhere in a United Europe'.[20] In March 1947 the Minister-President of North Rhine–Westphalia, writing to the Regional Commissioner about the future political structure of Germany, declared, 'It can be taken for granted that the overwhelming majority of the German people will be prepared in the future to forego part of its sovereignty in favour of European or other international constructions as a contribution to lasting world peace.'[21]

For the anti-Nazi conspirators inside Germany, this concept had been at the basis of the new government which they hoped to establish after they had eliminated Hitler and his regime. Former ambassador Ulrich von Hassell, in a document secretly transmitted to the British government in 1940, wrote that Europe represented neither a battlefield nor a power base but rather a fatherland of which a sane and strong Germany would be an indispensable part.[22] The Kreisau Circle – the secret think tank set up by Count Helmut von Moltke on his country estate – brought together representatives of a whole spectrum of political, social and religious opinion. They sank their differences to produce a constitution and the structure of a democratic state ready for the moment when they would achieve their liberation. But beyond Germany they envisioned a Europe resurrected after the war in a new spirit of cooperation. Prophetically, they had looked to a community of nations based on rejection of nationalism, even of sovereignty; a common economic policy leading to economic union; the abolition of customs barriers; the free movement of labour to eliminate unemployment; European courts of arbitration; and a government council drawn from the member states. A European army should be established under central leadership in which the German Army could participate. The members of the Circle also looked for an international forum for the whole world for the settlement of disputes and an international currency bank. The Kreisau Circle was wiped out by Hitler's executioners in 1944. 'We are to be hanged', wrote Moltke to his wife from prison, 'for thinking together.'[23]

In the early months of 1951 there began a series of meetings at Petersberg between Federal Chancellor Adenauer and the three High Commissioners. The aim of these talks was the ending of the Occupation and the replacement of the Occupation Statute by freely negotiated agreements and the bringing of the Federal Republic into the European Defence Community. In May 1951, at the Paris Conference of the Council of Foreign Ministers, the Federal Republic was accepted as a full member of the Council of Europe, West German sovereignty was formally restored, and the Federal Republic was invited to join NATO.

There was still some unfinished business. The Allies were still 'in a state of war' with Germany. At the beginning of 1950 the Foreign Office had issued a circular to all its representatives abroad. The British, French and US governments had agreed that ' it is psychologically and politically embarrassing as well as intrinsically absurd for Germany to continue to be formally regarded as the enemy' when the Federal government was being encouraged to associate itself with international organizations. But there could be no peace treaty with only half of Germany. A simple instrument of termination 'by omitting any reference to a peace treaty would maintain the legal basis for the Occupation and should avoid prejudicing any of the issues which arise in connection with present difficulties between the Western Powers and Russia'.[24]

At the Council of Foreign Ministers' meeting in New York in September 1950 formal agreement was reached on the termination of the state of war. On 9 July 1951 the Lord President of the Council, the Rt Hon. Herbert Morrison, announced to the House of Commons that 'the state of war with Germany was terminated from 4.00 p.m. this day'. The former wartime leader rose to mark the occasion. 'It is a tragic fact', declared Churchill, 'that six years have passed since the fighting stopped before the word "peace" can be spoken of between two great branches of the human family who were cast asunder by the terrible events of the past.'[25]

The British High Commissioner, Sir Ivone Kirkpatrick, notified Chancellor Adenauer formally by letter. At 4.30 p.m. on 9 July the Deputy High Commissioner called on the State Secretary to the Federal Chancellery, Professor Walter Hallstein and presented to him the note signed by the High Commissioner 'in terms instructed by the Foreign Office'. They then exchanged solemn handshakes and posed for photographs.[26]

At the Paris Conference in May 1952 West German sovereignty was formally restored. The Occupation was at an end. But in the British Zone, at least, the Occupation mentality lingered on. The Army was still a problem and had to be taught its new role. The Foreign Office produced a paper: 'Attitudes towards the Germans of HM Forces in Germany after the ratification of the Paris Agreements':

> Up to now the attitude of the Forces in general and the Army in particular towards the German population has been unsatisfactory. There has been remarkably little contact with German civilians. Little interest has been shown in the importance of the relationship. Several attempts made to improve the situation have met with only local success. The trouble seems to lie mainly with the unit commanders and the senior officers in the small formations. More particularly with the wives, who either will not or cannot give the necessary lead.

Good and constructive relations were now of very great importance, because very soon the Services would be stationed in Germany by agreement with a sovereign government and not by virtue of their victories in war. The Foreign Office concluded, a touch wearily, 'It is desirable to make one more effort to try to get the Army to co-operate fully in establishing better and more constructive relations with the German population.'[27]

An incident involving a senior officer demonstrated the problem of establishing good relations with the population where there was prejudice in high quarters. The Assistant Judge Advocate-General of the Army, Lord Russell of Liverpool, on his way to dinner one evening with his wife, found his route blocked by a village festival. Ignoring local police, he forced his car through the crowd, frightening pedestrians. Only when his driver was threatened was it discovered that he was a British officer. A furious Lord Russell insisted that he was *en route* to an important meeting, and the police escorted him on his way. Later that night Russell made two egregious errors as a public servant. First, he contacted directly certain British newspapers, giving an excitable account of the incident and claiming that Lady Russell had been 'assaulted'. Second, he openly criticized government policy. The behaviour of the villagers was the result of being 'too soft' on the Germans. He wrote to the High Commissioner demanding apologies from the German authorities and the police. Kirkpatrick reported to the Lord Chancellor, to whom as a law officer Russell was responsible, that the Army itself considered his behaviour 'foolish, arrogant and provocative'. The affair had 'done damage to relations which were going well in the area'. Russell was immediately recalled from Germany.[28]

The newspapers would probably have relished printing Lord Russell's account. A chronic problem for the Foreign Office was the post-Occupation attitude of the British media. Several newspaper correspondents confided to General Bishop, when he was head of Press and Information Division, that they had to work to special instructions from their editors. The *Daily Express* man was the most stringently controlled. He was told by his paper that nothing that was complimentary to the Germans was to be sent home, 'which of course obviously hampered his reporting'. One newspaper publisher also gave instructions to his correspondents in Germany that they were not to report anything favourable from the Federal Republic.[29] Sir Frank Roberts, who became in due course British ambassador to the Federal Republic, told the same tale (although he cited the *Daily Mirror* as 'a remarkable exception'):

> There was definitely a carping attitude. The British press were always picking out the unhappy incidents – complaints by the Germans – this, that or the other – in complete contradistinction to the Americans, who never published those kinds of articles. There was never anything good – and there were plenty of good things. And one discovered that this was in general the line which correspondents in Germany were expected to follow. But all this changed really with the Queen's visit to Germany in 1965.[30]

A former diplomat at the embassy in Bonn, Lance Pope (who had known Germany before the war, had spent five years as a prisoner of war and had served throughout the Occupation as a senior political officer), described in retrospect the attitude of the British press – and particularly of the BBC – as a nightmare:

> It was a real millstone round our necks for years – long after the Federal Government was formed. Indeed it reached its peak while Adenauer was being most successful. If a swastika was painted on a wall somewhere, the British press gave the impression that there was about to be a new Nazi movement. Almost none of the positive work being done by the democratic German parliament was reported at all. The *Manchester Guardian* was a special exception . . .
>
> It was an absolute nightmare to us, trying to improve relations with Germany, which it was our job to do. The press chief of the Federal Republic found that he literally had to cook the reports of the British press for Adenauer, otherwise it would have been so bad for relations if he'd read every day what the British press said. What was so noticeable was that the French, the Dutch, the Belgians, the Americans – all their reporting was much more favourable.[31]

In more enlightened circles there was a happier and more constructive legacy of the Occupation. One of those Germans selected to visit Britain was Frau Lilo Milchsack from the little town of Königswinter on the Rhine. She travelled with a group of teachers and local-government officers to study British methods. On her way home in the train an idea germinated in her mind. She had seen British and Germans together in England, exchanging ideas and engaging freely in discussion without animosity. Why should this not be continued as a regular event and on German soil?[32] This was the beginning of the Anglo-German Königswinter Conference, at which leading politicians, academics, journalists and businessmen from both sides come together every spring for free discussion. Frau Milchsack herself organized the meetings, for which in the early days there was no official money available. Such was the success and prestige of the conferences that, in addition to being awarded high honours in her own country, Frau Milchsack was created an honorary Dame Commander of the Order of St Michael and St George in the United Kingdom. The Königswinter Conference continues to be an established and influential annual event.

Gradually the rubble turned back into cities. The official estimate of the number of cubic metres of debris to be cleared at the end of the war was formidable. Berlin 60 million; Hamburg 43 million; Cologne 14 million; Essen 12 million; Dortmund 10 million. In the absence of manpower, women of all ages and classes set to work. Debris was passed in buckets from hand to hand in human chains and loaded on to the '*Trümmer*' trains – little trucks which shuttled to and fro through the ruins. In many towns each citizen was obliged to give up one day a week to clearing rubble. In Hamburg 8 million bricks were cleaned every month. In April 1947 the German Department for the Utilization of Debris put on an exhibition covering the whole zone showing how cheap brick houses and walls had been constructed from 70 million cubic metres of debris. A new kind of ceiling had been contrived from concrete and brick chips. New processes extracted steel, iron and non-ferrous metals from the rubble – usable even to the extent of making precision instruments. It was reported that thirty-five new firms were working. When at last building was allowed to begin, it was carried on around the clock, working by arc lamps at night. One British wife left on leave to England as the foundations were being dug for a block of flats; the flats were already finished when she returned.

The ravages of dismantling were eclipsed by the burgeoning of new plant. Because the Germans had had to be notified in advance that plant was to be dismantled and removed, they had worked day and night to construct replacements. Major-General Sir Alec Bishop recalled how they would set down the new piece of plant on the same seating and screw it on to the same bolts that were still sticking up out of the ground. Perversely, punitive

Allied policy had given German industry a head start on the road to modernization and the economic miracle.

When the dismantling crisis in the British Zone had been at its height, a Foreign Office spokesman had one day briefed the press in London. 'Most of the criticism we meet in Germany and the UK', he declared, 'is purely from the German point of view . . . What the Germans feel about it [dismantling] does not matter all that much.'[33] But did it? Five years after the end of the war, a senior clergyman appealed to the Allied Control Council on behalf of a small town in his diocese. The aluminium works was due to be dismantled, and there was no alternative employment. The workman did not understand high politics, the clergyman wrote: he could only see senseless destruction. To the politicians a few hundred workers might be of minor importance, but it should not be overlooked that each man had relatives, friends, acquaintances. 'If only', the writer concluded, 'the politicians of 1950 would learn from the mistakes of 1920.' Cutting aluminium production by a few thousand tons would not prevent a future war – 'only a proper appreciation of the fact that the Western world, for better or for worse, forms one single entity'.[34]

Notes

INTRODUCTION

1. PREM 240/46.
2. *Hansard*, 5th Series, Vol. 426, Col. 559.
3. *Hansard*, 5th Series, Vol. 426, Col. 533.
4. Stephen Spender, *European Witness* (London: Hamish Hamilton, 1946), pp. 11–12.

1. UNCONDITIONAL SURRENDER

1. Sir Vaughan Berry, interview, 25 July 1978.
2. *Hansard*, 5th Series, Vol. 414, Col. 2319.
3. FO 371/46785, 46786.
4. FO 371/50759.
5. FO 1014/180.
6. Ibid.
7. FO 371/50759.
8. FO 371/55965.
9. Ibid
10. Ibid.
11. Ibid.
12. FO 371/40615; FO 1032/750.
13. FO 371/12.
14. FO 1032/750.
15. Ibid.
16. Ibid.
17. FO 1030/22; FO 1051/491.
18. FO 1032/2099. The Select Committee's report appeared as *Parliamentary Papers*

1946–47. Report of Select Committee on Estimates (British Expenditure in Germany).
19. FO 1038/65.
20. FO 1038/170.
21. Ibid.
22. FO 371/64375.
23. FO 371/64374.
24. FO 371/64281.
25. FO 371/64375.

2. YEAR ZERO

1. Spender, *European Witness*, p. 23.
2. FO 371/45695.
3. FO 371/46730.
4. FO 1032/2099.
5. FO 371/26532.
6. Ibid.
7. FO 371/30928.
8. FO 371/39062.
9. Ibid.
10. AIR 48/70.
11. AIR 48/129.
12. AIR 48/223, 129.
13. FO 1051/799.
14. AIR 48/129; Martin Middlebrook, *The Battle of Hamburg* (London: Allen Lane, 1980).
15. *Statistical Digest of the War* (London: HMSO, 1951). (This is lesss than half the figure for deaths from

respiratory diseases in the same period.).

16. FO 371/46730.
17. Victor Gollancz, *In Darkest Germany* (London: Victor Gollancz, 1947), p. 70.
18. FO 371/55623.
19. APW (44)34.
20. *Hansard*, 5th Series, Vol. 426, Col. 601.
21. ORC (46)74.
22. FO 371/34462.
23. FO 1030/300; FO 371/50771.
24. FO 371/46729.
25. APW (45)5.
26. FO 371/46732.
27. FO 1032/383.
28. FO 1030/17.
29. Oliver Harvey, *The War Diaries of Oliver Harvey 1941–45*, ed. John Harvey (London: Collins, 1978), p. 365.
30. FO 1030/289.
31. FO 1032/1367.
32. FO 1032/383.
33. FO 1032/1465.
34. FO 1032/1367.
35. PREM 3194/12.

3. 'CHARLIE CHAPLIN'S GRENADIERS'

1. FO 371/46730.
2. Ibid.
3. FO 371/46971.
4. J. A. Cole, *My Host Michel* (London: Faber, 1955), pp. 22–3.
5. AIR 48/70.
6. FO 371/46730.
7. Christabel Bielenberg, interview, 5 September 1979.
8. Dr Walter Hensel, interview, 13 January 1978.
9. FO 1013/701.
10. Eugene Davidson, *The Death and Life of Germany* (London: Jonathan Cape, 1959), p. 385.
11. FO 371/40636.
12. FO 371/64240.
13. Lord Longford (formerly Lord Pakenham), interview, 11 September 1978.
14. Terence Prittie, *Konrad Adenauer, 1876–1967* (London: Tom Stacey, 1972), p. 131.
15. FO 1032/1462; FO 1032/531.
16. FO 1032/1465; FO 1032/1462.
17. FO 1032/531.
18. General Sir Alec Bishop, interview, 25 May 1978.
19. FO 1032/2099.
20. FO 371/55620.
21. FO 1049/71.
22. FO 1032/2099.
23. FO 371/64315.
24. FO 1030/320.
25. FO 371/55620.
26. Lance Pope, interview, 10 November 1978.
27. FO 1006/474.
28. Sir Vaughan Berry, interview, 25 July 1978.
29. Lucius D. Clay, *Decision in Germany* (Melbourne: Heinemann, 1950), p. 6.
30. *Hansard*, 5th Series, Vol. 426, Col. 575.
31. FO 936/1236.
32. FO 936/463.
33. FO 936/236.
34. FO 936/463.
35. *Manchester Guardian*, 21 September 1946.
36. FO 936/236.

37. PREM 8/524.
38. FO 936/236.
39. *The Times*, 28 November 1948.
40. FO 1030/97.

4. 'ABOUT AS BIG A MESS AS IT IS POSSIBLE TO GET INTO'

1. *Hansard* , 5th Series, Vol. 189, Cols. 1219–20.
2. FO 1060/240.
3. Beate Ruhm von Oppen, ed., *Documents on Germany under Occupation* (London: Oxford University Press, 1955), pp. 168–79.
4. FO 1005/1632.
5. CAB 134/596.
6. FO 371/70846.
7. *Hansard*, 5th Series, Vol. 426, Col. 617.
8. Interview with former officer of Recklinghausen CIC, 1978.
9. FO 1049/561.
10. FO 371/64881.
11. FO 1050/1611.
12. FO 1050/40.
13. *Hansard*, 5th Series, Vol. 425, Col. 2011.
14. FO 1005/1632.
15. FO 1050/38.
16. *Daily Mirror*, 8 June 1946, in FO 1030/304.
17. *Hansard*, 5th Series, Vol. 425, Col. 617.
18. FO 1030/304.
19. FO 1032/2100.
20. FO 936/366.
21. FO 1032/2009.
22. FO 1005/1632.
23. Ibid.
24. FO 1030/307.
25. FO 1050/38.

26. Ibid.
27. FO 1050/40; FO 1050/1610.
28. FO 1050/38.
29. FO 938/366.
30. FO 1032/82.
31. FO 1032/2230.
32. FO 371/70846.
33. Ibid.
34. Ibid.
35. FO 371/70828.
36. FO 1060/739.
37. FO 371/70830.
38. FO 1049/267.
39. FO 371/70846.
40. The Bad Nenndorf papers are contained in FO 371/70828, 70829, 70830. (Ten files are still closed.).
41. *Die Zeit*, 18 March 1948.
42. FO 371/70830.
43. FO 371/70828.
44. FO 371/70829.
45. FO 1050/38.
46. FO 371/109730.

5. NECESSARY BUT IMPOSSIBLE

1. FO 1006/101.
2. FO 800/317.
3. Ibid.
4. *The Times*, 29 September 1944.
5. Oppen, *Documents on Germany under Occupation*, p. 13.
6. Ibid., p. 102.
7. FO 1032/531.
8. CAB 118/50.
9. FO 1006/101 .
10. Private source.
11. *Die Zeit*, 20 July 1984.
12. *Hansard*, 5th Series, Vol. 467, Col. 1602.
13. Heinrich Fraenkel, *Vansittart's*

Gift to Goebbels (London:
Fabian Society, 1940), p. 50;
Left News, No. 71, May 1942.

14. FO 371/24389.

15. FO 371/24391.

16. Sebastian Haffner, *Germany:
Jekyll and Hyde* (London:
Secker and Warburg, 1940),
p. 132.

17. Heinrich Fraenkel, *Help us
Germans to Beat the Nazis*
(London: Victor Gollancz,
1941).

18. Ibid.

19. FO 371/23010.

20. FO 371/22975.

21. US National Archive, RG331
091.1–2 SHAEF.

22. Michael Balfour and Julian
Frisby, *Helmut von Moltke*
(London: Macmillan, 1972),
pp. 219–20.

23. *Left News*, No. 71, May 1942.

24. FO 371/39062.

25. FO 371/26528.

26. Ibid.

27. AIR 48/70.

28. Balfour and Frisby, *Helmut von
Moltke*, p. 219.

29. Joseph Goebbels, *The Goebbels
Diaries*, trans. and ed. Louis P.
Lochner (London: Hamish
Hamilton, 1948), p. 301.

30. FO 371/26528.

31. Goebbels, *Diaries*, p. 301.

32. Inge Scholl, *Six Against Tyranny*
(London: John Murray, 1955).

33. PREM 3/196/3A.

34. Peter Hoffmann, *The History of
the German Resistance 1933–45*
(London: Macdonald and
Jane's, 1977).

35. FO 371/26528.

36. FO 1013/2146.

37. Fabian von Schlabrendorff,
Revolt Against Hitler (London:
Eyre and Spottiswood, 1966),
p. 35.

38. *Hansard*, 5th Series,
Vol. 426, Col. 628.

39. FO 1032/2099.

40. Ibid.

41. Henry E. Collins, *Mining
Memories and Musings* (London:
Ashire Publishing, 1985),
pp. 39ff.

42. Private source.

43. FO 1038/61.

44. FO 1040/40.

45. FO 1013/2146.

46. FO 1050/1611.

47. FO 1049/1267.

48. FO 1030/288.

49. Dr Walter Hensel, interview,
13 January 1979.

50. F. S. V. Donnison, *History of the
Second World War. Civil Affairs
and Military Government, North-
West Europe, 1944–46* (London:
HMSO, 1961), p. 368.

51. FO 1038/782.

52. Haffner, *Germany: Jekyll and
Hyde*, p. 162.

53. *Hansard*, 5th Series, Vol. 430,
Col. 20.

6. 'THE CESSPOOL OF EUROPE'

1. Revd Geoffrey Druitt,
interview, 15 May 1978.

2. FO 1040/1868.

3. ORC (46)50.

4. FO 1036/92.

5. Ibid.; FO 371/70845.

6. FO 936/743.

7. *The Times*, 9 August 1946.
8. FO 936/741.
9. Ibid.
10. *Hansard*, 5th Series, Vol. 432, Col. 1779.
11. FO 1050/306.
12. Ibid.
13. *The Times*, 25 March 1947.
14. FO 1032/1170.
15. FO 1067/193.
16. FO 1067/192; FO 1067/193.
17. Ibid.
18. FO 1014/192.
19. FO 1067/193.
20. The Bückeburg papers are contained in FO 1032/1370, 1371, 1461; FO 1030/151, 171; FO 1046/201; FO 930/151; FO 936/563, 653, 738.
21. Interview, 1978.
22. FO 1032/146.
23. FO 936/425.
24. FO 936/741.
25. FO 946/743.
26. FO 1035/103.
27. FO 936/744.
28. FO 936/743.
29. *Hansard*, 5th Series, Vol. 427, Col. 1779.

7. 'A STRANGE PEOPLE IN A STRANGE ENEMY COUNTRY'
1. PREM 240/46.
2. FO 1030/188.
3. FO 1051/606.
4. FO 1050/1611.
5. *The Times*, 10 October 1946.
6. FO 1030/188.
7. FO 1051/150.
8. FO 1067/2.
9. FO 1032/1360.
10. FO 1014/891.

11. FO 1014/897.
12. FO 1014/892.
13. FO 1014/891.
14. FO 1051/849.
15. FO 944/892.
16. FO 1014/749.
17. FO 1014/894.
18. FO 371/56616.
19. FO 1014/891.
20. FO 1014/890.
21. FO 1032/2100.
22. *Hansard*, 5th Series, Vol. 427, Cols. 1165–7.
23. FO 1014/897.
24. Ibid.
25. FO 1050/1611.
26. FO 1051/799.
27. FO 1051/722.
28. FO 1032/1368.
29. All comments by former BAOR and Control Commission wives are taken from interviews conducted by the author in 1978–9.
30. FO 1032/531.
31. FO 1030/172.
32. FO 1030/176.
33. FO 1032/1465.
34. FO 371/70911.
35. FO 1014/26.
36. FO 898/178.
37. FO 1030/172.
38. FO 1014/26.
39. FO 1032/1095.
40. FO 1032/294.
41. FO 1014/26.
42. Ibid.

8. OUT OF THE DARK
1. FO 1014/26.
2. Michael Balfour, *Four-Power Control in Germany and Austria*

1945–46 (London: Oxford
University Press, 1956),
p. 231.
3. *Hansard*, 5th series, Vol. 416,
Col. 1073.
4. Edith Davies, interview,
25 January 1978.
5. FO 1032/479.
6. FO 1032/2101.
7. Edith Davies, interview,
25 January 1978.
8. Antje Boy, interview,
31 January 1979.
9. Ibid.
10. Ibid.
11. Ibid.
12. FO 1050/1611.
13. FO 371/64386.
14. Dr Hans Reimers, interview,
29 November 1978.
15. FO 1010/82.
16. Sir Robert Birley, interview,
31 May 1978.
17. David Phillips, ed., *German
Universities After the Surrender:
British Occupation Policy and the
Control of HigherEducation*
(Oxford: Oxford University
Department of Education
Studies, 1983), p. 78.
18. Ibid., p. 65.
19. Ibid., p.149.
20. Ibid., p. 112.
21. FO 1030/288.
22. Matthew Barry Sullivan,
Thresholds of Peace (London:
Hamish Hamilton, 1979),
p. 255.
23. Steel McRitchie, interview,
29 November 1978.
24. Lord Barnetson, interview,
25 July 1979.

25. Ibid.
26. FO 371/46728.
27. Ulrich Benthien, interview,
14 June 1979; Dr Schnapp,
interview, 7 February 1979.
28. Ulrich Benthien, interview,
14 June 1979.
29. Dr Schnapp, interview,
7 February 1979.

9. Make Germany pay
1. Salvador de Madariaga, *Neue
Zuercher Zeitung*, 1 November
1953. Quoted in Balfour,
Four-Power Control, p. 91.
2. FO 371/50867.
3. Balfour, *Four-Power Control*,
p. 89.
4. FO 371/55834.
5. FO 1049/245.
6. FO 1032/1231.
7. Ibid.
8. Details of Zonal Advisory
Committee meetings are
taken from notes provided by
Lance Pope, political officer,
CCG.
9. FO 1032/2103.
10. FO 371/70957.
11. FO 371/55834.
12. FO 371/65013.
13. Oppen, *Documents on Germany
under Occupation*, pp. 152–60.
14. *Hansard*, 5th Series, Vol. 427,
Cols. 1510–18.
15. CAB 134/595.
16. PREM 8/1210.
17. Ibid.
18. FO 1030/306.
19. PREM 8/1210.
20. Clay, *Decision in Germany*,
pp. 170ff.

21. Ibid.
22. FO 371/64275.
23. PREM 8/1210.
24. FO 1232/2101.
25. FO 371/64993.
26. CP (40)383.
27. FO 1030/329.
28. PREM 8/524.
29. FO 1030/343.
30. PREM 8/524.
31. FO 371/45695.
32. CAB 65/53.
33. CAB 134/596.
34. FO 371/45695.
35. Ibid.
36. FO 1030/17.
37. FO 1036/138.
38. FO 1025/15.
39. FO 1030/17.
40. FO 371/50867.
41. Oppen, *Documents on Germany under Occupation*, p. 76.
42. FO 371/70974.
43. Ibid.
44. FO 371/70943.
45. General Sir Alec Bishop's papers, Imperial War Museum 67/126/1–2.
46. FO 1056/553.

10. SPOILS OF WAR

1. Department of State Bulletin 13, No. 336 (1945).
2. PREM 8/524.
3. CP (46)384.
4. FO 371/45818.
5. FO 371/65012.
6. FO 371/65213.
7. FO 371/45818.
8. FO 371/64236.
9. Ibid.
10. FO 371/45695.
11. FO 1032/1231.
12. Ibid.
13. Ibid.
14. Ibid.
15. FO 371/70957.
16. CAB 134/598.
17. FO 371/45759.
18. The Salzgitter papers are contained in FO 371/45818, 65168, 65169, 65170, 65273; FO 1023/116; FO 1030/235.
19. FO 1030/235.
20. Sir Frank Roberts, interview, 23 October 1978.
21. The Leverkusen papers are contained in FO 371/65244, 65295; FO 1032/272; CAB 164/600.
22. The Henkel papers are contained in FO 1032/12, FO 371/65273, FO 1013/25, FO 1032/2345, FO 371/70925.
23. Details of Zonal Advisory Committee meetings are taken from notes provided by Lance Pope, political officer, CCG.
24. FO 371/65019.
25. FO 1029/61.
26. FO 1049/528.
27. General Sir Alec Bishop, interview, 25 May 1978.
28. Donnison, *History of the Second World War*, pp. 198–9.
29. Copy from Franklin D. Roosevelt Library, Hyde Park, New York.
30. FO 371/70927.
31. Ibid..
32. FO 371/64315.
33. FO 1050/483.
34. General Sir Alec Bishop,

interview, 25 May 1978.
35. Ibid.
36. FO 1014/842.
37. FO 1032/1814.
38. *Hansard*, 5th Series, Vol. 427, Col. 101.
39. FO 1032/1814.
40. FO 1014/842.
41. *Hafen-Nachrichten*, 15 October 1948.
42. Oppen, *Documents on Germany under Occupation*, p. 508.
43. FO 1032/2100.
44. FO 371/55616.
45. *Hansard*, 5th Series, Vol. 467, Col. 1599.
46. FO 371/70927.
47. FO 1032/2099.
48. FO 936/743.
49. Ibid.
50. FO 936/748; FO 371/55954;
51. FO 938/265; BT 211/169.
52. FO 371/65272, 65273, 70959;
53. FO 1032/2346; BT 211/241.
54. FO 371/65273.
55. Revd Alasdair McInnes, interview, 23 July 1979; Ivan Hirst, interview, 28 November 1978.
56. FO 371/65114.

11. **'LET GERMANY LIVE!'**
1. FO 1049/831; FO 1014/898.
2. FO 1014/38.
3. FO 1014/898.
4. FO 1050/1611.
5. FO 1030/306.
6. FO 1050/642.
7. FO 1032/2102.
8. *Hansard* ,5th Series, Vol. 420, Col. 500.
9. FO 1056/174.

10. FO 943/437.
11. *The Times*, 6 August 1946.
12. FO 1050/307.
13. FO 1014/954.
14. *Illustrated London News*, 5 January 1946.
15. FO 1032/1360.
16. Details of Zonal Advisory Committee meetings are taken from notes provided by Lance Pope, political officer, CCG.
17. FO 371/64820.
18. Ibid.
19. FO 1014/38.
20. FO 1014/408.
21. FO 371/70790.
22. FO 371/65295.
23. FO 1051/932.
24. *Hansard*, 5th Series, Vol. 244, Col. 528.
25. FO 1051/932.
26. Ibid.
27. Ibid.
28. Ibid.
29. F01035/103.
30. Ibid.
31. Ibid.
32. FO 1056/174.
33. FO 943/437.
34. Ibid.
35. *Hansard*, 5th Series, Vol. 425, Col. 2033.

12. **SEPARATION AND SOVEREIGNTY**
1. FO 371/55613.
2. Cole, *My Host Michel*, pp. 87–90.
3. Oppen, *Documents on Germany under Occupation*, pp. 290–91.
4. Ibid., p. 44.

5. Lord Annan, interview,
   31 July 1979.
6. Raymond Ebsworth,
   interview, 24 October 1979.
7. Oppen, *Documents on Germany under Occupation*, p. 192.
8. Ibid., p. 210.
9. FO 1050/1210.
10. FO 371/64628.
11. FO 1049/72.
12. FO 371/46827.
13. *Hansard*, 5th Series, Vol. 426, Col. 575.
14. FO 371/46791.
15. E. M. Cullingford, interview, 2 April 1979.
16. William Harris-Burland, interview, 26 July 1978.
17. FO 1032/1801.
18. Oppen, *Documents on Germany under Occupation*, pp. 390-92.
19. Ibid., p. 439.
20. FO 371/64315.
21. FO 1013/206.
22. FO 800/398.
23. Balfour and Frisby, *Helmut von Moltke*, p. 322.
24. FO 1049/1942.
25. *Hansard*, 5th Series, Vol. 490, Cols. 39–42.
26. FO 371/64383.
27. FO 371/93467.
28. FO 371/93484.
29. Major-General Sir Alec Bishop, interview, 25 May 1978.
30. Sir Frank Roberts, interview, 23 October 1978.
31. Lance Pope, interview, 10 November 1978.
32. Frau Lilo Milchsack, interview, 20 June 1978.
33. FO 1050/164.
34. FO 1023/116.

Bibliography

Annan, Lord, *Changing Enemies: The Defeat and Regeneration of Germany* (London: Harper Collins, 1995)

Balfour, Michael, *Four-Power Control in Germany and Austria 1945–46* (London: Oxford University Press, 1956)

Balfour, Michael, and Frisby, Julian, *Helmut von Moltke* (London: Macmillan, 1972)

Bielenberg, Christabel, *The Past Is Myself* (London: Chatto and Windus, 1968)

Bittenfeld, Hans Herwarth von, *Against Two Evils* (London: Collins, 1981)

Botting, Douglas, *In the Ruins of the Reich* (London: Allen and Unwin, 1985)

Brockway, Fenner, *German Diary* (London: Left Book Club, 1946)

Clay, Lucius D., *Decision in Germany* (Melbourne: Heinemann, 1950)

Cole, J. A., *My Host Michel* (London: Faber, 1955)

Collins, Henry E., *Mining Memories and Musings* (London: Ashire Publishing, 1985)

Crawley, Adrian, *The Rise of Western Germany 1945–72* (London: Collins, 1973)

Davidson, Eugene, *The Death and Life of Germany* (London: Jonathan Cape, 1959)

Donnison, F. S. V., *History of the Second World War: Civil Affairs and Military Government, North-West Europe, 1944–46* (London: HMSO, 1961)

Ebsworth, Raymond, *Restoring Democracy in Germany: The British Contribution* (London: Stevens, 1961)

Fraenkel, Heinrich, *Help Us Germans to Beat the Nazis* (London: Victor Gollancz, 1941)

——, *Vansittart's Gift to Goebbels* (London: Fabian Society, 1940)

Friedman, W., *The Allied Military Government of Germany* (London: Library of World Affairs, No. 8, 1947)

Goebbels, Joseph, *The Goebbels Diaries*, trans. and ed. Louis P. Lochner (London: Hamish Hamilton, 1948)

Gollancz, Victor, *In Darkest Germany* (London: Victor Gollancz, 1947)

Greene, Sir Hugh, *Third Floor Front* (London: Bodley Head, 1969)

Haffner, Sebastian, *Germany: Jekyll and Hyde* (London: Secker and Warburg, 1940)

Harvey, Oliver, *The War Diaries of Oliver Harvey 1941–45*, ed. John Harvey (London: Collins, 1978)

Hassell, Ulrich von, *The von Hassell Diaries, 1938–1944* (London: Hamish Hamilton, 1948)

Hearnden, Arthur, ed., *The British in Germany* (London, Hamish Hamilton, 1977)

Hoffmann, Peter, *The History of the German Resistance 1933–45* (London: Macdonald and Jane's, 1977)

Kordt, Erich, *Wahn und Wirklichkeit* (Stuttgart: Union Deutsche Verlagsgesellschaft, 1950)

Leber, Annedore, *Conscience in Revolt* (London: Valentine, Mitchell, 1957)

Meehan, Patricia, *The Unnecessary War: Whitehall and the German Resistance to Hitler* (Sinclair-Stevenson, London, 1991)

Middlebrook, Martin, *The Battle of Hamburg* (London: Allen Lane, 1980)

Mosely, Leonard, *Report from Germany* (London: Victor Gollancz, 1945)

Murphy, Robert, *A Diplomat Among Warriors* (London: Collins, 1964)

Oppen, Beate Ruhm von, ed., *Documents on Germany Under Occupation* (London: Oxford University Press, 1955)

Phillips, David, ed., *German Universities After the Surrender: British Occupation Policy and the Control of Higher Education* (Oxford: Oxford University Department of Education Studies, 1983)

Prittie, Terence, *Konrad Adenauer, 1876–1967* (London: Tom Stacey, 1972)

Ritter, Gerhard, *The German Resistance* (London: Allen and Unwin, 1958)

Rothfels, Hans, *The German Opposition to Hitler* (London: Oswald Wolff, 1961)

Schlabrendorff, Fabian von, *Revolt Against Hitler* (London: Eyre and Spottiswood, 1966)

——, *The Secret War Against Hitler* (London: Hodder and Stoughton, 1966)

Scholl, Inge, *Six Against Tyranny* (London: John Murray, 1955)

Spender, Stephen, *European Witness* (London: Hamish Hamilton, 1946)

Strang, Lord, *Home and Abroad* (London: André Deutsch, 1956)

Sullivan, Matthew Barry, *Thresholds of Peace* (London: Hamish Hamilton, 1979)

Weir, Cecil, *Civilian Assignment* (London: Methuen, 1953)

Index

disregard by their leaders of any form of decency or of honourable dealings: the same Germans whose brothers, sons and fathers were carrying out a system of mass murder and torture of defenceless civilians. You will have to remember that those same Germans are planning to make fools of you again and to escape the loathing which their actions deserve.

5. Our consciences are clear; "non-fraternisation" to us implies no revenge; we have no theory of master races. But a guilty nation must not only be convicted; it must realise its guilt. Only then can the first steps be taken to re-educate it, and bring it back into the society of decent humanity.

6. German discipline, though not our sort, is thorough. The people will judge you with no amateur eyes: and any slackness will be the cue for the resistance movements to intensify their efforts.

7. Be just; be firm; be correct; give orders, and don't argue. Last time we won the war and let the peace slip out of our hands. This time we must not ease off—we must win both the war and the peace.

B. L. Montgomery

Field-Marshal,
C-in-C 21 Army Group.

March, 1945.

PSS 1810 3.45

LETTER
BY THE
COMMANDER-IN-CHIEF
ON
NON-FRATERNISATION

MILITARY GOVERNMENT-GERMANY
SUPREME COMMANDER'S AREA OF CONTROL

NOTICE
CURFEW

From 16 June to 30 June 1945 no person within the occupied territory will be permitted to circulate on the streets or outside his own house without a permit of Military Government between the hours of **2245** hrs and **0500** hrs.

Any person found in the streets or outside his own house without such permit between those hours will be punished by fine or imprisonment.

All persons are further warned that military guards are instructed to shoot any persons seen outside their houses after hours who attempt to hide or escape.

BY ORDER OF MILITARY GOVERNMENT.

MILITÄRREGIERUNG-DEUTSCHLAND
KONTROLLGEBIET DES OBERSTEN BEFEHLSHABERS

BEKANNTMACHUNG
Ausgangsbeschränkung

Vom 16. Juni bis 30. Juni 1945 darf sich niemand im besetzten Gebiete ohne Erlaubnis der Militärregierung von **22.45** Uhr bis **5.00** Uhr im Freien oder ausserhalb des Hauses aufhalten.

Wer in der angegebenen Zeit ohne solche Erlaubnis im Freien oder ausserhalb des Hauses angetroffen wird, wird mit Geld- oder Freiheitsstrafe bestraft.

Warnung: Die Militärwachen haben Befehl erhalten, auf alle Personen zu schiessen, die während der Ausgangsbeschränkung ausserhalb ihres Hauses gesehen werden, falls sie sich zu verbergen oder zu entkommen versuchen.

IM AUFTRAGE DER MILITÄRREGIERUNG.